The Changing Scale of American Agriculture

John Fraser Hart

The
Changing Scale
of
American Agriculture

University of Virginia Press
Charlottesville and London

University of Virginia Press
© 2003 by the Rector and Visitors of the University of Virginia
Printed in the United States of America on acid-free paper
First published 2003

9 8 7 6 5 4 3 2 1

Library of Congress Cataloging-in-Publication Data

Hart, John Fraser.
    The changing scale of American agriculture / John Fraser Hart.
        p.   cm.
Includes bibliographical references (p.).
    ISBN 0-8139-2229-1 (alk. paper)
    1. Farms, Size of—United States. 2. Agriculture—Economic aspects—United
States. I. Title.
HD1470.5.U6 H37 2003
338.1'2'0973—dc21

                                                                    2003005504

To Dirk and Raina

Contents

List of Illustrations   viii

Preface   xi

Acknowledgments   xv

1. Background   1
2. Change in the Corn Belt   14
3. Beef   40
4. Dairying from Farm to Dry Lot   62
5. Dairying in Other Areas   80
6. Can Midwest Dairying Thrive?   96
7. Broilers   112
8. Broiler Areas and Broiler People   125
9. Eggs   146
10. Turkeys   169
11. Hogs   186
12. New Hog Farms   200
13. Critics   226
14. The Rim   239
    Conclusion   257

Notes   265
Bibliography   271
Index   277

Illustrations

Figures

1.1   Livestock on farms, 1900–1997   3
1.2   Shift in sales of farm products, 1949–1997   4
1.3   Farms per square mile, 1992   6
2.1   Average size of Corn Belt farms, 1850–1997   21
2.2   Acreage of farmland and average size of Corn Belt farms by tenure of operator, 1920–1997   22
2.3   Crops harvested in the Corn Belt, 1920–1997   24
2.4   Corn and soybeans as a percentage of Corn Belt cropland harvested, 1997   25
2.5   Sales of livestock as a percentage of Corn Belt farm sales, 1944–1997   26
2.6   Corn Belt share of farm sales, 1949 and 1997   27
2.7   Farmsteads in Cottonwood County, Minnesota, 1950 and 1996   29
2.8   Number of farms in the Corn Belt, 1860–1997   30
2.9   The Mather farms in 1999   31
2.10 The Magnus farm in 1999   36
3.1   Fed cattle sold, 1997   49
3.2   Panhandle feed yards, 1997   50
3.3   Aerial photograph of Brookover feed yard   52
3.4   Land use near Garden City, Kansas, 1998   53
4.1   Los Angeles milkshed, 1930   68
4.2   Incorporated dairy towns near Los Angeles   72
4.3   Chino valley dairy farms, 1997   73

5.1 Dairy farms with 500 or more cows, 1978 and 1997 81

5.2 Dairy cows in California, 1950 and 1997 82

5.3 Coolidge Dairy, 1998 87

6.1 Little Pine dairy, 2000 104

6.2 Tobkin farms, 2000 105

7.1 Per capita meat consumption, 1970–2000 121

8.1 Broilers sold, 1997 126

9.1 Laying hens, 1997 151

9.2 Cross section of cages for laying hens 154

9.3 Creekwood farms, 1990 165

10.1 Turkeys sold, 1997 171

10.2 Turkey brood barn 173

10.3 Turkey finishing barn 174

11.1 Hogs sold, 1997 188

11.2 Hogs sold in selected states, 1969–1997 189

11.3 Hog farms in eastern North Carolina, 1997 192

11.4 Layout of a farrow-to-finish hog operation 194

12.1 Premium Standard Farms hog farms in northern Missouri 203

12.2 A pork production system 204

12.3 Aerial photograph of hog farms in northern Missouri 205

12.4 Hog farms at Perico 207

12.5 Aerial photograph of Perico hog farms 208

12.6 Seaboard Farms hog farms near Guymon, Oklahoma 212

12.7 Aerial photograph of hog farms near Guymon 213

12.8 Hog sales in Minnesota and Iowa, 1987–1997 217

12.9 Hogs sold per square mile, Minnesota and Iowa, 1997 218

13.1 A hog farm as its critics see it 237

14.1 The nursery and greenhouse belt 240

14.2 Nursery and greenhouse crops sold, 1997 241

14.3 Cotton acreage in 1929, 1982, and 1997 244

14.4 Vegetable acreage, 1899 248

14.5 Acres of vegetables harvested for sale, 1949 248

14.6 Acres of vegetables harvested for sale, 1997 249

14.7 D'Arrigo Brothers farms 255

Tables

1.1   Number of farms and value of sales, 1997   7

1.2   Measures of farm size, East and West, 1949 and 1997   8

1.3   Largest farms, by commodity raised, 1997   9

1.4   Number of family-held and other corporate farms, selected states, 1997   10

2.1   Sales of farm products in Iowa, Illinois, Indiana, and Ohio, 1997   23

2.2   Sales of all farm products and of livestock in Iowa, Illinois, Indiana, and Ohio, 1949 and 1997   26

7.1   Average weight of broiler, feed required per pound of bird, and market age, 1935–1994   123

14.1   Average gross value produced by one acre of selected crops, United States, 1997   242

Preface

I have been visiting farms and talking to farmers for more than seventy years. During the 1930s I spent my summers on my grandfather's hardscrabble farm at the foot of Poorhouse Hill in Rockbridge County, Virginia. As a graduate student at Northwestern University in the late 1940s I began my serious study of farmers and farming when I did fieldwork in dairy farming areas in Wisconsin and when I wrote my doctoral dissertation on hill sheep farming in southern Scotland.

When I joined the faculty of the Department of Geography at the University of Georgia in the fall of 1949 it was already obvious that King Cotton was dead, and the question of the day was what was going to take its place. Ever since then I have been trying to learn more about the geography of agriculture in the United States, and about how it is changing.

Over the years I have published papers on various aspects of American agriculture and the rural landscape, and in 1991 I pulled together much of what I had learned when I published *The Land That Feeds Us,* which describes farming in the eastern United States by case studies of representative farms in the major agricultural regions east of the Great Plains.

I based those case studies on fieldwork I did during the early 1980s, and even as I wrote the book I realized that I was describing the high-water mark of the traditional small family farm. Farming was already in great ferment, because awesome technological innovations were forcing farmers to enlarge and modernize their operations to secure the economies and other advantages of scale.

Even earlier, in both editions of my monograph on the South, I had grappled with the question of how farmers might enlarge, restructure, and modernize their operations, and I had identified two possible strategies. Contracting for the use of machinery and equipment seemed better suited to crop farming, while contracting of production by vertical integration seemed more appropriate for livestock.

In central Florida the owners of small citrus groves were hiring contractors to do much of their grove work, because the contractors had the expensive machinery and equipment that small grove owners could not afford. This strategy did not pan out, however, because every grove owner wanted the machines at exactly the same time. Some got them too early, some got them too late, and farmers are properly reluctant to entrust their livelihood to others, no matter how reliable they may be, especially if they are serving too many masters.

Vertical integration, which broiler producers developed on the Eastern Shore of Virginia and Maryland and in north Georgia, worked much better. The integrator provided animals and feed, the farmer provided buildings and labor, and the integrator processed and marketed the fed animals in a tightly linked food-supply chain. Like any innovation, vertical integration has its critics, but it has provided reliable income for farmers, it has increased the scale of broiler production enormously, and it has made poultry our least expensive and most popular meat.

In the 1980s I was familiar with the modernization of broiler production in the South, I knew that turkey producers had adopted the broiler model, and I was aware that the scale of egg production had increased exponentially. I was also fascinated by the huge new highly specialized beef feed yards and dry-lot dairy operations in the irrigated oases of the West, but I kept wondering when hog production was going to modernize.

Why was hog production so laggard? The glib and easy answer was the threat of disease when so many animals were cooped up in close quarters, but that had not stopped the broiler, turkey, egg, beef, and dairy producers. Hog production was concentrated in the Corn Belt, and I began to suspect that part of the answer might lie in the enormous inertia of traditional Corn Belt hog farmers, a cautious and conservative lot who were quite content with things as they were and vigorously opposed change. They were not about to modify a corn/hog farming system that had flourished for 150 years or more; change had to come from outside the region.

That's why I pricked up my ears in the early 1990s when I began to hear rumblings that hog producers had started to modernize. Fellow named Wendell Murphy, they said, had developed large-scale modern hog production down in North Carolina. That's when I realized that the last major form of livestock production in the United States had been modernized, and that's when I realized that I had to write this book.

I first visited some of the new hog farms in Virginia and North Carolina in the fall of 1994, and I began seriously poking around hog farms in eastern North

Carolina in the summer of 1995. As time and funds permitted I have visited other parts of the country to refresh and expand my knowledge of the areas where each type of large-scale agricultural production has started, and to talk to the individuals who have started it.

I have sought out the entrepreneurs, the visionaries, the innovators, the leaders who have successfully pioneered new production systems. These are the people who have made things happen, instead of waiting for them to happen. Most of them are charismatic people, and as I have driven away after talking to them I have thought to myself, "I really wouldn't mind working for that person."

All of the people I have cited are real people, and I have used their real names. I cannot write notes as fast as I once could, so I taped our conversations, and they understood that I might quote anything they told me, as revealed by an occasional "Turn off that bleep tape recorder for a minute," which I promptly did. The only thing I have written that might surprise some of them is how much their operations have changed in the few short years since I talked to them. I have complemented my conversations with individual farmers by intensive quarrying of the vast treasure-trove of statistical information that is available in the various federal censuses of agriculture.

The farmers I have talked with are busy people, but they have given me of their precious time because they believe their story needs to be told. They are articulate, even eloquent, when they have talked with me one on one, but few are experienced at communicating to a larger audience, and they have trusted me to tell their story for them. I am honored and humbled by the responsibility they have placed on me.

They know the same media as you and I, and they fear that most of the American people are poorly informed about what is happening on our farms. They feel demonized by environmentalists like Robert F. Kennedy Jr., who has been quoted as saying that major hog producers are a greater threat to the United States and its democracy than are Osama bin Laden and his terrorist network.[1]

They know that few contemporary Americans have firsthand knowledge of farms, and even that knowledge probably is outdated, because the family farm of the 2000s is a far cry from the family farm of the 1980s. A modern family farm has become a business, a very big business indeed, with gross annual returns of hundreds of thousands of dollars and a capital investment of millions.

Witness the fact that fourteen of the twenty-seven farmers I described in *The Land That Feeds Us* had stopped farming by 2000 because they were too small to remain in business, and most of the rest had more than doubled the size of their operations, even though when that book appeared a few critics accused me of having chosen farms that were atypically large and successful.

My goal in this book is to speak for modern American farmers and to give you a better sense of what American farming is really like at the beginning of the twenty-first century. Perforce I must begin with the Corn Belt, because the midwestern agricultural heartland is still the engine that drives American agriculture by producing prodigious quantities of feed grains, but I have dealt primarily with livestock production, where the changes in scale have been greatest.

I have said little about government farm programs, because livestock farmers, apart from the complicated milk price support program, have been only indirect beneficiaries of the widely criticized federal farm subsidy programs, which have supported row crops. Row-crop farmers do have a right to feel aggrieved by the widely publicized statistic that the top 10 percent of farmers receive 61 percent of all subsidy payments; the top 8 percent of farmers produce 72 percent of the nation's agricultural sales, so the largest farmers actually are getting less than their share of these payments, but that's another story.

I have emphasized livestock farms and paid less attention to row crops, to fruit and specialty crops, and to "the exponential growth of organic farming," for which some people have high hopes. I have also steered clear of the intricacies of corporate acquisitions and mergers, which have treated feed mills, packing plants, even entire companies as mere pawns on a gigantic corporate chessboard, and even the very names of the corporations themselves seem to have kept changing.

I realize that attitudes toward large farms are passionately polarized. Some people see them as serious threats to the environment and to the very structure and existence of rural society, whereas others see them as the logical results of economic processes and technological innovation. I am in the latter camp, but I do believe that all change must be monitored and policed with the greatest possible care.

I am full well aware of the problems posed by large farms, and I have discussed criticisms of such farms in chapter 13, even though I am unsympathetic to some of these criticisms, because they seem based on an incomplete appreciation of actual farm operations and practices. I hope to give you a better understanding of how farming has changed, and to help you see these changes through the eyes of the farmers who have made them. My farmer friends have charged me to do so.

Acknowledgments

This book is based primarily on my conversations with farmers, complemented by intensive quarrying of the data published in the various federal censuses of agriculture. I owe a special debt of gratitude to each person I have quoted or cited in the text, because they have made my work not only possible but pleasant and rewarding.

I am equally grateful to those who have given me of their precious time and who have shared their insights and wisdom with me. In alphabetical order, they are Lew Aukeman, Bill Baxter, Charlie Beiser, Steve Beiser, Jim Bogart, Dennis Bottem, Don Buhl, Mark Campbell, Greg Carlton, Ennis Chestang, Paul Christ, Bruce Cuddy, John D'Arrigo, Don Devine, Tim Docheff, Rick Dove, Ron Durst, Don Forth, Frank Frazier, Taro Futamura, Phil Gersmehl, John Godinho, Steve Grady, Blake Gumprecht, John Howse, John Hudson, George Johnson, Kathy Klink, Jon Luikart, Cotton Mather, Chris Mayda, Rod McKenzie, John Morgan, Duane Nellis, Kathleen O'Reilly, Paul Orlopp, Ron Orlopp, Helen Palmer, Marlin Pankratz, James Parsons, Charles Perry, Larry Pickering, Joe Pires, Dave Preisler, George Raab, Bill Ramsey, Rebecca Roberts, Susan Schmidt, Richard Smith, Joel Splansky, Rod Squires, Harold Stanislawski, Jim Stocker, Mark Stoermann, Bob Stubblefield, Gary Tanimura, George Thompson, Tim Tracy, Arlen van Leeuwen, Ron Verhoeven, John Voris, Jim Wheeler, Dave Wood, Susy Ziegler, and all the other members and alternates of the GEIS CAC. I realize that no one else will recognize all these names, but for me simply reading this list brings back a host of delightful memories of some truly wonderful people, and I am sincerely grateful to each and every one of you.

I appreciate the patience, tolerance, and kind assistance of Julia Wallace, Lynne Beck, Eunice Johnson, Clarice Ostman, and Amy West of the Government

Publications Library at the University of Minnesota, which is virtually my second home.

Xuejin Ruan drew all the maps and graphs specifically for this book in the Cartography Laboratory at the University of Minnesota, under the direction of Mark B. Lindberg. I am grateful for their expertise.

I took all the photographs except for the vertical aerial photographs, which I acquired from the National Aerial Photography Service of the U.S. Department of Agriculture.

Jodi Larson has done a marvelous job of translating my text and an apparently interminable string of corrections onto computer disks. The unfailing good humor and crisp efficiency of Margaret Rasmussen have made the Geography Department at the University of Minnesota a pleasant place to work.

I followed an outstanding editor from another press to the University of Virginia Press, and I am jolly glad I did.

I greatly appreciate the careful copyediting effort of Barbara H. Salazar and the expert indexing of Galen Schroeder.

I can cheerfully attest that Meredith D. Hart, my wife of better than fifty-four years, is a saint. I am a very fortunate man.

The Changing Scale of American Agriculture

1
Background

At the dawn of the twenty-first century entrepreneurs were transforming American agriculture from a simple cottage industry into an efficient modern system of large-scale food production. Similar transformations wracked the steel industry and the automobile industry a century earlier, and more recently the grocery business has been transformed in the same way.

Massive transformations have serious consequences. They change the status of individuals, and they may deprive individuals and firms of some of their independence, if not their very existence. Some producers have gone under, whether from bad luck, poor management, or some combination thereof, but others have been able to find niches for themselves in the new system, and they have grown larger by consolidating smaller entities into prosperous new firms.

The scale of farming has changed so dramatically that farmers have had to add a zero or two to the way they once thought, whether it be dollars or acres, crops or animals, bushels or head. Once they thought in tens or hundreds, but now they must think in thousands; once they thought in thousands, but now they have to think in tens of thousands or even millions. This simple idea, "Add a zero or two," seems tough for city folk to grasp, but every farmer to whom I have talked has immediately understood what I meant, because it so neatly summarizes how the scale of American agriculture has changed.

Entrepreneurs have driven this change in scale. Many people seem to assume that things just happen, but things do not just happen, they happen only because someone makes them happen. Things happen, places are changed, and new systems are created by the decisions and by the initiatives of individual entrepreneurs. They have transformed American agriculture. Many of the entrepreneurs who have driven this transformation are still alive, and I have enjoyed the pleasure of listening to many of them while I was doing fieldwork for this book.

They have developed streamlined new organizational structures that reduce costs by securing economies of scale, and they have centralized control of production, processing, and marketing. These complex new organizations require a high order of managerial skill, because the effects of mistakes are magnified, and a large operation can lose money faster than a smaller one. They have reduced the cherished independence of farmers, because many of the major decisions that control the activities of modern farms are made in distant corporate boardrooms rather than in the farmhouse kitchen or in the barnyard.

In 1949 most American farmers sought to be as nearly self-sufficient as possible. They did a little bit of everything to produce most of what they needed. They grew a variety of crops, some of which they sold, some of which they ate, but most of which they fed to farm animals. Tractors were replacing horses and mules, but most farms had a milk cow or two, fed out a few steers and pigs to be butchered after the first frost of fall, and kept a flock of barnyard hens to produce meat for Sunday dinner and eggs that the farm wife could collect and barter for "store-boughten" delicacies (fig. 1.1). In summer she sweated over a boiling cauldron preserving vegetables from the garden and fruit from the orchard for winter consumption. In 1949 the average American farm sold only $4,097 worth of farm products.

In 1997 the average farm sold products worth $102,970. (I rely heavily on the *1997 Census of Agriculture*, even though rapid change has outdated a few parts of it, because it is our most up-to-date source of detailed and comparable geographical information for the entire nation, and it is consistent and comparable with censuses taken in earlier years.) Today most successful farmers have become specialists, and they are doing what their computers tell them they can do most efficiently and most profitably. They specialize in producing a single crop, maybe two, or a single type of livestock, and they buy everything else they need. Farmers and their wives stand in supermarket checkout lines just like the rest of us.

Specialization on producing a single commodity has spawned a new tripartite macrogeography of American agriculture: core, periphery, and rimland. To show this new macrogeography I calculated the percentage of farm income derived from sales of crops in 1949 and in 1997 in each county that equaled or exceeded the national value of farm sales ($85 an acre) in 1997 (fig. 1.2). In the midwestern heartland most counties gained more than 5 percentage points and shifted toward crops, because farmers in this area had changed from mixed crop-and-livestock farming to growing corn and soybeans for direct cash sale.

Counties in the periphery southwest and south of the midwestern core lost more than 5 percentage points and shifted toward livestock, because in the periphery entrepreneurs have developed highly specialized livestock operations that rely heavily on feed grains shipped from the core. The third major area is the rimland in California, in Florida, and in the Northeast, where most counties gained more than 5 percentage points, because farmers in these areas concentrated on producing vegetables, fruits, nursery and greenhouse products, and other highly specialized crops.

By 1997 most farms had gotten rid of their chickens and their milk cows and their hogs, but more than half of our farms still hung on to beef cattle (fig. 1.1). Small landowners and hobby farmers like beef cattle, which are a source of prestige rather than profit for their owners, because they prettify the place where the

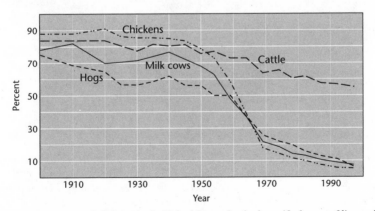

Figure 1.1. Percentage of all farms in the United States that had specified types of livestock, 1900–1997. (Data from relevant censuses of agriculture.)

hobby farmer likes to play cowboy on weekends. The digestive systems of cattle enable them to eat grass and other roughages that are unsuitable for other forms of livestock. They require relatively little time, so anyone with a small acreage of land may be tempted to run a few head on it. Despite the ubiquity of beef cattle, however, most of our beef actually is produced by a small number of large feed yards.

Most farms that once could comfortably support nearly self-sufficient farm families today are too small. Farms have had to get bigger or go under. This thought offends some people, because the Jeffersonian ideal of small owner-operated farms that are self-sufficient is deeply embedded in the American psyche. The idea that a family farm must be small and self-sufficient has died hard, but nowadays a family farm is a business that must gross at least $250,000 a year in order to remain in business and provide an acceptable level of living for a modern American family.[1]

Farmers who grossed less than $250,000 from their farms in 1997 received a paltry return indeed for their labor after they had paid their bills for machinery,

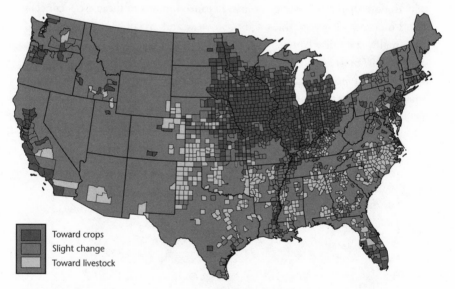

Toward crops
Slight change
Toward livestock

Figure 1.2. Counties whose sales of farm products shifted more than 10 percent toward crops or toward livestock between 1949 and 1997. Counties with less than the national value of farm sales ($85 per acre) are not included. (Data from *1950 Census of Agriculture* [Washington, D.C.: U.S. Department of Commerce, Bureau of the Census, 1952] and *1997 Census of Agriculture* [Washington, D.C.: U.S. Department of Agriculture, National Agricultural Statistics Service, 1999].)

fuel, seed, fertilizer, pesticides, feed for livestock, taxes, insurance, interest, utilities, and other farm expenses. Farming is no longer simply a way of life, although for many farmers it is still a very good life, and they would not swap it for any other. The old-fashioned, nearly self-sufficient small family farm is a thing of the past. Perhaps the old folks can gradually tighten their belts and still manage to hang on to little one-person farms on land they have inherited, but the younger generation are not willing to make the sacrifices necessary, and they have forsaken the farm in search of a better livelihood and lifestyle.

A successful modern family farm is a complex business that demands a wide range of management skills. It is a specialized commercial venture with greater gross sales and a greater capital investment than most of the businesses on Main Street. It has had to get larger in order to stay in business, but 95 percent of the farms in the United States still are operated by families, although many of them have had to hire nonfamily labor as they have grown larger.[2]

The number of farms has declined dramatically. Many undersized farms simply have dropped out of production, especially in environmentally constrained areas in the Northeast and in the South, but much of their land has been incorporated into larger farms. The number of farms in the United States fell from a peak of 6.8 million in 1934 to 5.4 million in 1949 and then to only 1.9 million in 1997, but the nation's cropland slipped only from 478 million acres in 1949 to 431 million acres in 1997.[3]

Nearly two million farms still sounds like quite a lot, but if they were spread evenly across the country there would be only one farm for every two square miles, and they would be hard to find. In 1992 fewer than half of the counties in the United States, mostly in the Midwest, could boast that they had at least one farm per square mile, and only a few intensively specialized (e.g., tobacco, dairy, poultry) counties had two or more (fig. 1.3). Most of the West and large areas in the South and the Northeast had less than the national average of half a farm per square mile.

Furthermore, most of the nation's 1.9 million farms are superfluous to the contemporary agricultural economy, and they are included in the census only by virtue of an official definition of a farm that is extremely generous: a farm, according to the U.S. census of agriculture, "is any place from which $1,000 or more of agricultural products were produced and sold, or normally would have been sold, during the census year." At least a million of the places included by this definition could not be considered real, honest-to-God farms by the wildest stretch of anyone's imagination.

In 1997 61 percent of all our "farms" sold less than $20,000 worth of farm products, but they produced a mere 3 percent of the nation's food and fiber (table 1.1). Half of all "farm operators" reported that they had off-farm jobs, and nearly half admitted that farming was not their principal occupation.[4] Operations such as these might properly be described as nonfarm farms, because they must have nonfarm income to support their farm activities.

Although the official census definition of a farm is extremely permissive, it should not be changed, because it has the great advantage of allowing the census to report a wonderfully complete and detailed accounting of the nation's agriculture. Even those of us who grumble about it would object vigorously to any proposal for making it less liberal. Simply remember that more than four-fifths of the "farms" included in the census are actually nonfarm farms, and they contribute little or nothing to the nation's agricultural economy.

The size of farms has increased. The number of farms and the size of farms are merely two ways of saying the same thing, because the size of farms increases when the number of farms decreases unless the acreage of farmland changes significantly. The average size of farms in the United States increased from 215 acres

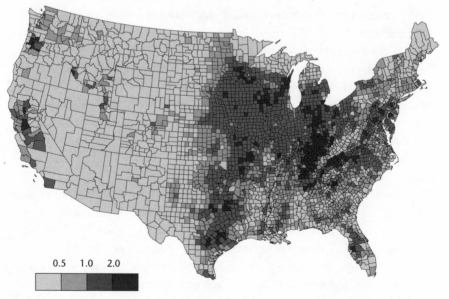

0.5   1.0   2.0

Figure 1.3. Farms per square mile, 1992. (Data from *1992 Census of Agriculture* [Washington, D.C.: U.S. Department of Agriculture, National Agricultural Statistics Service, 1994].)

in 1949 to 487 acres in 1997 (table 1.2), while the number of farms was dropping from 5.4 million to only 1.9 million. National averages are inflated, however, by the large farms and ranches in the dry West; east of the Missouri River the average farm increased from 115 acres in 1949 to 250 acres in 1997.

The total acreage of farmland also can be misleading, because much of the farmland of the West is rangeland of only limited agricultural value, and much of the farmland of the East is woodland of equally limited value. The acreage of cropland harvested is a better indicator of productive agricultural land, and on the average farm in the East it nearly tripled, from only 46 acres in 1949 to 127 acres in 1997 (table 1.2).

Individual farmers have had many reasons for deciding to enlarge their farms. Increased specialization, greater commercial orientation, and technological innovations have forced them to grow larger to achieve economies of scale. Some new technologies, such as improved fertilizers and hybrid seeds, can be used on farms of any size, but many innovations require larger farms, because they have extremely high unit costs at low volumes of production but low costs at high volumes. For example, a $250,000 tractor (yes, there are such!) would cost $2,500 an acre on a 100-acre farm but only $25 an acre on a 10,000-acre farm.

Farmers have had to increase the volume they produce in order to stay in busi-

Table 1.1
Number of farms and value of sales, 1997

| Sales categories | Farms | | Sales | |
	Number	Percent	Amount ($000,000)	Percent
All sales	1,911,859	100.0%	$196,865	100.0%
$500,000 or more	68,794	3.6	111,476	56.6
$250,000–499,999	87,777	4.6	30,505	15.5
$100,000–249,999	189,417	9.9	30,143	15.3
$20,000–99,999	390,785	20.5	18,806	9.6
Less than $20,000	1,175,086	61.4	5,934	3.0

Source of data: *1997 Census of Agriculture*, vol. 2, pt. 1 (Washington, D.C.: U.S. Department of Agriculture, National Agricultural Statistics Service, 1999), 12.

ness. They have no control over the price they receive for their products, and when the price drops, they can maintain their income only by reducing their costs or by producing more. They have watched their profits per head or per bushel shaved thinner and thinner, and they have had to produce more head or more bushels in order to stay in business.

The farm business has gone the way of the grocery business. Once nearly every corner had a small ma-and-pa grocery store that eked out a living by taking a high markup on a small volume of sales, but today the grocery business is dominated by supermarkets that make their profits from a large volume of sales with razor-thin markups, just as the farm business is dominated by large operations that produce huge volumes with tiny profit margins.

American agricultural production has become increasingly concentrated. In 1997 less than 4 percent of the farms in the United States produced 57 percent of our farm products, while 61 percent of the farms produced only 3 percent (table 1.1). One-third of a million farms that each sold more than $100,000 pro-

Table 1.2
Measures of farm size, East and West, 1949 and 1997

	1949	1997
Average total acreage per farm		
United States	215	487
East	115	250
West	527	1,100
Average acreage of cropland harvested per farm		
United States	64	219
East	46	127
West	122	426
Average value of farm products sold per farm		
United States	$4,097	$102,970
East	3,291	90,700
West	6,613	123,841

Source of data: *1950 Census of Agriculture,* vol. 2 (Washington, D.C.: U.S. Department of Commerce, Bureau of the Census, 1952), chap. 1, p. 32, and chap. 9, p. 752; and *1997 Census of Agriculture,* vol. 1, pt. 51 (Washington, D.C.: U.S. Department of Agriculture, National Agricultural Statistics Service, 1999), 184–92.

duced more than four-fifths of the nation's crops and animals, while the other 1.6 million farms did not contribute very much.

The concentration of production of individual crops and types of livestock is even more striking. The largest size category of farms producing most commodities includes fewer than 1,000 farms, and these farms account for less than 1 percent of all farms producing that commodity, but they produce ten, twenty, even one hundred times their share (table 1.3). For instance, 640 feed yards that sold 5,000 fed cattle or more produced three-quarters of our beef in 1997. Fed cattle are the extreme example of concentration, but laying hens and turkeys are not too far behind, and even the major field crops show a remarkable concentration.

The largest farm operations are massive. One thousand acres of corn or soybeans, for example, is four times the size of the average farm in the East, or more than six times the size of an original 160-acre homestead, and the scale of the

Table 1.3
Largest farms, by commodity raised, 1997

Commodity	Number of farms	Trait	Percentage of Farms	Percentage of Products
Fed cattle	640	5,000 sold	0.6%	74.7%
Laying hens	606	100,000+	0.8	65.9
Turkeys	868	100,000 sold	14.4	63.2
Sugarcane	58	2,000 acres	6.0	53.8
Hogs	2,462	7,500 sold	2.6	50.1
Cotton	3,173	1,000 acres	10.1	39.7
Vegetables	604	1,000+ acres	1.1	36.4
Potatoes	220	1,000+ acres	2.1	31.4
Orchards	614	1,000+ acres	0.6	28.6
Broilers	1,319	750,000 sold	5.5	26.4
Milk cows	878	1,000+	0.8	17.5
Soybeans	6,962	1,000 acres	2.0	16.1
Wheat	2,783	2,000 acres	1.1	14.2
Corn	6,535	1,000 acres	1.5	13.7

Source: *1997 Census of Agriculture*, vol. 2, pt. 1 (Washington, D.C.: U.S. Department of Agriculture, National Agricultural Statistics Service, 1999), 28–43.

largest livestock operations is equally staggering. Such huge operations demand an extraordinarily high order of managerial skill, and successful modern farmers, like other business people, must know how to obtain and manage capital and how to keep the farm in the family, on top of everything else they need to know and be able to do.

A successful modern farm is a tightly integrated operation that cannot be broken up and partitioned among the heirs when its owner dies. One child must continue to operate it as a unit, and the other children are not willing to donate their inheritance to him or her, so family farms have been forced to incorporate to facilitate the transfer of assets from one generation to the next. Incorporation is simply a legal strategy for keeping the farm in the family when multiple ownership becomes necessary.

Some people have ideological and emotional objections to the very idea of corporate farms, and some states have passed laws to restrict them, but in 1997 only 4.4 percent of the farms in the United States were incorporated, and 90 percent of these were family-held corporations (table 1.4). Only 8,000 corporate farms were not family-held, and one-quarter were in California, Florida, or Texas. Nonfamily-held corporate farms are so heavily concentrated in the irrigated oases of the West that easterners cannot understand why westerners are concerned about them, and westerners cannot understand why easterners are not.

A family-held corporation can keep a farm operation intact after the death of

Table 1.4
Number of family-held and other corporate farms, selected states, 1997

	All farms	Corporate farms Family-held	Other
United States	1,911,859	76,103	7,899
California	74,126	4,473	779
Florida	34,799	3,881	635
Texas	194,301	4,659	610
Iowa	90,792	5,733	395
Illinois	73,051	2,790	253

Source of data: *1997 Census of Agriculture,* vol. 2, pt. 1 (Washington, D.C.: U.S. Department of Agriculture, National Agricultural Statistics Service, 1999), 300–308.

its owner, but nonfamily-held corporate farms generally have not been too successful, because farms, especially livestock farms, need the constant attention of an owner to a greater degree than most other businesses, and it is hard to find managers who have the dedication of owners.

Crop farmers and livestock farmers have different needs when they enlarge the scale of their operations.[5] Crop farmers need to farm more land in order to increase their volume of production, but farmland has been too expensive for them to buy and too valuable for the owners to sell. Crop farmers thus have elected to enlarge their farms by renting land rather than by buying it, and they have invested their capital in the machinery wherewith to work it.

Livestock producers want to own the land before they invest in buildings, fences, watering ponds, loading and handling facilities, and other necessary structures. Many livestock producers do not need large acreages, because they can buy feed more cheaply than they can grow it themselves, and they house their animals in special purpose-built facilities, many of which look like conventional factories. These facilities are not cheap.

Livestock producers have been forced into new patterns of organization that have deprived them of some of their cherished independence. They are driven by the demands of meat-processing companies, who in turn are driven by the demands of consumers. Contemporary Americans are reluctant to spend time in their kitchens preparing food, and they are concerned about their health. They demand cuts of meat that are leaner, of predictably uniform quality, and in convenient ready-to-use packages. Processors are happy to satisfy this demand, because they make far greater profits from selling value-added products that have been specially prepared and packaged in plastic than they do from selling raw meat.

In order to manufacture standard products the processors must have a steady supply of animals of nearly identical size, shape, and quality. They have kept animal geneticists working overtime to develop prolific breeding stock that grow faster and produce leaner meat with less feed. Generally it is easier to produce these superior animals on large farms, because they require a greater capital investment and more specialized management. Furthermore, the processors prefer to deal with a few large producers, who can regularly deliver large numbers of standard animals, than with many small farmers, who deliver small lots of highly variable quality on an irregular and unpredictable schedule.

Entrepreneurs have modernized meat production, which has six major stages: (1) growing the grain, (2) milling the grain into feed, (3) breeding the animals, (4) feeding the milled grain to the animals, (5) butchering the animals, and

(6) selling the meat. Many years ago farmers did it all themselves, but grain farms, feed mills, feeding farms, processing plants, and marketing companies evolved into more or less separate firms as agriculture became more specialized and more commercially oriented.

Today the various stages have been pulled back together by vertical integration and streamlined into more efficient meat-producing systems called food-supply chains. A firm is vertically integrated when it takes control of two or more stages, whether by outright purchase of other firms or by contract with them. Feed mills, for example, have tried to increase their sales of feed by forward integration: they have contracted with farmers to feed animals for them, and then they have marketed the animals. Processors have integrated both ways: backward, by contracting with farmers to deliver the steady supply of animals they need to keep their production lines running, and forward, by developing marketing and distribution systems for their products.

The farmer who contracts with an integrator is expected to provide the facilities and labor. The integrator provides the animals and feed, supervises the farm operation, and handles processing and marketing. Farmers appreciate the income they are guaranteed by the integrator, but they resent being supervised on their own farms. Furthermore, the integrators prefer dealing with large farms, and many small farmers fear that integration will squeeze them out of business.

Gary Benjamin of the Federal Reserve Bank of Chicago undoubtedly spoke for many small farmers when he said that large producers are "cannibalizing" small farmers,[6] but the large producers retort that the small farmers are shooting themselves in the foot by refusing to accept and adopt modern technologies.

"Vertical integration" has become a dirty word in the minds of many farmers, because they associate it with the loss of their independence. The term has become virtually synonymous with large-scale modern livestock production, and those who are trying to halt the development of large new agricultural systems have seized upon it as a potent political weapon. They have secured the passage of state laws forbidding it, and the integrators have been forced to find creative ways of circumventing these laws, or to move their operations to other states that are more permissive.

Different commodities are at different stages of the integration process. Broiler production, which led the way, was almost completely integrated by 1960, but turkeys were not integrated until around 1990. The integration of hog production started late but it is catching up rapidly. Packing companies have integrated vegetable production, but the major field crops, such as corn, soybeans, wheat, and cotton, do not lend themselves well to integration. The farmer sells most of them himself, although processors have contracted with some farmers to produce special crops, such as white corn grown for tortilla chips.

Vertical integration into food-supply chains is the way to the future of American agriculture, which entrepreneurs have transformed from a cottage industry into a streamlined modern system of food production. This transformation has forced most farmers to specialize in producing a single commodity, and it has forced them to enlarge their scale of operations. It has marginalized the "small family farm," which did many different things, none of them particularly well. A modern family farm must be an efficient business with gross sales of at least $250,000 a year in order to provide an acceptable level of living for a contemporary American family.

2
Change in the Corn Belt

The seedbed of American agriculture was the fertile limestone plains of south-eastern Pennsylvania, which are the only extensive tract of inherently good farm-land on the eastern seaboard of the United States. By happy coincidence, some of the best and most advanced immigrant farmers from Europe settled this su-perb farmland. The German farmers in southeastern Pennsylvania developed a system of mixed farming that was so sound ecologically and so successful eco-nomically that their descendants have practiced it for three centuries in what is still one of the finest farming areas in the United States.

Mixed farming integrates crop and livestock production. The farmers grew corn, small grains (wheat or oats), and clover in regular rotation. They used these crops to put good solid flesh on lean hogs and cattle, and they hauled manure from the animals to their fields to enrich the soil and maintain its fertility. They raised their own hogs, but they bought cattle from drovers.

Professional cattle drovers ranged far and wide through the valleys and hills of western Pennsylvania, Maryland, and Virginia. They bought lean cattle, a few at a time, from individual settlers, and assembled them into large herds that they drove to the sales rings of southeastern Pennsylvania. They sold the animals to local farmers, who took them home to their barnyards to fatten them up for market. ("Fat" has become such a dirty word that nowadays farmers prefer to say that they "feed" lean cattle instead of saying that they fatten them.)

Migrants from southeastern Pennsylvania transplanted their farming system to the Miami Valley of southwestern Ohio, where the Corn Belt was born, and whence it spread westward across the Middle West.[1] The Corn Belt farming system was based on a standard three-year rotation of corn, small grains, and hay. Corn is the quintessential American crop. The small grain that followed corn was winter wheat in the south, oats in the colder areas farther north. Clover was the principal hay crop in the early days, but eventually alfalfa almost completely replaced it.

Clover and alfalfa both are hard to establish on bare ground, so farmers planted the hay seed with their small grain, and the grain served as a nurse crop that sheltered the tender young hay plants. Both clover and alfalfa are legumes. They extract nitrogen from the air and store it in nodules on their roots; the nitrogen enriches the soil for the corn crop that begins the next cycle of the rotation.

Farmers modified the standard rotation in response to environmental conditions on individual farms and in individual fields. On better ground they might extend it by planting two or more crops of corn before they planted the small grain, and on steep or hilly land subject to erosion they might leave their fields in hay for several years before plowing them up to plant corn.

Corn Belt farmers fed most of their crops to livestock. Corn is the world's finest feed for putting good solid flesh on lean hogs and beef cattle. It also commands a good cash market, and farmers were closely attuned to the corn/hog ratio; they sold their corn for cash if the price of corn was higher, but they fed it to hogs if the price of hogs was higher. They took most of their wheat to the mill to be ground into flour, but they fed some to animals. Oats were important feed for their workhorses, and farmers also fed their hay to their animals.

Hogs and beef cattle were the money animals, but most farms also had a milk cow or two, a flock of chickens that had free run of the barnyard, and other domestic animals. The type of livestock fed varied with the size of the farm. Small farms concentrated on hogs, which required but repaid lots of attention. Hogs attained a market weight of "two and a quarter," 225 pounds, in only six months. Farmers had to breed their own sows, because they could not afford to pay others to produce baby pigs for them to feed.

Beef cattle need much longer to grow to market weight, and the Corn Belt farmers who fed cattle bought lean "feeder" animals from producers in other areas, mainly from ranchers in the West. After harvest in the fall farmers figured how much corn they had, subtracted the amount they would need to feed their hogs, and bought enough feeder cattle to use the rest.

As a general rule, the size of farms increased westward in the Corn Belt. Ohio and Indiana, which were settled first, had small corn/hog farms with relatively few cattle. Improved technology enabled farmers to cope with larger acreages in areas that were settled later. Iowa had larger farms, and many Iowa farmers fed lean feeder cattle from ranching areas in the West for the urban markets of the East, in addition to feeding their own hogs.

The exception was the Grand Prairie of east-central Illinois, which was settled late because its vast level plains were so hard to drain. The farms of the Grand Prairie were so large that the farmers were fully occupied with their crops, and they had little time for livestock. They sold all of their crops, and thus they were cash-grain farmers rather than mixed farmers.

The rural landscape reflected these differences in types of farming. Every farmstead had a wooden corncrib with open slatted sides through which air could pass to dry the ears of corn and keep them from molding, and most farmsteads had a general-purpose barn for hay, work animals, and equipment. Many cattle-feeding farms in the western Corn Belt had a second barn to shelter cattle, and next to it was the stoutly fenced feedlot, but cash-grain farms on the Grand Prairie often had no farm buildings other than corncribs.

Efficient crop rotation required that the fields of a farm should be as nearly identical as possible, because each field was used for each crop at some time during the rotation cycle. In livestock areas each field had to have a fence of hogproof woven wire, because in any given year the animals might be turned into it to "hog down" the crop to save the expense of picking it or to glean what the pickers had missed. Livestock areas had interchangeable square fields of ten to twenty acres enclosed by woven wire fences, but cash-grain areas needed no fences because they had no livestock, and their fields were long and narrow to reduce the expense of turning equipment at the ends of rows.

Corn Belt farming was completely transformed in the last quarter of the twentieth century. Farmers were caught in a cost/price squeeze. The costs of producing crops and livestock rose much faster than the prices farmers received for their products, and the profit per bushel or per head was sliced thinner and thinner. Farmers had to increase their total volume of production to compensate for their shrinking profits per unit. They had to produce more from each acre they farmed, and they had to farm more acres. They increased their production per acre by using better seeds, more chemicals, and bigger and better machinery, and by specializing in what they have learned they can do best.

The transformation of the Corn Belt actually began in 1933, when hybrid seed corn became available. Farmers have always saved seed from their very best plants to sow in future years, but selective breeding by plant scientists produced varieties that were far more productive. Back in the pre-hybrid days farmers went to church and boasted about corn yields of 50 bushels an acre, and even in the 1950s they marveled at the idea of 100-bushel yields, but today they feel sorry for themselves if they do not get well over 125.

In the old days farmers and plant breeders occasionally lucked out when a natural genetic mutation in the reproductive process produced a valuable new variety of a crop. Some of our best crop varieties are the results of such mutations. Today we no longer have to wait and hope, because biotechnology enables plant breeders to borrow a useful genetic code from one organism and transfer it to another.

For example, for more than thirty years farmers have used insecticides based on synthetic *Bacillus thuringiensis* (Bt) to suppress caterpillars, beetles, and other pests. In the 1990s biotechnologists transferred the Bt gene to corn and produced a variety that is toxic to corn borers, which can chew up an entire crop in a few days. In 1995 borers destroyed $285 million worth of corn in Minnesota alone, but now farmers who plant Bt corn no longer have to worry about them.[2]

Biotechnologists have also produced soybean varieties that resist certain herbicides, and in 2000 more than half of our soybeans and one-third of our corn grew from genetically modified seed. Farmers like these new transgenic crops because they greatly reduce the need for synthetic chemical pesticides and are friendlier to the environment.

Not everyone is happy with genetically modified organisms (GMOs). Some people are uneasy about the mysterious science of biotechnology, which works its miracles at submicroscopic levels, and small but intensely passionate and highly vocal groups of activists have played on their fears. The activists have used the news media extremely well, while the biotech companies have smugly assumed that they only had to sell their seeds to farmers and could ignore consumers.

Attacking GMOs is also a socially acceptable way of attacking large corporations and demonstrating anti-Americanism, and some countries have even embargoed imports of GMOs. In April 2000 a careful study by the National Academy of Sciences concluded that they pose no apparent threat to people who eat food made from them, but the arrogant biotech companies may be losing the battle of public opinion. One is forced to wonder how hybrid corn might have fared if it had been developed in today's activist climate.

The development of hybrid corn enabled Corn Belt farmers to double and even triple their yields, but it also forced them to start using a whole arsenal of agricultural chemicals. The soils of the Corn Belt are so inherently fertile that they can produce forty bushels of corn to the acre with no additives but leguminous crops and barnyard manure, but farmers had to start pouring on chemical fertilizers to take full advantage of the potential productivity of hybrid corn.

One of the finest chemical fertilizers is anhydrous ammonia, a dangerous chemical that is a superb source of nitrogen if it is injected into the soil properly. Long rows of gleaming white tanks of anhydrous ammonia are a common springtime sight in dealers' yards at the edge of nearly every small town in the Corn Belt. The dealers, often elevator operators, also sell insecticides to control insects and diseases, and they sell herbicides to kill weeds so farmers no longer have to cultivate between the rows of crops to eradicate them.

Increased yields and greater use of agrichemicals have been associated with larger, more sophisticated, and much more expensive machinery. As late as 1950 some people argued vehemently that tractors would never completely replace workhorses, but few contemporary Corn Belt farmers would even know how to start hitching up a team. The modern farmer has three or four tractors, maybe more, at $50,000 or more a pop, a combine with a list price well over $200,000, and a total machinery inventory of $500,000 to $1 million or more. You could have equipped an entire farm in 1950 for the price of the electronic monitor on a modern corn planter.

The self-propelled combine harvester has revolutionized corn picking. Much of the crop was picked by hand back in the days of 40-bushel corn, and husky young farm boys liked to boast that they had picked 100 bushels in a day, but not everyone believed them. During and after World War II mechanical pickers replaced hand picking. They tore the entire ear from the stalk, but the farmer had to shell the kernels from the ears after they had been picked. Combines, which both pick and shell corn, began to replace mechanical pickers in the 1960s. An early four-row combine could pick and shell 100 bushels of corn in less than ten minutes, and now six-, eight-, and even twelve-row models are common.

Combines have two harvesting heads, which a farmer can easily change in half an hour. The farmer harvests soybeans with the revolving reel-type head, then changes to the corn head, which has large blunt metal prongs that nose between the rows of corn. The loose beans or corn are stored on top of the combine in a large bin. They are unloaded through a tubular spout that swings out to one side over the metal tractor-drawn wagon or truck that hauls them back to the farmstead.

Traditional wooden corncribs with open slatted sides cannot hold loose shelled corn, and they are disappearing rapidly. Combines have forced farmers to invest in new cylindrical grain storage bins of gleaming corrugated metal. Most farms have nests of several bins, with a tall metal "leg" housing a bucket elevator towering above them. The elevator lifts loose corn and soybeans to the distributor head, which directs them through a spider-like aerial network of six-inch metal tubes to the desired bin. Most bins have some kind of drying system, because grain in an enclosed bin must be dried to keep it from becoming moldy.

Farmers in the Corn Belt have started to put global positioning systems (GPS) on their combines, tractors, and other machinery to enable them to farm more precisely. GPS, which were developed by the military but have been made available to the public, use orbiting satellites to pinpoint locations on the earth's surface to within a few feet.

In the past farmers had to treat each field as though it were completely uniform throughout, even though they knew better, because they were not able to adjust their equipment to compensate for variations in soil fertility, drainage, slope, and other factors that affect their yields. They blanketed the entire field with uniform applications of fertilizers and pesticides, too much in some parts of the field, not enough in others.

The development of variable-rate applicators now enables farmers to place chemicals precisely where they are needed, just the right amounts in just the right places. They no longer waste money putting chemicals where they are not necessary, they make more money by increasing their yields, and they avoid any possible undesirable environmental effects of excessive application.

Combines now have digital yield monitors that measure the force of the harvested grain beating against a fixed plate to estimate the yield of grain at one-second intervals. The GPS pinpoints these measurements to within a distance of a few feet to produce a detailed yield map of the field. The farmer compares this yield map with a detailed soil map of the field to determine which parts need more fertilizer next year, and how much more.

While the crop is growing the farmer hires a pilot to fly across the field and take infrared aerial photographs, which clearly show healthy plants and weeds. The GPS on the variable-rate pesticide applicator uses this information to spray herbicides on the weedy patches and to avoid wasting it on healthy plants that do not need it.

The integration of GPS, variable-rate applicators, yield monitors, and infrared aerial photographs has enabled Corn Belt farmers to tailor their operations much more precisely, but this new technology does not come cheap, and it takes awhile for the farmer to learn how to use it effectively. The expense must be spread over such a large acreage that smaller farmers simply cannot afford it, and even some of those who can afford it are not sure that it will ever pay for itself.

Some older farmers think the new GPS-based technology is unnecessary, "because I already know every rock on the place by its first name," and they dismiss GPS as just an expensive toy for the younger farmers who do not know the land as well. Even the older farmers may be forced to use it, however, when they have to rent additional land in order to expand their operations, because they need it to help them on land with which they are not familiar.

Bigger and better machines have enabled Corn Belt farmers to farm more land, and the cost of the machines has forced them to farm more land because they need to spread the cost over as many acres as possible. For example, a $200,000 combine would cost $1,000 an acre on a 200-acre farm, which would be completely unrealistic, but only $100 an acre on a 2,000-acre farm, which would be within the ballpark.

The average size of farms in the four Corn Belt states has been escalating furiously since 1950, after having been remarkably stable for nearly a century (fig. 2.1). The eastern states, which were settled first, when the technology available limited the acreage a family could handle, have persistently had smaller farms than the western states that were settled later.

Every farmer in the Corn Belt needs to increase the size of his farm, but the intense competition for land has driven the price so high that few farmers can afford to buy it, and most have enlarged their farms by renting land rather than by buying it. The farmer who owns part of the land he farms and rents the rest is called a part owner, and part ownership has been the preferred strategy for farm enlargement in the Corn Belt since World War II.[3]

(It is in no wise sexist to refer to Corn Belt farmers as "he" or "him," because 91 percent of them are male.[4] A few women make a living as full-time farmers, and I yield to no one in my awe and admiration of what they are doing, but most of the female "farmers" in the Corn Belt are widows who have inherited the farm from their husbands and are having it worked by a son or nephew.)[5]

Part owners farmed less than one-quarter of the farmland in the Corn Belt in

1949 but nearly two-thirds in 1997, and the average size of part-owner farms shot from 205 acres to 545 acres (fig. 2.2). Part ownership has increased at the expense of tenants and full owners. Tenant farmers who own no land at all are increasingly rare, and most probably are sons or nephews who expect to buy or inherit the farm when an elderly parent or relative dies.

Some people completely misunderstand the true character of full-owner farmers. They simply assume that it would be nice if farmers owned all the land they farm, and fail to realize that full-owner farmers are older, close to retirement, and scaling back on their farm operations. They are emotionally attached to land that has been in the family for several generations and they are reluctant to sell it, but they are doing precious little farming on it.

The part-owner farmer on the other side of the fence is reluctant to buy land; he would rather rent it. He knows that the price of land is so high that it will never

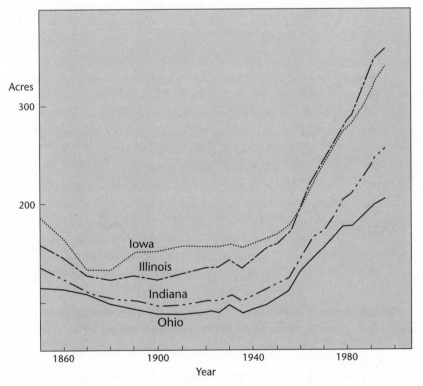

Figure 2.1. The average size of farm in four Corn Belt states increased steadily during the second half of the twentieth century. (Data from relevant censuses of agriculture.)

pay for itself as an agricultural investment. He does not want to tie up in land capital he could invest more productively elsewhere, although he might be willing to buy a neighboring farm or even a parcel of land that would help to round out his property, and perhaps even pay a premium for it. The average acreage actually owned by part-owner farmers is surprisingly close to the average acreage owned by full-owner farmers, which reinforces the notion that part-owner farmers have not bought much land (fig. 2.2).

As farms have grown larger, they have needed better management, because larger farms can make more money, but they can also lose more money, and they can lose it faster. The grandfather of today's farmer was a jack-of-all-trades who did many different things on the farm. The modern Corn Belt farmer can no longer hope to succeed by doing many things more or less adequately. He has to concentrate on doing what his computers tell him he can do best, and he must ruthlessly extirpate the less profitable aspects of his operation.

A modern family farm has become a highly specialized business, with a

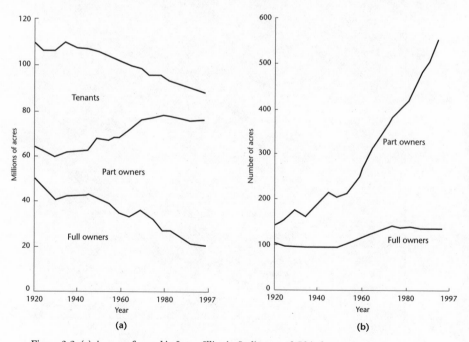

Figure 2.2. (a) Acreage farmed in Iowa, Illinois, Indiana, and Ohio by tenants, part owners, and full owners, 1920–1997. (b) Average number of acres farmed in the same states by part owners and full owners. (Data from relevant censuses of agriculture.)

greater capital investment and greater gross sales than most of the businesses on Main Street. It must sell at least $250,000 worth of farm products each year to provide an acceptable living for a contemporary American family, and many farmers say that even this number is far too low, because they must pay for seed, chemicals, machinery, fuel, taxes, interest, insurance, repairs, depreciation, and all other farm expenses before they can spend any money on themselves. As one farmer said to me, "An awful lot of money passed through this place last year, but not much of it stuck."

Only 11 percent of the farmers in the Corn Belt sold farm products worth $250,000 or more in 1997, but they produced 57 percent of all farm sales (table 2.1). The rest are undersized, part-time, niche, or hobby farmers. Many do not expect to make a living from their farms, but simply enjoy living in the countryside. Some have identified niche markets for specialized products, such as organic or ethnic vegetables. Some older farmers are eking out an existence on last-generation ma-and-pa farms. (The farm population is aging, but only slowly; the average age of Corn Belt farmers was 48.4 years in 1950 and 52.9 years in 1997.)

Many Corn Belt farmers supplement their farm income appreciably by taking jobs off the farm, and the percentage who do so is increasing. In 1950 only 16.5 percent worked off their farms 200 days or more (which is tantamount to a full-time job), but the figure had risen to 36.8 percent by 1997, and it was even higher in the more heavily urbanized eastern part of the region, where off-farm

Table 2.1

Sales of farm products in Iowa, Illinois, Indiana, and Ohio, 1997

	Number of farms	Value of sales ($000,000)	Percentage of Farms	Sales
All farms	290,350	$30,419	100.0%	100.0%
Farms with sales of				
$500,000 or more	10,317	11,039	3.6	36.3
$250,000 to $499,999	21,132	6,218	7.3	20.4
$100,000 to $249,999	45,982	7,418	15.8	24.4
Less than $100,000	212,919	5,744	73.3	18.9

Source of data: *1997 Census of Agriculture*, vol. 2, pt. 1 (Washington, D.C.: U.S. Department of Agriculture, National Agricultural Statistics Service, 1999), 193–201.

jobs are more plentiful.[6] Many a farmer has told me, "My son is making more money from his off-farm job than I've ever made on the farm, even in a good year."

Most of the full-time farmers in the Corn Belt have shifted from mixed crop-and-livestock farming to cash-grain farming. They no longer feed livestock, but specialize in producing corn and soybeans for direct cash sale. As late as 1940 farmers used most of the cropland in the Corn Belt for the traditional rotation of corn, small grains, and hay, and few had even heard of soybeans (fig. 2.3). By 1997 soybeans had completely replaced small grains and hay, and the Corn Belt had become one vast field of corn and soybeans that reached 800 miles east and west from Sioux City to Cincinnati and spread up to 200 miles north and south (fig. 2.4).

The percentage of Corn Belt farm income derived from sales of livestock has decreased with erratic regularity since World War II (fig. 2.5). The sharpest drop was around 1970, when beef cattle feeding relocated from the western Corn Belt to the southern High Plains of Kansas and Texas. Between 1949 and 1997 the four Corn Belt states lost market share of all major farm commodities except soybeans (fig. 2.6). It might seem a bit odd to talk about the declining importance of livestock in four states that produced and sold $11.6 billion worth in 1997, but the share of farm sales derived from livestock in these states cascaded from 69 percent in 1949 to only 38 percent in 1997 (table 2.2).

Some states in the Midwest have encouraged this change by imposing restrictive regulations on animal agriculture. In March 2000, Roger Gilland, who has a 2,000-head beef feedlot near Redwood Falls, Minnesota, told me, "We are

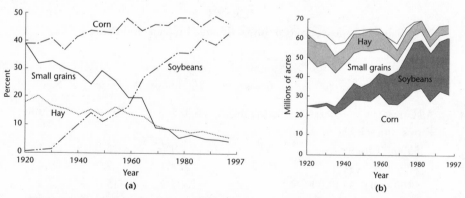

Figure 2.3. Crops harvested in Iowa, Illinois, Indiana, and Ohio, 1920–1997. (a) Percentage of total harvested cropland represented by individual crops. (b) Millions of acres of individual crops harvested. Soybeans have largely replaced small grains and hay in the Corn Belt cropping system. (Data from relevant censuses of agriculture.)

just marking time here. We need to expand, but it is almost impossible with all the rules and regulations in Minnesota. After trying for two years we still have not been able to get permission to upgrade our present facilities, and we plan to move to Nebraska when the facilities have outlived their usefulness."

The decline in livestock production has reduced the supply of fed animals for processing plants, and some plants have had to shut down. "We have lost three in the last six months," Roger said, "and there is only one left in this area. We used to be able to do all our hauling with just one truck, and we could make several round trips a day, but now we need four or five."

Many Corn Belt farmers have had difficulty adjusting to the way American agriculture is changing. Their forebears settled in an area that has been singularly blessed by nature. The soils are so productive and the climate is so propitious that it was almost impossible to fail as a farmer if you were to work long and hard and to live frugally. The person who could do nothing else could always make a living as a farmer, or so it seemed.

The mixed farming system flourished for a century and a half, with little change and little need to change. Farmers did what their fathers and grandfathers

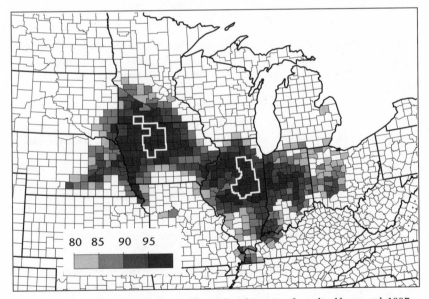

Figure 2.4. Corn and soybeans as a percentage of total acreage of cropland harvested, 1997. Some traditional cash-grain counties grew no other crop. Areas outlined in white = 100% or more. (Data from *1997 Census of Agriculture*.)

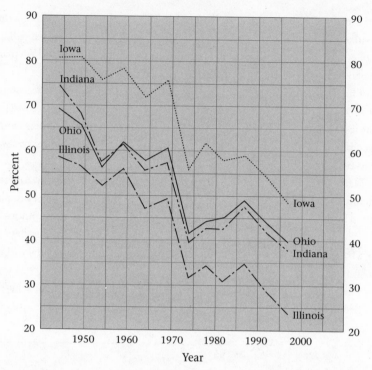

Figure 2.5. Sales of livestock as a percentage of all farm sales declined erratically between 1944 and 1997 in Iowa, Illinois, Indiana, and Ohio, reflecting the steady shift from mixed crop-and-livestock farming to cash-grain farming. (Data from relevant censuses of agriculture.)

Table 2.2
Sales of all farm products and of livestock in Iowa, Illinois, Indiana, and Ohio, 1949 and 1997 (millions of dollars)

	All sales	Livestock sales	Percent
1949	$4,441	$3,055	68.8%
1997	30,419	11,590	38.1

Source of data: *1950 Census of Agriculture,* vol. 2 (Washington, D.C.: U.S. Department of Commerce, Bureau of the Census, 1952), chap. 9, pp. 752, 753; and *1997 Census of Agriculture,* vol. 51, pt. 1 (Washington, D.C.: U.S. Department of Agriculture, National Agricultural Statistical Service, 1999), 193–210.

had done before them, and they grew smug and complacent, even arrogant, in their success. They were always willing to tinker with new ideas, but they saw no need for any significant change in a system that was working so well.

The old ways are no longer good enough, because the scale and organization of American agriculture have changed dramatically since the 1970s. Today Corn Belt farmers must compete in a global economy, and they have to risk huge investments to stay in business. Successful modern farming requires new thought patterns, but some conservative farmers have tried to mobilize their political muscle and pass laws to thwart change instead of trying to learn how to cope with it.

A modern cash-grain farm in the Corn Belt needs 800 to 900 acres of cropland to produce $250,000 worth of corn and soybeans, and that is hardly enough to keep the farmer busy. Bill McCue, who works full-time as a CPA in Minneapolis and has a part-time farm near Belle Plaine, Minnesota, told me in August 1998 that 700 acres of corn and soybeans was about all he could handle, because he could farm only on weekends.

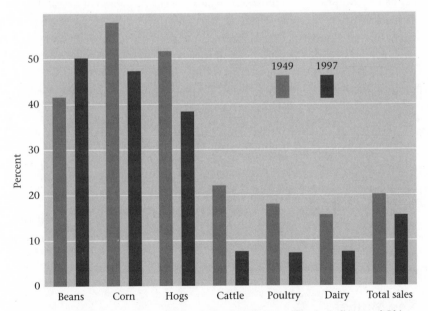

Figure 2.6. Corn Belt share of farm sales, 1949 and 1997. Iowa, Illinois, Indiana, and Ohio lost share of national sales of all major farm products except soybeans. (Data from relevant censuses of agriculture.)

Eight hundred acres, though, is the equivalent of more than five 160-acre homesteads, which means that four of every five original homesteads are redundant to the needs of contemporary agriculture. The Corn Belt landscape is littered with abandoned farmsteads and with undersized last-generation ma-and-pa farms (fig. 2.7). The land is paid for, the old folks can survive on their accumulated capital, and some politicians erroneously assume that such places are "family farms," but the children of the family would not be foolhardy enough to accept a lifetime of arduous physical labor with almost no income on such "farms." Neither would the politicians.

The number of farms in the Corn Belt actually has been declining at a surprisingly smooth and steady rate ever since the Great Depression of the 1930s, with little apparent sign of such perturbations as the "farm crisis" of the 1980s (fig. 2.8). Most farmers can tell you which of their neighbors will be next to stop farming. As in any other line of work, some farmers are good managers, but others are not, and their peers know who is headed for trouble, who is already there.

Large-scale farming requires skillful management and close coordination of the entire food-production process, usually by major corporate entities, and small farmers are wont to excoriate all farms larger than their own as "corporate farms." Some farmers like to hedge their risks by contracting with the corporation to lock in a guaranteed price for some or all of their products. Contracts are especially useful for those with low equity positions who need to borrow operating capital. Other farmers feel that contracts threaten their cherished independence, and they prefer to take their chances on the open market.

Farmers in the Midwest generally dislike vertical integration, when a single entity controls the entire production process, and many states have enacted laws that severely restrict or prohibit it. They are more comfortable with vertical coordination, when many producers cooperate to achieve a common goal, although sometimes it is hard to tell the difference.

Ken Mather and Doug Magnus are Corn Belt farmers who have shifted from mixed crop-and-livestock farming to specialized cash-grain farming of corn and soybeans.[7]

Ken Mather

Ken Mather has actively participated in the transformation of Corn Belt agriculture. In 1851 his great-great-grandfather, Samuel Mather, rode west from Ohio

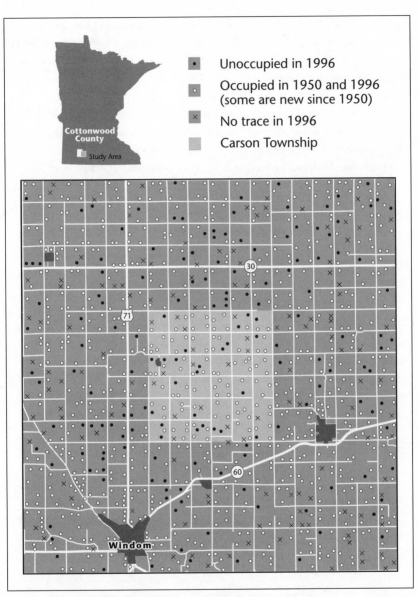

Figure 2.7. Farmsteads in eastern Cottonwood County, Minnesota, 1950 and 1996. In 1950 the central township had 132 farmsteads, 3.7 per square mile, for an average farm size of around 180 acres. Ninety-two of these farmsteads were still occupied in 1996, but 48 by nonfarm families, 9 by part-time farmers, and only 35 by full-time farmers, for an average of less than one farm per square mile and an average farm size slightly greater than 640 acres. (1950 data from aerial photographs and topographic quadrangles; 1996 data from field survey; used by permission of *CURA Reporter* [University of Minnesota].)

on horseback and bought a 250-acre farm a mile east of Springdale, Iowa, which is fourteen miles east of Iowa City (fig. 2.9). The next year he and his wife loaded their fourteen children and everything they owned into two ox-drawn covered wagons and moved to the new farm, which has been farmed by Mathers ever since.

In 1910 his oldest son, Samuel Jr., bought another 140 acres south of Springdale. During the Great Depression an insurance company foreclosed on a loan it had made to him, and it held title to the farm for ten years before he was able to pay off the loan and reclaim the farm. His son, Anders, rented the farm from his mother after his father died, and he bought it from her estate after she died in 1938.

Anders Mather was an excellent judge of beef cattle. At first he bought feeder cattle from a local dealer, but by the early 1940s he had decided he could do bet-

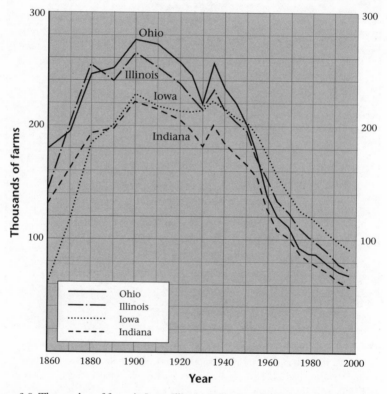

Figure 2.8. The number of farms in Iowa, Illinois, Indiana, and Ohio peaked in 1900, had a secondary peak in 1935, and has declined dramatically ever since. (Data from relevant censuses of agriculture.)

ter, so he began making regular trips to ranching areas in the West to buy feeders. His neighbors admired what they saw in his feedlots, and they paid him to buy feeders for them too. By 1950 he was taking orders for feeder cattle from farmers all over eastern Iowa.

Anders bought cattle for fall delivery after farmers had harvested their crops. For his own farm each year he bought 300 calves at 400 to 450 pounds and 200 yearlings at 650 to 700. At first he fed them alfalfa hay to help them adjust to the full concentrated feed of corn, with a protein supplement of cottonseed meal, which was shipped in from the South by the boxcar load. The yearlings reached a market weight of 1,200 pounds in nine months, and the calves took twelve to fourteen months to reach their market weight of 1,100 pounds. Anders always had a couple hundred head of hogs to clean up the fields after harvest and to clean up what the cattle wasted in the feedlot, but hogs were always incidental to cattle.

In 1960, when he was 68, Anders began renting the farm to his grandson, Ken, who was born in 1940. Ken had gone to the University of Iowa for a year but

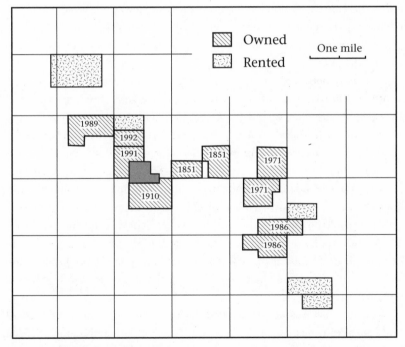

Figure 2.9. The Mather farms in 1999, showing the date each farm was bought and the farms that were rented in 1999. (Based on data provided by Kenneth Mather; used by permission.)

hated it; he wanted to farm. He really should have gone to Iowa State, the ag school, but his grandfather would not let him, because Iowa State never had a winning football or basketball team. Ken's father, Andy, who had always farmed rented land, bought the farm from the estate for $350 an acre after Anders died in 1964. He continued to rent it to Ken until 1980, when Ken bought it from him for $525 an acre.

"In 1960, when I married Jan and started farming," Ken remembers, "all I owned was $20,000 worth of machinery. Back in those days it was all four- and five-year rotations, corn, corn, oats, and a year or two of meadow. You fed it all. You ran it through the livestock, and nobody even thought of selling grain. Nobody grew soybeans. They were a poor farmer's crop. You could count all of the fields of soybeans in the community on one hand and still not use all your fingers."

In the late 1960s Ken realized that his cattle were not making him any money, because a small Iowa farm feedlot could not compete with the huge new feed yards that were being developed in irrigated areas in the West. In 1971 he had a chance to buy a 250-acre farm a mile east for $1,400 an acre (fig. 2.9), so he liquidated his cattle operation for the down payment on it. He realized that he had to build expensive new facilities or get out of hogs, so he got out of hogs. "My grandfather would turn over in his grave," he said, "if he knew there were no livestock on the place."

Ken was a bona fide cash-grain farmer when I first visited his farm in 1982. He owned 400 acres and rented 600 more for $150 an acre. He was growing more soybeans, because they were a good cash crop, and they broke the buildup of corn diseases in the soil when he grew continuous corn. His corn yields were running 150 to 160 bushels per acre and beans were running 50 to 55, but low prices were killing him. His cost of producing corn was $2.75 to $2.80 a bushel, but that day the price, which fluctuates daily, even hourly, was only $1.85, and the price of beans was only $4.85 when it had cost him $6.00 to produce them.

All he could do was hope that the price would improve before he went broke. "Marketing is the hardest thing about grain farming," he said. "Your goal is to hit the top half, and if you can manage that you're doing pretty good. I spend more time sitting at my computer than I spend sitting on a tractor, ten to fifteen hours a week, at least."

Ken obviously was fairly concerned. "I can't take on any more debt," he said, "and I am already pushing my labor supply. I am full-time, and Randy, 19, Alan, 16, and Mike, 14, help me after school. Dad is retired, but he helps me whenever

I need him, say two weeks in spring, a month in the fall. He doesn't charge me anything, just donates his help. Jan runs the grain drier and does most of the bookwork." Jan, who topped her class at the University of Iowa, is also the family historian.

"Our busy times are planting in May and June, and harvest from mid-September to Thanksgiving. We don't have to work as hard the rest of the year, but in the spring we have to fertilize, till, and spray herbicides to get the land ready to plant crops, and we are always busy getting equipment ready for jobs that have to be done.

"What do I do in winter? Make management decisions about seed, chemicals, and fertilizer. Buy equipment. Read newsletters and farm magazines. Spend two to four weeks attending meetings, seminars, and study groups. Worry about tax management. And Jan and I like to get away to Aspen once or twice each winter for a week-long skiing vacation. This winter there's a farm seminar in the Alps that we are thinking about attending.

"We formed a family-held corporation in 1976 for tax purposes. If we hadn't incorporated, we'd have a desk full of tax receipts instead of a farm. You incorporate either for tax purposes or for estate planning, and I don't have to think about that for a while. I'm not sure I want any of my sons to farm. It's a tough row to hoe, tough to get started, a financial struggle all your life. Jan and I sacrificed financially for fifteen years, and these days it's a lot tougher. I can see it stretching to an entire lifetime for one of the boys."

Things were looking better when I went back to visit Ken in the fall of 1983. When I pulled up to the farm, Jan asked me if I had seen him out on the road. I must have looked a bit puzzled, because she said, "Oh, he runs five to seven miles three days a week, and he's out running." When he came loping up in a few minutes I started to tease him, and he bridled. "Now wait a minute!" he expostulated. "I spend my life sitting on farm machinery, sitting at my desk, and I don't get enough exercise. I need it. Now that I'm running, I feel better, I eat better, I sleep better, I don't have any more trouble with ulcers.

"Things are a lot better this year," he said. "I'm looking to get bigger now, because Randy is starting to get interested in farming. I'll use profits to expand. A year ago I didn't expect to, and maybe I'll change my mind next year, but right now looks like a pretty good time to buy land. The price has fallen off the table.

"The prices are about $1,000 an acre lower than they were last year, and when it gets down to these prices, you can buy it to make money. I'm ready to buy if I can find land I like at a reasonable price. I'd like to keep everything in a ten-mile circle. I really would like to keep it all in five miles, but I don't think I can manage that, because too much land is in strong hands."

In 1986 Ken helped Randy buy a 150-acre farm. In 1958 his grandfather had looked at this farm and declared that it was not worth the asking price of $275 an acre, and a doctor bought it as an investment. In 1978 the doctor sold it for $2,500 an acre, which Ken said was way too much, and the guy that bought it went broke. In April 1986 Ken bid $1,700 an acre for it, but was turned down.

The farm was still for sale in August. Ken offered $1,300, the owner asked for $1,400, and they settled on $1,350. "I paid cash," Ken remembers. "I probably should have taken on some debt and bought more, but the early 1980s still scared me. I took on more debt when I bought 80 acres than I had paid for my first 250-acre farm, and I was still kind of overwhelmed by it."

When Alan graduated, they bought another farm for $1,100, and both boys have bought additional farms in the $1,400 to $1,500 range. They also rent land, and in 1999 they grew about 1,250 acres of corn and 750 of soybeans (fig. 2.9). Ken said the average lease in the county in 1999 was probably around $120 an acre, but some owners were asking $150, "and that's pretty tight with grain prices the way they are now."

Ken said, "The boys had to form their own farm business corporations for tax purposes, same as I did. They started farming when the 1985 Farm Bill had a $50,000 limit on payments to individual farms, so they each had to have their own corporation. Our corporation owns the pool of equipment and they lease it from us, but they pretty well manage it. I told 'em, 'If you need something, go for it, you don't have to consult me,' but they always do."

Ken and Jan semiretired in 1998, and they spend most of the summer at their lakeshore cottage in northern Minnesota. The fish sticks Jan makes from the fish Ken has just pulled from the lake are fit for the gods, far too delicious for mere mortals. Ken and Jan drive home for a week or so each month in summer, and in the spring and fall Ken works with the boys. "You can see that the land is all sort of in a line," he said, "and if the weather lets us, we just start at one end and go to the other, but a lot of the time it will rain more on one end or in the middle, so we work where we can, and nobody's fields are always first or always last."

They plant corn the last week of April and the first week of May. There's an optimum window of three weeks, and Ken said you can always count on it to rain at least half the time. Alan operates the planter, Randy operates the sprayer, "and

I'm the gopher," Ken said. "I spend all day going for this or going for that." They plant beans after they have finished planting corn, and they plant varieties of corn and beans with different maturities to spread out the harvest.

They start to harvest around September 20 and hope to finish by November 10. "You need six weeks to get thirty good harvest days," Ken said. The boys have bought a large tractor-trailer grain truck that can haul grain in from distant fields faster than farm tractors pulling wagons. "Three of us can harvest more grain now than four of us could with tractors and wagons," Ken said. At the farm they have a drier that can handle the grain as fast as they can haul it in and six large metal storage bins with a total capacity of 120,000 bushels.

"Right now the boys are using their labor and equipment to the max," Ken said. "They could take on a little bit more land, but not much. They would like to buy land if they could find some for sale, but it's in pretty tight hands right now. If you own it you know what you've got, but if you lease it you might not have it three years down the road. My real estate agent urged me to be cautious. He said there are about thirty farms in the county for sale, but only about four pockets of cash big enough to buy them, so we can afford to be pretty choosy."

Ken is uneasy about the corporate takeover of American agriculture and the concentration of control in fewer hands. "One company's chemicals won't work with another company's seeds," he said, "so you're trapped into buying the whole package from a single company at the price they set. Corporations don't like the way the price of crops fluctuates, five-dollar corn one year, dollar corn the next. They want to squeeze the price as close to the cost of production as they can get it.

"They want you to sign a contract, but they're in business for their benefit, not for mine. The only contracts I have seen would increase my risk and lower my income. The profit will be gone out of production agriculture when there's only one buyer and we can't call several different terminals to get competitive bids for corn and soybeans. That's when I would urge the boys to hang out the 'For Sale' sign on their farms."

Doug Magnus

Doug Magnus, who grows 1,400 acres of corn and soybeans near Slayton in far southwestern Minnesota, has helped to globalize the American soybean industry. I first met him in 1973 when I gave my annual lecture at the South Dakota State

Geography Convention. He was then a 22-year-old majoring in agronomy. He had discovered that geographers have so much more fun than agronomists that he was minoring in geography, and we became good friends.

Doug had attended South Dakota State for two years, then was called into the army for two years, including a tour in Vietnam, farmed for a year with his father, Clarence, and decided to return to SDSU to finish his degree. Clarence thought it was a mistake, but Brenda, Doug's wife, who is trained as a medical technician, strongly supported him by taking a factory assembly-line job. "I still couldn't have done it without the GI Bill," Doug said, "and it probably cost me a lot of money, because farm prices were exceptionally good when I was in school."

In 1976 he graduated and started farming by renting a 160-acre farm from Clarence, who owned 440 acres. Both of them also rented land from others, and by 1983 they were farming 1,400 acres, alternating corn and soybeans (fig. 2.10). "The price of soybeans normally should be two to two and a half times the price of corn," Doug said. "If it drops lower we plant more corn, and if it gets higher we plant more beans. We are really stretched for planting in spring and harvest in fall, and we couldn't handle any more land. Even now my retired uncle helps us out, and so does Brenda." I asked Brenda what she did on the farm, and she said, "Oh, I just help Doug out when he needs me."

Doug and Clarence are big on John Deere equipment, which is painted green, so I was surprised to see on Doug's farm an enormous red six-bottom plow with huge moldboard blades. "Well," Doug said, "you wouldn't know it wasn't a John

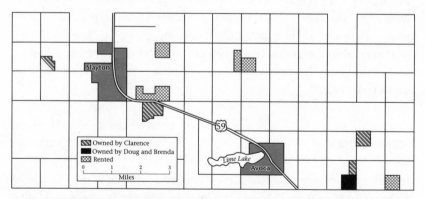

Figure 2.10. The Magnus farm in 1999, showing parcels owned by Clarence and Alice, parcels owned by Doug and Brenda, and rented parcels. (Based on data provided by Doug Magnus; used by permission.)

Deere if I painted it green, but the real reason I have it is that Brenda likes it better than a John Deere."

"Brenda?!" I expostulated.

"Yep," Doug said. It turned out that Brenda did all of the plowing, 500 acres a year. She also chopped silage, hauled grain in from the fields, chopped stalks, drove the disk cultivator, and drove the truck that hauled grain from the farm to the elevator. And this was the lady who modestly admitted that she just helped Doug out when he needed her!

Doug and Clarence sold all of their beans and most of their corn, but they like beef cattle, and they fed out 500 head a year. They bought 500-pound feeders from ranchers at auctions in South Dakota, fed them corn for ten months, and sold them to local packers at 1,150 pounds. I impolitely wondered if they were making any money feeding cattle, and Doug said, "Some years you do, some years you don't. The cattle business is not for the faint of heart. But they are my babies!"

In 1983 Doug was also feeding 600 hogs a year. In 1980 he had bought a "bare quarter" (160 acres of land with no buildings) for $2,100 at 8 percent interest, and he fed hogs under contract to meet his payments on it. "Hogs are less risky than cattle," he said, "and when you contract you know the profit you are going to make on each one, so I feed enough to make my quarterly payments."

Buying that bare quarter was a mistake, because Doug paid far too much for it, and he was relieved when he decided to forfeit it. He was equally relieved to be able to get rid of the hogs, "because their manure is too acid, and everything has to be stainless steel, even the feeders. I don't want 'em on the farm!"

The early 1980s were tough for farmers. Prices were terrible, and the papers were full of stories about farmers who had lost their farms. Every time I talked to Doug I was worried until he reassured me that he was still in business. "Somebody is going to farm the land," he said, "even though they are not making any money on it. They've just got to hope that a good year is going to come along and pull them out."

It helps to have a sense of humor. "This spring," Doug said, "we spent a lot of time just standing by the tractors waiting for it to get dry enough to get out into the fields. Then the crops were drowned out, and we had to replant. Then they were damaged by a severe hailstorm, and many plants were knocked down by high winds. This summer we had bad drought conditions combined with high temperatures. We got hit hard by corn borers, which eat through the stalk and make it topple over, and beans have been hit by woolly bear caterpillars. I guess it's been a pretty normal year."

Doug's cheerfulness is contagious. In addition, he is outgoing and articulate, and he has always been involved in public affairs. He started on the boards of local co-ops. In 1988 he was elected to the state soybean council, and he served three terms as chair, in 1991, 1992, and 1993. In 1992 the governor of Minnesota appointed him to the state Environmental Quality Board, where he served two four-year terms. He is also a consultant for a major farm machinery manufacturing company.

In 1993 the U.S. secretary of agriculture appointed Doug to the United Soybean Board, which is responsible for using check-off funds to promote research, marketing, and the development of new uses for soybeans. In 1994 the board elected him chair of its International Marketing Committee, and in the next six years he led nine trade delegations to sell American soybeans in Europe, Russia, Turkey, Southeast Asia ("It was eerie to go back to Vietnam"), China, Brazil, and Argentina.

In 2000 the board told him, "Two terms on the marketing committee is enough. Now you've got to become chairman of the entire board." One of his first official actions as chair was to welcome to his farm a delegation of twenty feed manufacturers from seven European countries, even though he was properly concerned that they might bring hoof-and-mouth disease with them. He wanted to show them how we grow and handle soybeans in an effort to allay their fears about GMOs.

In 2002 he ran for and was elected to a seat in the Minnesota House of Representatives. I asked Doug how he could find the time for all of his outside activities, and he said, "I figure it takes me about three and a half months of full six-day weeks to grow 1,400 acres of corn and soybeans. I need forty-five to fifty days in spring to plant and spray, forty days starting around the first of October to harvest, and ten to fifteen days to haul the grain to the elevator. I can fit in other things around my busy seasons.

"I talked to Dad and Brenda before I made any commitment, and both of them strongly support me. Dad is semiretired now. He and Mom bought a camper van in 1984, and each fall, before the snow starts to fly, they head for the same campground in Phoenix, where they spend the winter, and they come home when the weather turns nice. Brenda now works full-time as a medical technician in Slayton, but she loves to help on the farm. When she gets home from work she can hardly wait to change her clothes and get out onto that tractor. Both she and Dad are here to help me when I need them."

As an agricultural leader, Doug is concerned about the number of farmers who are willing to sit around in the coffee shop and complain that it's all "their" fault, and are not willing to recognize the necessity of change. "Farmers must shift from production-based thinking to consumer-based thinking," he said. "We must give consumers what they want, instead of expecting them to take what we give them.

"We are going to have to figure out how to add value to the commodities we produce, because bulk commodities, such as corn and beans, produce low returns. We are going to have to learn to partner with the companies that add value, even though it is going to cost us some of our independence. I want to sell at least 40 percent of my crops by contract for future delivery at a guaranteed price, because I want the premium price I will get as a preferred supplier/producer."

Doug Magnus and Ken Mather both reflect the shift in the Corn Belt, the nation's agricultural heartland, from mixed crop-and-livestock farming to cash-grain farming, even though they differ in degree. Ken has gotten rid of cattle completely, but Doug still has a sentimental attachment to them, and he lives closer to the ranch areas from which he buys feeder cattle. Doug would like to contract for the sale of part of his crops, but Ken is leery of contracts. They both specialize in growing corn and soybeans for sale, like most farmers in the contemporary Corn Belt. These feed grains are shipped to the huge new livestock operations that entrepreneurs have developed around the peripheries of the Midwest (fig. 1.2).

3
Beef

Cattle have complex digestive systems that enable them to eat grass, leaves, and other parts of plants that many other animals, including the human animal, cannot digest. We depend on cattle to convert these plant parts into food we can eat. Most beef cattle are born and raised in areas that are too dry or too rough for crops. In the western United States most beef cattle are bred on large ranches in areas that are too dry to grow crops without irrigation. Ranches are so large they are described in sections (square miles) rather than acres, they have hundreds of cattle, and the sale of cattle is their primary and usually only source of income.

Farms in the East now produce more beef cattle than the traditional ranching areas of the West. In the East farms and herds generally are much smaller, and the cattle often are of dubious quality and even more dubious ancestry. Many farmers who have cut back on their farm operations and taken jobs in town can still raise cattle in their spare time, and cattle often are a sideline or a hobby for people who have other income. Anyone with a few acres of grass can run cows on it, and on many farms cattle are little more than lawn ornaments for city folk who enjoy playing cowboy on weekends.

Greg Schmidt is vice president for production of Carroll's Foods, one of the leading turkey- and hog-producing companies in eastern North Carolina. "I have a small farm with seventeen cows," he said when I visited him in July 1997. "One time a cattle buyer, more honest than most, told me, 'I make my living, unfortunately, buying cattle from people like you for less than they are worth.' But cattle are prestigious. It is status to have them. It's also therapeutic. You pull up in your pickup truck and watch them graze. It's comforting. Of course a real commercial cow/calf operation is a lot of hard work. You would probably need at least four hundred cows to make a living on it."

A cow/calf operator of whatever size keeps a herd of cows and expects each cow to drop a calf each spring, just when the lush new growth of grass is starting to shoot up. The calves stay on pasture with their mothers all summer and are weaned in the fall, when they weigh 350 to 400 pounds. The breeder may keep them over the winter, if he has enough feed, or he can sell them as "stockers" to someone who does have the necessary feed. The stocker farmer will keep the young cattle, now known as "yearlings," on pasture the following summer and sell them in the fall at a weight of 600 to 700 pounds.

Cattle can keep growing on roughages, and some cattlemen sell grass-fed beef, but you probably would not be willing to buy it a second time. Grass can produce "4-H cattle—all horns, hoofs, hide, and hair," but it cannot put on the good tender flesh that American consumers demand. Lean "feeder" cattle must be "finished" to a market weight of 1,000 to 1,200 pounds by feeding them concentrated feed, such as corn and other grains.

Historically it has been cheaper to move cattle to feed than to haul feed to cattle. In medieval Europe herds of lean cattle were droved from the North German Plain to feeding areas in the Low Countries, and Scots droved herds of cattle to London. Before the American Revolution drovers bought lean cattle from farmers in Appalachia and droved them north through the Great Valley to be finished by farmers in southeastern Pennsylvania.

The ranchers who settled the American West used railroads rather than drovers to move their lean feeder cattle east to farmers in the Corn Belt, which fortuitously was en route to the major market for beef in the cities of the East. Up until 1960 most of the nation's fed beef was produced by small farmer feeders in the western Corn Belt, where most feedlots held only a few hundred head of cattle, and for no more than five months of the year.

Ranchers depended on Corn Belt farmers to feed their cattle, and Corn Belt farmers depended on ranchers for a steady supply of cattle to feed. Few farmers had time to wander around ranch country looking for cattle to feed, so they placed orders for their feeder cattle with specialized order buyers. The order buyer bought large lots of cattle from the larger ranches, and assembled large lots by buying many small lots at local livestock auction barns.

Small farmer feeders in the Corn Belt shipped in feeder cattle after they had harvested their crops in the fall, fed them for 120 to 150 days, and shipped them off to the stockyards before it was time to begin crop work in the spring. They used feed produced on the farm and family labor that otherwise would have gone unused.

Corn, which is produced in abundance on Corn Belt farms, is the standard against which all other cattle feeds are measured. It is high in fats and starch, high in digestible nutrients and net energy, and easily digestible, and cattle love it. It must be balanced by roughages, and alfalfa hay, which is produced as part of the traditional Corn Belt rotation, is one of the best. Alfalfa is highly palatable, has high protein and mineral content, and is a good source of vitamin A.

The major meatpacking companies (Swift, Armour, Wilson, Morrell, Cudahy, Hormel) had plants at the stockyards at the terminal markets (Chicago, Omaha, Denver, Kansas City). The farmer did not sell his cattle directly, but turned them over to a commission man, who sold them to a buyer from one of the packing companies.

The beef cattle business was highly fragmented, with ranchers, order buyers, farmer feeders, commission men, and meatpacking companies, and each had to make a profit. Too many people were trying to outfox, outsmart, outtrade, and get the better of each other, and too much sharp dealing by too many people created an industry-wide climate of distrust. Even today this situation has not improved. In 1998 an article in *Beef Today* by Nita Effertz lamented that "this segmented industry is full of people who make their living fostering and then feeding off the mistrust between producer, processor, and retail customer."

Warren Monfort

Despite its fragmentation, the beef business vies with the broiler business for the honor of having led the way to an enormous increase in the scale of livestock production in the United States. Warren Monfort of Greeley, Colorado, who was born in 1892 and died in 1978, is the entrepreneur who is generally given credit for having pioneered large-scale beef feedlots. His son, Kenneth, who took over the business in 1970 and sold it in 1987, retired to a palatial condominium near Sarasota, Florida.

"In the 1950s my dad's feedlot was one of the wonders of the world," Ken said, "and we had a steady stream of visitors, but I didn't get to meet many of them, because it seems like I spent all my time building more corrals." In 1998 Ken's health had deteriorated, and he said that his memory was also failing badly. He suggested that the best source of information about the early days of the Monfort operation was his father's good friend W. D. Farr of Greeley.

Mr. Farr is a wise and perceptive gentleman who has been feeding cattle in the Greeley area since the early 1930s. He has played a major role in national cattlemen's associations and is widely recognized as one of the most astute elder statesmen of the business. Warren Monfort had an almost father-and-son relationship with him, and they knew each other as members of the same bank board of directors for more than twenty years in addition to their shared interest in cattle.

Monfort was teaching school in Illinois when his father died in 1930, and he came back to Greeley to take over his family's eighty-one-acre farm. "He had seen how they were feeding cattle in the Midwest," Farr said, "and he thought he could do better. What they were doing wasn't really cattle feeding at all. The only reason they had cattle was to use their surplus corn. If they had more corn than the hogs could eat, they bought some cattle, and they kept them until the corn was eaten up. Warren knew he could do better. His whole life became focused on the cattle business, and he always wanted to be the biggest and best at whatever he did."

Monfort started feeding a few head of cattle and kept adding more. Farr was also feeding cattle, and they loaded them at the same railroad siding. They had long talks about the cattle business while they were sitting on the corral fence waiting for the trains that would haul their cattle to the stockyards. They had been selling in April and May, when everybody was selling and the price was low, and decided to shoot for the better summer market, which nobody had ever done. Their experiment turned out well, because they found an excellent market in the summer resorts in the Rocky Mountains, and it was a step in the direction of year-round feeding.

In the early days nothing was mechanized. The cattle pens had inside feed bunks that farmers filled with scoop shovels from horse-drawn wagons loaded with feed. They dumped hay along the outside of one side of the pen, and the cattle would stick their heads through to eat it. Financing was a problem. "My dad always told me that raising cattle was a sure way to go broke," said Farr, "and the bankers wouldn't lend us any money. Cattle had a bad reputation. They went bust after World War I, and all through the twenties and thirties seems like every cattle person in the United States went broke in one way or another. The ranchers went broke, the feeders went broke, the packers went broke, the banks went broke. Everybody was gun-shy about cattle."

Ken said, "My dad just made the decision to borrow as much money as he could, and he did the most he could do with the bad credit he had. When he made a little money, he reinvested it. Some others did that off and on, but when we hit a bad market they'd either go broke or at least decide not to expand. He just tightened up when we hit a bad market, but he always wanted to grow."

Monfort also was constantly trying to learn more about the cattle business. In 1940 he organized a T-bone Club that met every other Friday night just to talk about cattle. This club included Farr and a few other feeders, a butcher, an order buyer, a commission man, the county agent, and the local radio announcer. "Monfort was an extremely intelligent man," Farr said, "and he was the student of the group."

Monfort just kept building more pens and feeding more cattle, and all of a sudden people realized that he had pens enough to feed 3,500 cattle. "It was unheard of," said Farr. "Nobody was supposed to have more than one or two hundred, maybe three." Monfort also had learned to smooth out the swings in the cattle market by buying a pen of new feeder cattle every time he sold a pen of fat cattle, so price fluctuations did not trouble him.

Price controls kept him from expanding much during World War II, and there were some poor crop years when it was hard to get corn, but he enjoyed a real bonanza when price controls were lifted as soon as the war ended, because he had the experience and was ready to move easily to year-round feeding, and there was a huge demand for beef.

"People had jobs and they had money," said Farr. "They had all come home from the war, and everybody needed a new suit, a new pair of shoes, a new automobile. They had discretionary income, and they thought they were entitled to a nice juicy steak every Saturday night. It was just one hell of a good time, and Monfort made the most of it." Per capita beef consumption in the United States rose from sixty pounds in 1950 to ninety-five pounds in 1970.[1]

The government grading system that had been mandatory during the war helped to ensure that consumers got beef of consistent quality. Before the war the big packers had merely assigned their own top house grades to the best cattle they bought each day, no matter how good or poor they really were, so the individual brand grades did not mean very much, because they actually varied from day to day.

Chain grocery stores, which had just gotten started in major cities before the war, could not tolerate these variations. They required consistent beef quality, because they were advertising for multiple stores all over the city, and their customers had begun to tell them what they would buy, when, and how much they were willing to pay for it. Small packing companies, which had built modern new plants in the rural areas where beef was produced, were able to deliver standard quality products, and by the 1980s the small flexible packing companies had put the big old terminal packing companies out of business.

Monfort continued to expand. "It was just gradual growth over the years," Ken said, "with no particularly noticeable spurt, but it always seemed like a real big job when he put in another string of pens. He just kept adding pens, adding pens, adding pens! He was not much bigger than a lot of other feeders before the war, but they pretty much stayed put, and eventually they were so small that they had to get out of the business." John Anderson, who farms a few miles north of Greeley in an area where feedlots once were common, summed it up succinctly in 1998 when he told me, "You just don't see no more small feedlots no more. Seems like 'Sell it off' is your only salvation."

Feedlots today are larger, but their basic layout and design have not changed much since the early postwar years. They have many individual pens enclosed by sturdy wooden fences. Most pens cover about an acre and hold around 400 cattle. They have a good steady supply of water for the cattle to drink, but they are called dry lots because they have no grass or other plant life. Cowboys on horseback patrol the pens daily and move the cattle as necessary. The pens are separated by driveways wide enough for the trucks that automatically unload feed twice a day as they drive past the concrete troughs that line the outside edge of each pen. A large revolving screw in the bed of each truck mixes the feed as the truck hauls it from the squat feed mill next to the towering grain elevators.

A nutritionist at the feed mill measures the proper ration of flaked grain, roughage, and protein and mineral supplement for each pen, based on the age and weight of its cattle. Those fresh from the range get 50 to 60 percent corn silage or alfalfa hay, because they have been raised on grass, but the nutritionist steadily increases the percentage of grain, which is made more palatable by flaking (steaming and rolling) it. The cattle prefer grain once they get used to it, and the finishing ration is about 90 percent grain. The feeder expects each animal to gain an average of 2.5 pounds or more a day for a feeding period of 120 to 150 days, and he expects to put two and a half lots of cattle through each pen each year. Each animal also presents him with about 22 pounds of manure each day, so he has to scrape out the pens periodically. He sells the manure to neighboring farmers, who are happy to buy it for fertilizer.

Monfort always wanted to be the best as well as the biggest, so he began sorting his fed cattle into uniform lots before he shipped them to market. Packers were willing to pay premium prices for them, and in the early 1960s he established a national reputation as an outstanding feeder when his cattle received the top price in the Chicago market more often than those of any other feeder. He also realized that the packers were paying by the dressing percentage, or the percentage of usable meat they could get from a live animal, so he shipped cattle that were a little light on water and on hay. They dressed a few percentage points higher, and thus gave him a better price per live-weight pound.

Greeley was a good location for feeding cattle in the early days because it had good railroad connections to all the major terminal markets. After World War II, trucks began to take over the business from railroads. They could haul cattle equally easily in all directions, so feeders in Texas and Oklahoma could compete with feeders on the railroads. Warren Monfort used independent truckers, but he was always looking for ways to save a few pennies, Farr said, and he hated to see other people making money at his expense. If he thought they were making too much, he wanted to get into their business and have the profits for himself, so in 1970 he decided to start his own trucking company.

Trucks could haul beef carcasses more cheaply than they could haul live cattle, and the old terminal packing plants were antiquated, inefficient, and plagued by high labor costs, so in 1960 Monfort decided he could make more money if he had his own packing plant in Greeley. The plant also enabled him to slaughter cattle precisely when they peaked. He no longer had to keep feeding them until some plant could take them, and thus kept down his feed costs. Warren told Ken, "I have built a large cattle feeding business, and now it's up to you to build a large packing plant business."

Ken tackled the task with gusto, although when he talked to groups of cattle feeders he used to joke, "Those of you who don't like me because I am a packer should know that my father doesn't like me as a packer either." He had difficulty developing a market for his meat until he brought in Maurice Feldman, a New York City beef salesman who knew the retail beef business intimately and was able to develop good market ties through his contacts in supermarket chains.

Feldman also encouraged Ken to shift to boxed beef production. Traditional packers had shipped whole carcasses or sides of beef that had to be butchered at the retail store, and parts of the carcass were hard to sell. Boxed beef was deboned, trimmed of fat, and cut to the store's specifications at the packing plant. Supermarkets no longer had to employ expensive butchers, and they could buy only the cuts they knew they could sell. Customers could select what they wanted from refrigerated cases, without waiting for a butcher to cut their meat.

Boxed beef production also reduced labor costs at the packing plant, because each worker had to make only the same identical cut on each carcass as it passed, and far less skill was necessary. Many Americans consider packing plant work distasteful and dangerous, as indeed it is, but the plant was able to attract large numbers of cheap willing workers from impoverished areas in Mexico.

The packing plant enabled Monfort to move from commodity production to value-added production. Commodity products are all alike, their prices are erratic, and profits are low. Further processing of commodities adds disproportionately to the value of products that are sold to consumers. The ultimate goal is to produce attractively packaged products with recognized brand names for which consumers will pay a premium, products that are specifically tailored for particular market segments. In some parts of the United States supermarkets sell Monfort branded beef, although it is not nationally distributed.

In 1970, when Warren retired and Ken took over, Monfort opened a 125,000-head feedlot southwest of Greeley, and in 1974 it opened another a few miles to the east. The suburbs of Greeley were creeping ever closer to the old original lot north of town and residents were complaining about its odor and dust. In 1973 Ken became a hero by closing it voluntarily, although he probably would have been forced to close it eventually anyhow. "By 1973," Ken said, "we had saturated the Greeley area, and we had to develop new feedlots and new packing plants in other areas."

The 1970s and '80s were tough years in the beef business. Per capita consumption had started to drop because people were concerned about their health and disappointed in the quality and price of beef. Cattle prices were low, costs were rising, and interest rates were exorbitant. Monfort did not have ready access to the immense amount of operating capital it needed. Ken realized that the operation had grown too big for a family corporation, but it was too small to compete with the big companies, so in 1987 he sold the company that Warren Monfort had founded to ConAgra for $365.5 million. The name has been retained, but the subsequent history of Monfort is a tangled tale of corporate restructurings, mergers, acquisitions, openings, closings, and the like, and corporate ConAgra is so rude and uncivil that it won't let you get anywhere near one of its feedlots. I wonder what it is trying to hide.

Warren Monfort was a quiet and reserved person. He did not talk much, and he had few interests outside the cattle business. He was constantly challenging himself and looking for ways to make more money. Farr said, "He probably would be turning over in his grave if he knew that his grandson had bought a professional baseball team. I don't think Warren even went to the movies!"

"That's probably an exaggeration," Ken retorted, "but he certainly was a very hard worker. He worked constantly, and he was exceptionally good at a lot of things. He was an excellent judge of cattle. He kept better books, accounting-wise. He was good at mechanics; he got the idea of putting screws in the bottoms of the feed trucks to mix the feed. And he was wise enough to hire the smartest people he could find, and strong enough not to be threatened by them."

Earl Brookover

The Colorado Piedmont and the South Platte River valley north of Denver, where Warren Monfort flourished, is still a major cattle-feeding area, but in the early 1960s the center of gravity of cattle feeding in the United States began to shift from the small farm feedlots of the western Corn Belt to huge new commercial feed yards on the southern High Plains (southwestern Kansas and the panhandles of Oklahoma and Texas), an area that was the very heart of the infamous Dust Bowl of the 1930s (fig. 3.1). The new commercial feed yards on the southern High Plains were highly specialized mass-production operations. They bought their feed and concentrated on producing beef. They were large, with a capacity of 20,000 to 50,000 head. Their volume enabled them to prosper with relatively low profit margins per head, and they minimized their overhead costs by operating year-round rather than seasonally.

The new feed yards used the latest technology and they required a high level of management. The small general farmer-feeders in the Corn Belt, who used cattle to market their grain and had other farm business to think about, were not able to compete with the highly skilled professionals who managed the large new feed yards. Today more than half of our beef is produced by fewer than 500 commercial feed yards that market 50,000 head or more a year. Most of these feed yards are in the triangle marked by Denver, Omaha, and Lubbock, Texas, with the greatest concentration on the southern High Plains (fig. 3.2).

Earl C. Brookover, of Garden City, Kansas, was the entrepreneur who initiated the tectonic shift of cattle feeding from the Corn Belt to the southern High

Plains. He was born on a farm forty miles north of Garden City in 1906. After he graduated from Kansas State in 1934, he bought his own farm, raised cattle, and irrigated potatoes. He was fascinated by irrigation, and seized an opportunity to work for the W. R. Grace Company installing irrigation systems on sugar plantations in Peru. When he returned, he became a pioneer in developing irrigation in southwestern Kansas.

Brookover saw the potential for using irrigated crops to feed cattle, and in 1951 he built the first commercial feed yard on the southern High Plains at the northern edge of Garden City. Its initial capacity was 1,500 head; he doubled it to 3,050 by 1953, and the local newspaper marveled at its "huge size," but within a decade he had expanded it to its present capacity of 40,000. The original Brookover feed yard has become pretty much surrounded by the residential growth of Garden City and it probably will have to be relocated eventually, but in 1999 it was still a major urban landmark. Towering above its pens are four enormous grain elevators spanned by a monumental billboard with bold white block letters on a blood-red background adjuring all and sundry to "EAT BEEF KEEP SLIM."

Early irrigators dammed and diverted streams to flood fields, and of neces-

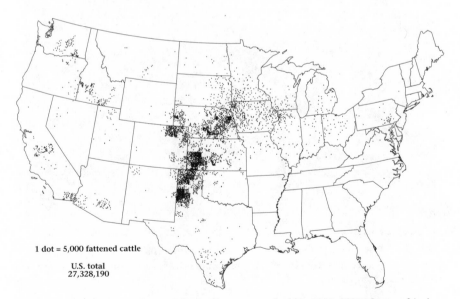

1 dot = 5,000 fattened cattle

U.S. total
27,328,190

Figure 3.1. Cattle fattened on grain and concentrates and sold in 1997. (*1997 Census of Agriculture*, vol. 2, pt. 1 [Washington, D.C.: U.S. Department of Agriculture, National Agricultural Statistics Service, 1999].)

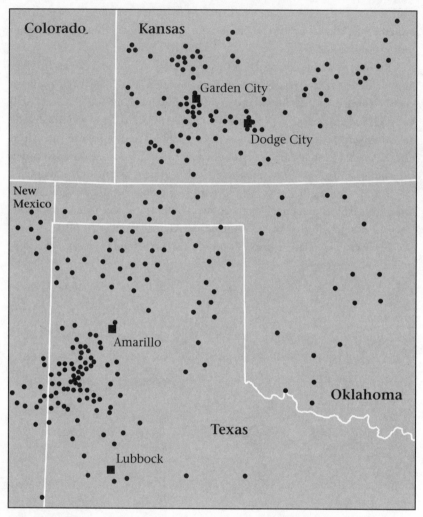

Figure 3.2. Beef cattle feed yards in the Panhandle area, 1997. (Based on data provided by the Texas Cattle Feeders Association, the Kansas Livestock Association, and the Oklahoma Cattlemen's Association.)

sity they were limited to level alluvial bottomlands. The development of deep wells and powerful pumps after World War II enabled them to raise water hundreds of feet from the underlying Ogallala aquifer, and center-pivot sprinkler irrigation systems enabled them to irrigate rolling upland areas where gravity systems will not work. A center-pivot system is a sprinkler-studded aluminum tube that is supported eight feet above the ground by A-shaped towers. Each tower is on wheels, and it moves slightly faster than the next tower closer to the water source at the center. The whole system sweeps slowly in a circle, like the hand of a giant clock, and the towers can climb gentle slopes, so center-pivot systems are not limited to level areas.

Earl Brookover realized that the new technology would work wondrously well in the belt of sand dunes, ten to twenty miles wide, that parallels the south side of the Arkansas River valley, and in 1977 he bought 10,000 acres of sandy ranchland in the dune belt (fig. 3.3). He leveled 6,000 acres, enough to install twenty-one center-pivot irrigation systems, and had corn yields of 230 bushels per acre. He needed fuel for his irrigation pumps, so he became involved, with great success, in developing gas and oil wells. He built a second feed yard with a capacity of 35,000 head in the dune belt.

Brookover was a true visionary. Where most people saw only a sea of sand dunes speckled with sagebrush, he saw a championship golf course, and then he surrounded it with a handsome residential development (fig. 3.4). When he died, in 1985, the Brookover Companies had interests in feed yards, farms, a feed manufacturing company, gas and oil, the golf course, and real estate. His heirs were wise enough to hire professional management, and the Brookover Companies have earned an enviable reputation as an extremely well managed operation.

Like most of the other cattle feeders on the southern High Plains, Brookover operates custom feed yards, which might be described as boardinghouses for other people's cattle. More than 90 percent of the cattle in a Brookover yard actually belong to someone else, and it is feeding them for a fee, but it does keep around 2,500 cattle of its own in a "shelf" program. On the basis of a telephone call it will sell cattle from the shelf to and feed them out for anyone who wants to take a chance on the vagaries of the cattle market. A custom feeder is a specialist who sells knowledge as much as feed. He puts the desired finish on a beef animal for the lowest possible cost. He must be able to judge when the cattle have made their most efficient gain and acquired their desired finish, because thereafter they become more expensive to feed and they make less money for their owner.

Most custom feed yards have a heterogeneous mixture of every conceivable variety and breed of cattle, because the yard is in the business of feeding whatever its customers pay it to feed. This heterogeneity highlights the excessive fragmentation of the cattle industry and the difficulty it will have in trying to produce the consistent product of uniform quality that contemporary consumers demand. Feed yards developed the idea of custom feeding to help them obtain the large-scale financing they needed, because the total financing necessary for 100,000 cattle on feed can easily exceed $50 million. They got an unintended boost from the capital gain and depreciation provisions of federal income tax regulations, which made cattle feeding an attractive tax shelter for nonfarm investors in the 1960s.

Bill Baxter, president of the Brookover Companies, said, "Custom feeding is a highly competitive business, and we have to work hard to keep our yards full.

Figure 3.3. Vertical aerial photograph of the Brookover Ranch beef cattle feed yard, circles of cropland irrigated by center-pivot systems, and unirrigated sand dunes covered with sagebrush. This area is to the right in Figure 3.4. (U.S. Department of Agriculture, National Aerial Photography Program exposure 8965-100, August 11, 1997.)

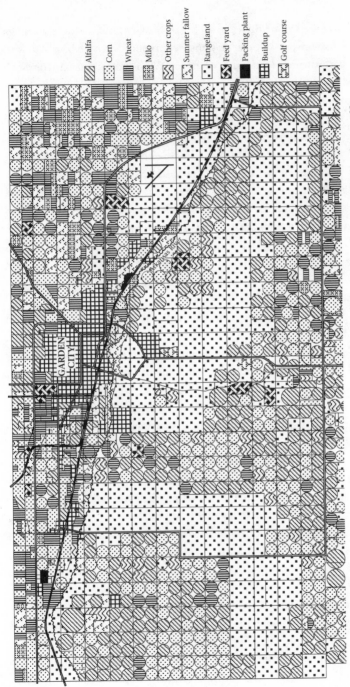

Alfalfa

Corn

Wheat

Milo

Other crops

Summer fallow

Rangeland

Feed yard

Packing plant

Buildup

Golf course

GARDEN CITY

Figure 3.4. Land use near Garden City, Kansas, in 1998. The area shown in Figure 3.3 is to the right center. The Brookover golf course and residential development are three miles west of the feed yard, and the grazing areas are sand dunes too choppy even for center-pivot irrigation systems. (Redrawn from Saito et al., "Changes of Crop Combination Regions and Land Use in the Kansas High Plains," *Science Reports of the Institute of Geoscience, University of Tsukuba*, sec. A, vol. 21 [January 2000], 107–129; used by permission of the Institute of Geoscience, University of Tsukuba, Japan.)

We travel all over the United States in search of business, attend cattle meetings and trade associations, make presentations, set up booths, give talks about feed yards, cattle performance, marketing, whatever. We visit the home farm or ranch and try to get our customers to visit us. Most have been here. We depend a lot on word of mouth and referrals by satisfied customers."

Brookover charges the cost of feed and pen rent of 5 cents per head per day. The company produces much of its feed but has to import corn from Nebraska. Pens vary in capacity from 60 to 500 head, but the ideal size is two truckloads, or 140 animals. Each pen is 150 feet deep and has 10 to 12 inches of feeder bunk space per head. "The typical feeding period is 120 to 150 days," Bill said, "and we try to turn the entire yard around two and a half times a year. We bring them in at six and a half to seven hundred pounds and ship them out at eleven to twelve hundred. We tell the meatpacking companies when we think a pen is ready, and each company sends a buyer to bid on it. We notify the owner when we get a bid we think is good enough, but the owner must decide whether to accept it or to wait and hope for a better one."

During the 1960s many others on the southern High Plains followed Earl Brookover's lead and opened large commercial feed yards, even though cattle feeding is a risky business, and not all of them prospered. Initially they had plenty of local feed because government farm programs had restricted the acreage of cotton and wheat, and many farmers were using their idled land to grow grain sorghum, or milo, a coarse feed grain that is well suited to the dry-land environment. The growing demand for feed and the new technology of irrigation enabled farmers to shift up to corn, which is a better feed than milo but needs more water. The continued growth of feed yards eventually outstripped the ability of the area to produce its own feed, however, and the southern High Plains has become a feed-deficit area that has to buy grain from the Corn Belt.

The growth of feed yards and the increased production of feed grains on the southern High Plains in the 1960s coincided with a dramatic shift in the location of the American meatpacking industry. Interstate highways and refrigerated trucks reduced the cost of shipping processed meat and enabled the industry to move away from the old terminal markets, which were saddled with tradition-bound companies, aging plants, and high labor costs.

Innovative new companies built modern packing plants in rural areas close to the source of fed cattle. Eight new plants increased the processing capacity of the southern High Plains from 0.4 million head in 1960 to 2.6 million head in 1969,[2] and in 1981 IBP opened the world's largest beef packing plant just seven miles west of Earl Brookover's original feed yards in Garden City. The new companies have turned beef packing into one of our most concentrated industries. The Big Four (IBP, Excel, ConAgra, and Farmland) increased their slaughter share 80 percent in 1998.[3] Many older plants are now closed down, and any attempt to revive cattle feeding in the Corn Belt, if one were to be considered seriously, would be enormously handicapped by the lack of processing facilities.

Some of the new packing plants have generated social stress in local communities. The plants are perilous places to work, because the knives and saws that dismember carcasses can slice human flesh just as easily, and blood-drenched floors are slippery, but the companies have controlled their labor costs ruthlessly. Most Americans refuse to work in such dangerous conditions for low wages, so the companies have had to recruit minority and immigrant workers, mostly Hispanic and Southeast Asian. Traditional rural communities often do not know how to deal with people who are so different from themselves, and race-based tension seems inevitable.

The Harris Ranch

After World War II large-scale cattle feeding also spread from the Colorado Piedmont to other irrigated oases in the West. Its spread was fostered by the growth of the population, the increased demand for beef, and the availability of a wide variety of agricultural by-products that could be used for feed. Corn, grain sorghum, and barley were the preferred grains, and alfalfa hay and corn silage were the most desirable roughages, but the cost of feed was such a major factor in the success of feedlots that their operators fed almost anything they could buy cheaply and their cattle were willing to eat.

Cottonseed cake and hulls were staples in the southern oases, as were sugar beet tops and the pulp from which the juice had been extracted in more northerly areas, but even a partial list of feeds that have been used is mind-boggling: surplus raisins, prunes, carrots, and cantaloupes; citrus pulp from juice-concentrating plants; grape pumice from wineries; waste from other vegetable- and fruit-canning plants; grain by-products from bakeries and cereal factories; spent mash from distilleries and breweries; restaurant waste and garbage; blood, bones, viscera, and other slaughterhouse wastes; rendered animals; and litter from broiler houses.

Many oasis feedlots in the West have closed because farmers have shifted up to specialty crops that pay better than feed grains, and these oases are too far from the principal feed-grain-producing areas in the Midwest (fig. 3.1). One of the notable exceptions is the innovative Harris Ranch feedlot northeast of Coalinga, California, which is the largest and most sophisticated cattle-feeding and beef-processing operation on the West Coast. The Harris Ranch is a showplace and has been a leader in developing branded microwaveable beef products.

Jack A. Harris was born in 1914 in west Texas, where his father, Alex, operated a cotton gin.[4] Jack always acted like a good old boy from Texas, even though in 1918 Alex moved his family to the newly developed cotton-producing area in the Imperial Valley of Southern California. There he opened one of the first cotton gins, and he soon opened four more. Back in those days bankers did not lend money to farmers, so farmers had to borrow from the people who processed and marketed their crops. Cotton farmers borrowed from ginners. Then in 1925 the Imperial Valley suffered a severe drought and farmers could not repay their loans, so Alex decided to pull up stakes and move all his equipment and 200 mules north to the Central Valley, first to Tulare, then to Chico, to raise cotton.

At first they were lucky and had hot summers, but Chico really is too cool for cotton, and then in 1937 they were flooded out. Jack called a man near Coalinga who had worked for Alex and told him he needed work. "Come on down," the man said, so Jack loaded his mules and equipment on a train and brought them to Coalinga to try to grow cotton. Jack rented 160 acres of sagebrush and desert shrub that had been good only for grazing sheep and cattle until the recent invention of the centrifugal pump had made the land irrigable. The old sheep rancher who owned it told Jack he would sell it to him cheap if he could make a crop on it, because that would increase the value of his other land, which probably was worth no more than 50 cents an acre.

Jack drilled a 500-foot well that pumped 1,200 gallons a minute, and he talked the pump company into letting him pay for the pump after he had ginned his cotton. When he was not working cotton he worked part-time in the oil fields for extra income. His cotton did so well that he rented 640 acres in 1938, and he spent the rest of his life looking for ways to expand his operation and make more money. By 1945 he was farming 3,000 acres, had built a cotton gin, and was growing cantaloupes as well as cotton.

Not all of his efforts were successful. In 1940 he bought 1,800 feeder pigs to fatten, but hog cholera wiped them out. His only comment in the face of such disaster was, "Well, it looks like we missed this one." Don Devine, senior vice president for finance of the Harris Ranch Feeding Company, said, "I have never known a man with stronger nerves. Nothing bothered him. The money he had to have to run us was tremendous, but it didn't seem to bother him at all. I wouldn't have been able to sleep at night for worrying about it."

In 1951 Jack began buying cotton land in Arizona. He became increasingly exasperated with the government's price support and acreage control program for cotton, and he managed to catch the eye of the national news media when he showed how silly it was. In 1957 he planted 4,600 acres of cotton outside the program, which was perfectly legal, but he was required to pay a penalty of 18 cents a pound. His cost of production was 16 cents a pound, and he sold his crop at the going market price of 34 cents a pound, so he broke even, even though he had to pay a total penalty of $965,595.[5] And those were 1957 dollars, back in the days when the Sunday *New York Times* cost only a quarter.

One of Jack's farms in Arizona had a 4,000-head feedlot, and that might have given him the idea of starting one in California. Don Devine said, "Jack was a sponge, always absorbing new ideas. We always dreaded it when he came back from a trip, because the first thing he would say was, 'Those guys are doing this; how come we're not doing it?'" Jack had an abundance of feed in California, because the water he was pumping was slightly salty, and he had to grow crops that were salt-tolerant. About a quarter of his land was planted to cotton; much of the rest was in barley or wheat, which did not require a lot of water, and in a wet year they needed none at all. Cattle were an efficient way of marketing the grain he had to grow.

In 1964 Jack opened the Harris Ranch feedlot with a capacity of 10,000 head, but almost immediately he realized that it was too small to capture the economies of scale he desired, so within a decade he had expanded it to its present capacity of 100,000 head. Don Devine said, "Jack was the epitome of an entrepreneur. He was not a sophisticated businessman by today's standards, but he had an instinctive understanding of what it took to make things work. He just had a great sense of what needed to be done, and he was right more often than he was wrong."

In 1974 he realized that he needed to build his own slaughterhouse near the feedlot. A bluff old boy named "Red" Diamond, who was a lot like Jack, came over and said to him, "Why are you going to spend all that money to build a slaughterhouse? Hell, I've got one in Selma that I'll sell you. You get the plant, and you also get the customers and the trained employees." So Jack bought it. Later he had to enlarge it, but it worked just fine. Don suggested that they change the name from Diamond to Harris, but Jack said not to bother. "I won't say Jack was modest," Don said, "because he really wasn't, but he just didn't feel any need to have his name plastered over everything he owned. He was just as comfortable sitting around a campfire bullshittin' with the cowboys as he was with the most important people in the world, and it wasn't an act, either. He was just comfortable with himself, and he could be at home with anybody. He was real."

Jack's dislike for government subsidy programs definitely did not extend to huge subsidies for irrigation projects. He and other big growers pressured state and federal legislators to construct an enormous irrigation canal, the California Aqueduct, to bring fresh water from Northern California to the semiarid western side of the San Joaquin Valley, site of the Harris Ranch. The whole farming system changed when the federal water project was completed in the late 1960s. Farmers could grow fruit and vegetable crops that were more valuable than grain, and feedlots had to cope with declining grain supplies just when large packers in the East were starting to ship boxed beef to the West. Most California feeders and packers went out of business, but Jack Harris persisted, and in 1998 his feedlot finished 250,000 cattle, one-third of the total for the entire state.

The Harris Ranch feedlot used local barley and wheat on a seasonal basis, but for nine or ten months of the year it got feed from the Midwest in 110-car unit trains. It used local alfalfa, but corn accounted for three-quarters of its feed costs. It bought cattle mainly from California, Nevada, and Oregon at a weight of 500 to 800 pounds and fed them to a weight of 1,100 pounds. "On average," said Don, "we feed 120 to 130 days, but it depends on the price of grain and the cattle market, and it changes every year. What works this year doesn't work next year. Agriculture is not a business you can do with a lot of MBAs working for you. They're gonna calculate return on investment and income growth and revenue growth and all that kind of thing, but agriculture just does not produce a steady flow of earnings. It's a commodity business that does not lend itself to the way corporations are run now.

"For example," he explained, "beef generates about 75 percent of our gross income, but it can vary from 90 percent to negative." In addition to its beef operation, the Harris Ranch had 15,000 acres of cropland in 1998. Cotton was the key crop, and the ranch had its own cotton gin, but it produced thirty-three different crops, including field grains (barley and wheat), fruits and nuts (almonds, oranges, lemons, apples, olives, peaches, plums, and walnuts), wine and table grapes, cantaloupes, and vegetables (lettuce, tomatoes, garlic, onions, and broccoli). The ranch also had an operation that bred and boarded thoroughbred racehorses, because the Harris family loves horses.

In 1975 Jack Harris saw another opportunity when Interstate 5, the principal north-south highway on the West Coast, was completed across the western corner of his ranch. This stretch of I-5 passes through a sparsely populated area with few services, so Jack bought an 80-acre parcel at the closest interchange and developed an attractive motel and a restaurant that serves 2,000 meals a day. The restaurant is a wonderful showcase for Harris Ranch branded beef products, and it provides valuable customer feedback.

Jack Harris died in 1981, and his son, John, took over the business. "We only process 750 cattle a day," John said in 1998. "We realized that we were too small to complete with plants that produced three or four thousand, but we saw a lot of niches we could fill. We knew we could not produce the cheapest beef, so we decided to produce better beef, and to put the Harris Ranch name on it. We produce branded beef, and we guarantee its quality and consistency. We have become strongly service-oriented and customer-oriented."

Dave Wood, chairman of the beef division, added, "The beef industry has not produced a consistent product that has given the customer a pleasant experience. We guarantee our product. A customer who has had a bad experience can take it back to the retailer, and we guarantee to replace it one hundred percent, no questions asked, but we do try to find out whether it was miscooked, mishandled, or just a bad piece of meat.

"We needed a different mind-set," he said. "We had to become consumer-driven, not production-driven. We had to stop thinking about what we wanted to feed and to start thinking about our customers, the retailers and the restaurateurs, and about what they could sell that their customers would want to continue buying." In the early 1990s retailers were becoming concerned that they were losing their market to fast-food outlets and chains of family restaurants, so the Harris Ranch began to develop a line of "home replacement meals," fully cooked entrées ready to pop into the microwave and eat in seven minutes. Dave explained, "At four-thirty in the afternoon 75 percent of Americans don't know what they are going to fix for dinner, but they want to spend less than fifteen minutes fixing it."

John added, "In the beef-packing business you need to sell all the cuts. Some are undervalued, and using them in precooked items allows us to make them more valuable." In 1998 *Beef* magazine awarded its prestigious annual Trailblazer Award to John and Dave for their efforts in bringing microwaveable beef products to the marketplace.

The Harris Ranch must have feeder calves of consistent quality in order to produce beef of consistent quality, and it works closely with ranchers to help them upgrade their herds. It has identified the genetic traits in beef bulls that result in calves that are ideal for the consumer and work well for the rancher. It encourages ranchers to buy the right kinds of bulls, and it pays a premium price for their calves. In 1998 it was using only Angus bulls, because the Angus Association was the only beef breed association that had adequate carcass data.

The Harris Ranch, with its emphasis on consistency and quality, might well serve as a model for the beef industry, which originally led the way to modern, large-scale animal agriculture but now has been left in the lurch by other kinds of livestock because it is too fragmented to produce beef of the consistent quality that consumers can depend on and are willing to pay for. Beef has disappointed too many people too many times.

W. D. Farr said, "Beef is the Cadillac of foods, but we have too many mixed breeds, too many mongrel cattle. We have 104 breeds of cattle, and we probably don't need more than about four. We need controlled breeding for consistent quality. Most ranchers know nothing about beef or the dressed carcass. All they've ever done is sell live animals, and they have this fixation that everybody is an enemy unless they are raising cattle."

The entire beef industry is based on a philosophy of independence, and cattle ranching is the last redoubt of rugged individualism in the United States. Ranchers are fiercely independent and almost ferociously far to the right politically. "You've got a million cow/calf producers in this country," said Don Devine, "and you're lucky if you can get even three of them to agree on anything, much less a million."

Small producers in the East who have fewer than 100 cows produce half of the calves born in the United States, and meatpackers have no effective way of telling them what the consumer wants because the price of cattle is based on their live weight rather than on their quality, so producers have no incentive to produce quality calves. A better pricing system would be based on the quality and the yield (percentage of edible meat) of the carcass, but cattlemen have been reluctant to accept it. Government inspectors determine the quality of a carcass, and that's fine, but the packer determines the yield grade, and ranchers and feeders know for sure that the packers adjust the yield grades to their own advantage.

The beef industry has also failed to educate consumers about how to buy beef. People want beef that is tender and tasty, but they refuse to buy it when they see it. The best prime beef is well marbled. It has streaks of fat running through it. Some people refuse to buy it because they think it is "too fat," and they are worried about cholesterol. Others balk at the price, and cattlemen have learned that it does not pay to produce it.

Fragmentation also has hampered the efforts of the industry to promote beef consumption, even though $1 goes into a check-off fund to promote beef every time an animal is sold. "Some guy from Podunk, Nebraska," said Dave Wood, "who markets maybe three hundred cattle a year, will complain, 'Whatever happened to all my check-off money? I ain't never seen nothin' on TV.' You try to explain to him that Podunk, Nebraska, is not our market. Our market is Los Angeles, San Francisco, New York, Boston. A lot of these ranchers are really wonderful people, but they don't come in to town very often."

Better integration of the beef industry, no matter how desirable it might be, probably is a long way off, both because of the enormous amounts of additional capital that would be necessary and because cow/calf production requires such extensive acreage that it offers few significant economies of scale for operations with more than about fifty cows. The quality of beef probably will remain inconsistent and beef probably will continue to lose its share of the consumer's meat dollar, which dropped from 48 percent in 1975 to 32 percent in 1997.[6]

Many former feed yards west of the Rockies have closed down because oasis farmers have shifted up to the production of specialty cash crops that pay far better returns than feed grains, and the Harris Ranch is the last remaining large beef cattle feed yard in California. Warren Monfort was the entrepreneur who developed the first large modern feed yard on the Colorado Piedmont north of Denver, but in 2002 the greatest concentration of feed yards was on the southern High Plains of southwest Kansas and the panhandles of Oklahoma and Texas, where Earl Brookover pioneered large-scale cattle feeding based on crops produced by deep-well irrigation. Even the southern High Plains have become a feed-deficit area, and feed yards must ship in corn and soybeans from the Corn Belt.

4

Dairying from Farm to Dry Lot

The traditional dairy belt of the United States reaches across the northern tier of states, from Minnesota and Wisconsin eastward to New England.[1] During the nineteenth century dairy farming followed the wheat frontier westward across these states. Wheat was an especially important pioneer crop in three areas, each of which later became a major dairy area. The first was the Genesee country of western upstate New York. The second was the "backbone counties" in northeastern Ohio, so called because they were the height of land between streams flowing north to Lake Erie and those flowing south to the Ohio River. The third, largest, and ultimately most important area was southern Wisconsin and Minnesota.

Wheat was the principal source of income for the first farmers in these areas and livestock was secondary, although most farms had a flock of chickens, a pen of hogs, and a few milk cows. The farmer turned the cows loose to graze the natural grass pastures and fed them as little as possible. For most of the year the cows did not produce much milk, but in spring and summer, when the grass grew lush, they produced more than the family could drink, and the women and girls of the farm had the task of preserving the surplus by making it into cheese or butter in the farmhouse kitchen.

They put rennet, the lining membrane from a calf's stomach, in milk to co-agulate it into thick curds and watery whey. They salted, molded, and cured the curds to make cheese, and they fed the whey to the hogs. They also fed the hogs the thin milk that remained after they had skimmed off the thick cream to make butter. They agitated the cream in a churn until it coagulated into globules of but-ter, which they removed with a wooden paddle, salted to keep it from spoiling, and packed in wooden kegs. Some people liked to drink the thick buttermilk re-maining in the churn, which still contained small blobs of butter, but others fed it to their hogs.

In the early days the farm wife bartered cheese, butter, eggs, lard, and other surplus farm products for groceries at the crossroads country store, but farmers became more interested in butter and cheese when their wheat yields began to plummet. Continuous cultivation of the crop had depleted the soil of the nutrients wheat needs, and it had also fostered a variety of insects and diseases that gorge on wheat. Normally farmers would have expected the price of wheat to rise when production declined, but actually the price dropped, because farmers on the next wheat frontier farther west had already started to flood the market with their crop.

Some farmers gave up, sold their farms, and moved west. Those who stayed had to adopt a new farming system that was based on the Corn Belt system but adapted to the dual environmental constraints of glacial topography and short cool summers. The youthful glacial topography has extensive areas that are too poorly drained or too steep to be cultivated successfully, but such land can sup-port good pasture. Summers north of the Corn Belt are too short and too cool to ripen corn, a subtropical plant, into grain, so farmers had to harvest the entire plant for fodder when it was still green.

Pasture and fodder crops cannot fatten cattle and hogs, but they can sustain dairy cows, and farmers north of the Corn Belt began to specialize in producing milk, even though they were well aware of the relentless drudgery of dairy farm-ing. A dairy cow produces so much milk that the farmer must relieve her every twelve hours, seven days a week, fifty-two weeks a year, with never even one day off, much less a vacation. As dairy cows became more important, farmers realized that they needed a new and better kind of barn.

Traditional barns on wheat farms had been hollow rectangular shells with large double doors on either side that led to a transverse floor where wheat was threshed. Farmers never allowed animals in the barn, even in the worst weather, because it was used only for threshing, but they realized that their dairy cows needed shelter. Eventually some clever farmer in the Genesee country of upstate New York got the bright idea of jacking up his barn and building a solid masonry ground floor beneath it for his cows. This novel two-level barn, with livestock on the ground floor beneath a huge hollow loft that held hay for their winter feed, became the standard barn of the dairy belt.

Farmers near railroads could ship fresh milk to urban markets, but milk spoils quickly, and few milksheds extended out more than one hundred miles or so. Comedians joked about poky milk trains, which seemed to stop every few miles to pick up cans of fresh milk. Many city people still got their milk from town dairies, whose owners kept a few cows in sheds behind their houses. Most notorious was the shed in which Mrs. O'Leary's cow allegedly kicked over a lantern and started the great fire that destroyed much of Chicago in 1871, but all cities had many small dairies.

Farmers beyond the urban milkshed had to process their milk into butter and cheese, which make less money than fresh milk but have a far longer shelf life. Farmhouse kitchens began to get too cramped as production increased, and the quality of farmhouse butter and cheese often left much to be desired, so groups of farmers formed cooperatives to build and operate creameries for making butter and cheese. They set a pattern of cooperative marketing that still persists in dairy areas, and the tradition of cooperation has carried over into the political arena, where dairy groups have been singularly effective, perhaps too effective for their own good.

Around 1900 dairy farmers in Wisconsin started to harvest their corn as silage, which they could feed their cows in winter, when milk prices were highest, instead of feeding corn as dry fodder in summer, when prices were lowest. They cut off the entire plant before the grain had ripened, chopped it into pieces no larger than your little finger, and blew them into a tall cylindrical silo. Concrete silos towering over two-level barns with large haylofts above masonry ground floors for livestock have become the hallmarks of traditional dairy areas in Wisconsin. Since World War II farmers have added blue metal silos to the dairy landscape. These silos are lined with glass, which makes them airtight, so they keep corn silage and hay crops fresh and succulent, but they cost far more than conventional concrete silos.

By 1920 Wisconsin had passed New York to become the nation's leading dairy state, and it held first rank until California passed it in 1997. Traditional dairy farms in the Midwest remained small, because farmers could grow enough corn and alfalfa on 80 to 120 acres to feed twelve to sixteen cows, and that was all they could milk by hand, even if they had large families to help them. They liked to keep their farmsteads looking nice, with neatly mowed lawns, bright beds of flowers, and handsome name signs, because they could rarely be away from them for more than a few hours at a time.

Dairy farms were so small that the better dairy farming areas were densely populated, with six to eight farmsteads per square mile. They were served by dense networks of paved roads to enable the milk truck to get to each farm every day, no matter what the weather. The dense rural population supported a closely spaced system of small market towns and villages, and dairy farming areas had an air of complacent prosperity.

Dairy farming began to change when plant breeders developed new varieties of corn that yielded more and matured earlier. Heavier yields enable dairy farmers to fill their silos from only half as much land as they once had needed, and earlier maturity allowed them to wait safely for the rest of their corn to ripen into grain. Short-season corn has allowed some farmers in the southern part of dairy country to get rid of their cows and sell all of their corn for cash, but their farms are so small that they have had to supplement their income by taking off-farm jobs. Some of them run small herds of beef cattle, which are far less work than dairy cattle, but they produce less than one-tenth as much income as dairy cows.

In the 1940s many dairy farmers remodeled their barns to install pipeline milking machines and to make stalls for more cows. A milking machine looks like an octopus, with four long rubber arms and a suction cup at the end of each arm. The farmer carries a milking machine to each cow, attaches a suction cup to each of the cow's four teats, and clamps the other end of the machine to an overhead pipeline. The pipeline has a partial vacuum that gently sucks the milk out of each teat and carries it to the milkhouse, where it is cooled and stored until the tank truck comes to collect it. Milking machines enabled dairy farmers to expand their herds to forty to sixty cows.

Dairy cows are mammals and, like all other female mammals, they produce milk to nourish their offspring. A cow does not start to give milk until she has a calf, when she is said to be "fresh." Modern dairy cows, paradoxically, are such high-powered milk-producing organisms that they produce enough milk to strangle their calves. The calf needs the first flush of colostrum, which has high protein content and antibodies essential for its immunity, but then the farmer must remove it from its mother and feed it by hand. Dairy farmers keep their best calves and raise them to replace older cows that are worn out. The other female calves and all of the male calves have little value, except possibly for veal, and dairy farmers get rid of them in any way they can.

Dairy cows have a 283-day gestation period, and farmers try to keep them in nearly constant production by breeding them 60 to 90 days after they come fresh. Once farmers used bulls, but dairy bulls are notoriously mean and dangerous, and now most dairy farmers use artificial insemination, which has greatly improved the quality of their herds, because they can buy frozen semen from much better bulls than they can afford to buy and maintain.

The cow's milk production eventually begins to tail off, and after a standard 305-day lactation period the farmer stops milking her to "dry her off," cuts back on her feed to keep her from getting too fat, and gives her two months to rest before she has her next calf. After four or five lactation periods she is pretty well worn out, so the farmer gets rid of her and replaces her with a young heifer. A farmer milking fifty cows normally also has to feed eight to ten dry cows and twelve to twenty-five replacement heifers, even though not one of them is bringing in as much as a single penny.

Dairy farmers in the Midwest have been slowly pushing up the size of their herds and their milk yields. The average size of a milking herd in Wisconsin, for example, increased from around twenty cows in 1960 to around forty in 1980 and to around sixty in 2000, while the average milk yield per cow for a standard 305-day lactation went from 8,000 pounds in 1960 to 12,300 pounds in 1980 and 17,000 pounds in 2000.[2] In 2000 the best dairy cows were producing more than 30,000 pounds per lactation, or nearly 100 pounds a day, but good dairy farmers are quick to remind you that high yields alone are no guarantee of high profits if the cost of producing them is too high, and their goal is to keep their cost per pound as low as possible.

Dairy farmers are sensitive to changing American tastes in consumption of their products. We have been shifting from whole milk to low-fat milk or even to soft drinks, and from ice cream to yogurt, because we are worried about our bulging waistlines. We have been buying less butter and more margarine, which is cheaper, but at least we are eating more cheese, especially mozzarella on pizzas. Not too long ago poor transportation restricted urban milksheds, and in more distant areas many small crossroads creameries made butter and cheese, but now most milk goes to large central plants that process it into fluid milk, butter, cheese, or whatever product the market demands that day.

The milk processors are important, because they are the key to the dairy price support program. In the early days dairy farmers were whipsawed by seasonal fluctuations in the price of milk, which was high in fall and winter, when their production was low, but they could hardly give their milk away in spring and summer, when their pastures were green and their production was high. In 1937 they finally exercised their political muscle and secured passage of a law that has been the basis for the price support program ever since, although Congress has rarely been able to resist the temptation to tweak it and tinker with it and treat it like a political soccer ball.

The dairy price support program is extremely complicated, and it is indirect, because dairy farmers get their monthly milk checks from the processing company, not from the government. The processors sell as much fresh milk as they can, and convert the rest into butter, cheese, powdered milk, and other storable products. If they cannot sell these products, the government buys enough of the surplus to enable the processors to pay farmers the guaranteed minimum price.

The dairy price support program divides the United States into areas of highly variable size that, for some obscure reason, are called "milk marketing orders." The minimum price of milk is the same throughout each order. The national minimum price is based on the cost of producing milk near Eau Claire, Wisconsin, which had the lowest cost of production in 1937, when the program began, and the minimum price in each order is sufficiently higher to cover the cost of shipping milk from Eau Claire by train. Tanker truck transport has rendered this pricing system completely obsolete, but everyone seems reluctant to change it for fear they will be worse off if it is modernized.

The federal milk price support program has cosseted traditional dairy farmers in the Midwest in a comfortable cocoon and given them a false sense of security. They are cautious and conservative, risk-averse and reluctant to change. The monthly milk check has been a steady, reliable source of income. They hardly noticed the "farm crisis" of the early 1980s in the Corn Belt areas south of them, and they pretty much ignored the revolution in the technology of dairying that began brewing near Los Angeles after World War II, and thence has spread to other parts of the country. When they have become aware of it they have claimed that the price support program has given an unfair advantage to milk producers in distant parts of the country, whereas in fact these producers have become intensely competitive because they have become more efficient and reduced their costs of production.

Before World War II more than two thousand small dairies produced milk for the residents of the Los Angeles area (fig. 4.1).[3] Many had no more than eight or ten cows in a shed behind the house on a residential lot. They bought all of their feed, and family members milked the cows by hand. They bottled and sold the milk directly to customers. Some had regular home delivery routes, and some had drive-in cash-and-carry sales outlets next to the street in front of the house. Some of these small dairy stores also stocked bread, butter, cheese, and other convenience items.

Larger dairies, with 50 to 100 cows, were at the edge of the built-up area, where land was relatively cheap and taxes were lower. The two principal clusters were in then-remote agricultural areas, one near Artesia and Norwalk in southern Los Angeles County and northern Orange County, the other some forty miles inland in the Chino Valley at the southwestern tip of San Bernardino County (fig. 4.1). Nearly all the dairymen in these areas were recent immigrants from Holland or the Azores.

The dairymen near Artesia specialized in producing large amounts of milk on small acreages. They bought all their feed and used all their land for the un-

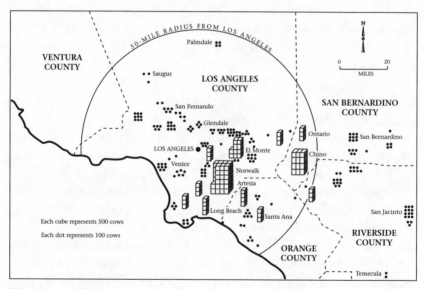

Figure 4.1. In 1930 the Los Angeles milkshed had many small dairies. After World War II the industry concentrated near Artesia until residential development forced it to migrate to Chino. (Redrawn from L. B. Fletcher and C. O. McCorkle Jr., *Growth and Adjustment of the Los Angeles Milkshed: A Study in the Economics of Location,* Bulletin 787, California Agricultural Experiment Station, 1962.)

paved corrals where they kept their cows. Their principal roughage was rectangular bales of alfalfa hay, which they trucked in from irrigated oases in the desert and stacked in piles twenty to thirty feet high beside the corrals.

Artesia is near the port at Long Beach, which was convenient for importing copra from the Philippines and other concentrated feed for the cows. Martin Verhoeven, whose father had a dairy near Artesia, said, "We used to think you couldn't dairy without coconut meal, but World War II put a stop to that in a hurry, and we found we could feed a lot of different things, like grain, cottonseed, orange pulp, sugar beet pulp, and almond hulls from California, and corn from the Midwest.

"The war also forced my father to put in a milking machine in 1943," Martin added, "because labor was scarce and he couldn't find anyone to milk by hand." He was on three different places, each one a little bit bigger than the previous one, because, like the other dairymen in the area, he needed to keep increasing the size of his herd to increase his milk production and to reduce his overhead costs per cow.

After World War II the Artesia area was the beneficiary of the first great relocation of dairies in Greater Los Angeles. The explosive growth of residential subdivisions put enormous pressure on small neighborhood operations. New residents complained about their flies, odors, and unsightly manure heaps. Taxes on dairies were escalating rapidly to pay for municipal improvements that they did not want and did not need. Zoning regulations would not allow them to make necessary improvements, but they could not maintain required health standards with outdated facilities and equipment.

Small neighborhood dairy operators saw the handwriting on the wall, so they sold their properties to developers for handsome prices. Some retired, but farmers had to pay heavy capital gains taxes on their windfall profits if they did not reinvest them in agricultural enterprises, and many younger dairymen moved to the Artesia area, where they developed large new state-of-the-art facilities. The loss of farmland to urban encroachment actually rejuvenated the dairy business, because it provided a massive infusion of urban capital.

The new dairies in the Artesia area became models of efficient large-scale production that have been emulated by modern dairies everywhere else. They concentrated on producing milk, shooting for the highest production per cow and the lowest cost per gallon, and they depended on others to produce their feed. They needed no cropland, and became known as dry-lot dairies because they kept their cows in unpaved corrals with abundant feed and water but not so much as a single blade of grass. Many did have a small patch of pasture, but it was only a settling area for disposal of washwater from the milking barn.

One of the biggest headaches of a dry-lot dairy is what to do with all the manure that the well-fed cows keep producing. Traditional farmers spread manure on their cropland as an excellent fertilizer, but dry-lot dairies had no cropland, and some of them just stacked it up until they could pay someone to haul it away. At one time a manure stockpile near Artesia contained more than 400,000 cubic yards of the stuff, which is more than enough to fill a football stadium to overflowing.[4]

The corrals were separated by paved lanes for walking the cows to and from the milking barn twice a day and for the trucks that automatically unloaded feed on the pavement alongside the corral as they drove slowly down the lane. The corral was fenced with vertical metal stanchions through which the cows could poke their heads to eat. Some sets of stanchions had headlocks that could be levered shut to hold the cows firmly in place when they had to be inspected or treated. Down the middle of the corral were north-south shades of flat corrugated metal where the cows could take shelter from the heat of the midday sun, and close by were enormous stacks of rectangular hay bales under peaked metal roofs supported by long slender poles.

The heart of a dry-lot dairy was the milking barn. In traditional flat barns milkers had to lug an awkward milking machine to each cow, attach it, and remove it, tasks that required an inordinate amount of lifting, bending, and stooping. The development of the double-herringbone milking parlor probably did more than any other innovation to facilitate the evolution of modern large-scale dairies. Milking 100 cows a day in a traditional flat barn was a full-time job, but a milker in a parlor can easily handle 500 cows a day or more.

Down the middle of a milking parlor is a pit three feet deep in which the milkers stand upright and do not need to bend and kneel. Milking machines are permanently installed along each side of the pit. The cows walk into the parlor on the upper level at either side and back into the milking stalls, which are angled herringbone-wise to the pit. Early milking parlors were double-fours, with four stalls on either side, but double twenty-fours and larger have become common.

The milker standing in the pit deftly attaches and removes the milking cups. A pipeline carries the milk to the tank in which it is cooled and stored until the truck comes to collect it. The entire operation is computerized. Each cow has attached to her neck or ankle a transponder that electronically records the amount of milk she has given.

Technological innovations enabled dairymen near Artesia to expand their herds, and the minimal size for a viable dairy was 250 to 300 cows on 20 acres. The area that had initially seemed so remote almost immediately began to feel the pressure of the rapid population growth of Greater Los Angeles. In 1956 three communities near Artesia actually incorporated as the municipalities of Dairyland, Dairy Valley, and Dairy City, with 75,000 cows and 6,000 people on 11,500 acres of land, in an attempt to keep people out and to preserve the land for dairying (fig. 4.2).

These places hoped to keep taxes down because dairies did not need such urban niceties as sewers, sidewalks, and street lights, but property taxes in Dairy Valley rose from $19.25 an acre in 1951 to $277.50 an acre in 1965, and those who had bought land for $10,000 to $20,000 an acre in the 1950s were selling it to developers for $50,000 to $60,000 an acre in 1970. Pressures for urban development triggered the second great relocation of dairies in Greater Los Angeles. By 1980 Dairy Valley had changed its name to Cerritos, Dairy City was Cypress, and Dairyland was La Palma. They had a combined population of 109,000 people but no dairy cows, because all the dairies had relocated, mainly to the Chino Valley.

By the time it had reached its peak in the early 1990s, the 19,000-acre Chino Valley dairy area could boast that it had the most awesome assemblage of dairy cows the world has ever known.[5] In 1992 it had 308,743 cows on 379 dairies, an average of 815 cows per farm, 16 cows per acre (fig. 4.3). Chino dairymen strove for ever-larger operations, higher-yielding cows, and low costs of production. They fed all the concentrates the cows' stomachs could digest, and their milk production per cow was close to double the national average. The construction of freeways reduced their transport costs for feed to and milk from the area, and Chino spawned an impressive array of feed dealers and other ancillary businesses to serve its needs.

Arlen van Leeuwen's father grew up on a dairy farm in Holland, came to California when he was 16, worked for a while on a dairy farm near Tulare, then moved to Artesia, married a Dutch girl, and started his own dairy with twenty-five to thirty cows on eighteen acres. At first the two of them did all the work, but during World War II they expanded to sixty cows and could afford to hire a helper. By 1958, however, Arlen said, "the place was too small. The houses around the side would catch our runoff water every time it rained, there was a high school across the street, and a restaurant and a market on the other side. Dad was feeling a lot of pressure, the land had appreciated enough that it was worth a pretty good piece of money, and it was financially feasible, so he decided to move here to Chino.

"Why did he pick Chino? His milk marketing association served this area as

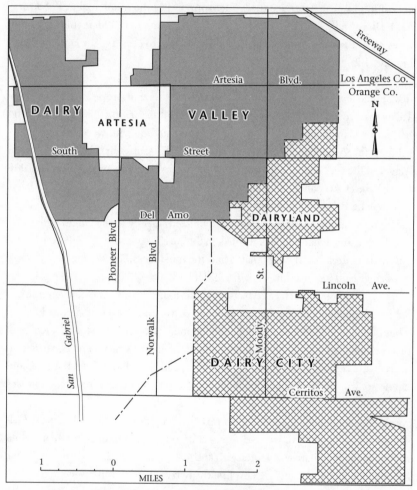

Figure 4.2. Incorporated dairy areas, Los Angeles and Orange counties. Three cities south-east of Los Angeles incorporated in a futile attempt to preserve themselves as dairy farming areas. (Courtesy of the Association of American Geographers. Fielding, Gordon J., 1962. *The Professional Geographer*, p. 13.)

well as Artesia. A lot of family and friends had come out here already, and there was a whole sense of community. A real big factor was church and school. He and Mom wanted to send us kids to a Christian school. The Dutch Reformed Church had started one here. They have had to open it up beyond the smaller community to make it work, because people don't have as many kids as they used to, but they still pick their teachers from colleges that are affiliated with the church."

Martin Verhoeven added, "The Dutch Reformed are very devout people. On Sundays we only do the minimal. I can remember we always ate cold meals on Sundays because my mom prepared them on Saturday so she wouldn't have to cook on the Sabbath, and Dad always shaved Saturday night to avoid having to shave on Sunday."

Arlen's father was milking 300 cows in a flat barn when he first moved to Chino, but when Arlen came into business with him in 1973 they remodeled the barn into a double-ten parlor and started milking 450 cows with two hired milkers. In 1998 they had built up to 800, where they were maxed out, and kept the barn busy pretty much around the clock. Three workers did the milking, a fourth worked outside on feeding, a fifth moved the cows and helped the milkers, a sixth raised the baby calves, and a part-time veterinarian also bred the cows.

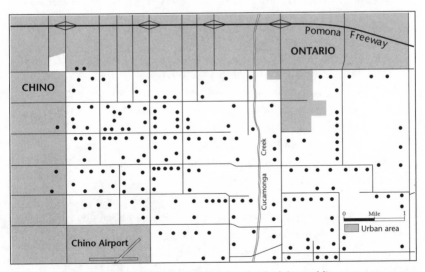

Figure 4.3. In 1997 the Chino Valley, east of Los Angeles, had the world's greatest concentration of dairy cows. Each dot represents one dairy; the average dairy had 880 cows. (Used by permission of Joel Splansky.)

Arlen fed the cows a veritable smorgasbord of "commodities," which is what dairymen call concentrated feeds such as rolled corn, canola meal, wheat bran, corn gluten, cottonseed, sugar beet pulp, and almond hulls. He contracted with a feed dealer for anywhere from three to twelve months, and the dealer brought a load and dumped it in Arlen's commodity barn whenever he needed it, so it was always fresh. He bought some alfalfa hay directly from a farmer in the Imperial Valley and some from one of the hay dealers who hauled it in by the truckload to the sales lots for baled hay that dot the Chino dairy area.

A man who does some farming took away the manure, and Arlen paid him 50 cents a ton for the privilege. The back part of Arlen's land, which does not have corrals, was a disposal area for washwater from the milking barn. He had to put dry cows on it for a week or so just to keep down the weeds. "Dad thought this place was great when he bought it," he said, "because there's enough slope that rainwater just runs off into the creek. You wouldn't even dare to think that way anymore, and we have had to retrofit the place by building retaining ponds to hang on to the water."

The creek is at the headwaters of the Santa Ana River, which flows westward through Orange County. The county plans to raise its flood control dam on the river, which will flood Arlen's property, so in 1997 the county bought it from him and gave him a lease to stay on it for seven years. "We can leave any time we want," he said, "but the plan is to stay here for seven years and then probably retire, even though I will be only sixty, because neither of our two children want to dairy.

"We can't stay in Chino. The dairies moved out here in the fifties and sixties, they are all thirty to forty years old, they are small in acreage, there's a lot of urban pressure, and the land is becoming expensive, so they are moving out again. There's no future for dairy here. A new dairy that milks 800 cows would probably cost $2 to $3 million, but today you can't build a place and milk only 800 cows, because the overhead's too high. A lot of them that are moving are building much larger than that, and they also need hundreds of acres of land because of new regulations on water and manure and those kinds of things."

In 1998 Lewis Aukeman was already half-packed and getting ready to leave. His father immigrated to this country from the Netherlands, and by 1958 he had worked up to a 100-cow dairy farm, which was big back in those days, in a Dutch area in Michigan. That was the year Lew came to Chino to visit two of his uncles, and he never went back to Michigan. He started milking eighty cows on a twenty-acre place. He had one helper and they did the whole thing, feeding, milking, everything.

Then he thought it sure would be nice if he got a little bigger, say 120 cows, so he could have two guys working and he could do the relief work. Then pretty soon it was 160 cows, then 200, then pipeline milking machines came in, so he kept growing, and by 1977 he was milking 400. Then the developers showed up.

"When I came here in '58," he said, "there was not even talk of a freeway, only the 10 freeway up in Upland. Then they built the 60 freeway, and I was only a quarter of a mile from that. Then the developers were there, so I sold the place and bought this 65 acres, where I am milking 1,500. Then they built the 15 freeway, and the developers are offering $100,000 an acre, even more near the freeway, so I sold the place, and in another year I'll be gone. My 65 acres and my neighbor's 38 acres have been approved already for 413 houses, and the prices on 'em start at $200,000."

Lew said that half of the dairymen who sell their land in Chino are moving north in California, to Bakersfield, Tulare, even as far as Modesto. A quarter are moving out of state to Idaho, Arizona, New Mexico, or Texas, and the other quarter are retiring. Arlen van Leeuwen said, "We have looked at New Mexico and Arizona, more out of curiosity than anything else. In Texas the combination of heat and high humidity is too hard on the cows. If we moved I think we would pick an area in California. We are too soft, and we like the California lifestyle."

Lew Aukeman said, "I am 72 years old, and I would be hanging it up myself if I didn't have my son in with me. We are going up north, where my other son is already milking 800 near Tulare. I am buying land for $3,000 an acre, but it will cost three and a half to four million bucks for facilities just to milk these same cows. What we do here on 65 acres you need at least 400 there just to spread the manure and the excess water."

In 1998 Ron Verhoeven had not decided what he was going to do. His father, Martin, moved from Artesia to Chino in 1955. Martin rented for ten years, but in 1965 he built his present place for 540 cows on twenty acres. Ron has a dairy in Chino, another son has one in the Central Valley, two sons-in-law also have dairies, and "I've only got one maverick son-in-law," said Martin. "He's a cabinetmaker."

Ron moved to his present place in 1997 because urban sprawl was going to take over the one he had. This one came up for rent because its owner had just built a 3,000-cow dairy near Tulare. This place was larger and more modern, and it gave Ron a chance to expand from 600 to 900 cows. He wanted to expand because his son, Dennis, had just graduated from school and started working with him.

Ron said that a reasonable rent for the place, which has twenty acres of corrals and twenty acres of pasture for spreading waste washwater from the milking barn, would be $9 to $15 per cow per month. He has first option to buy it if the owner ever wants to sell it, but it would lock him out of any future growth, because he already has as many cows on it as he can get and still be environmentally safe.

Ron had to buy cows for around $1,500 a head when he expanded, but he prefers to raise his own replacements. He sends his newborn heifers to a specialized local nursery for four months, and then they go to a specialized replacement heifer raising ranch, with a capacity of 16,000 head, amidst the hay fields of the Imperial Valley. "Two or three weeks before they're gonna calve we bring 'em back here where we can keep an eye on 'em. We keep 'em in those maternity pens over there."

Suddenly his voice rose. "Hey, there's a cow having a calf right now! Just to the right of the first pole under that shade you'll see a black cow facing that way with a calf hanging out of her. Looks like she needs help, Dennis! Just try to sneak up behind her and get ahold of it." Dennis loped down the lane, vaulted over the corral fence, and helped to pull the calf into the world. Later, when I was leaving, he wondered whether he should shake hands with me, because he had not had a chance to wash, but I insisted.

Ron figures on having to replace about 30 percent of his cows each year because they don't get bred or they don't produce enough milk. "Forty pounds a day was a pretty good milk average back when I started," said Martin, "but today you'd go broke on forty pounds. Today the average is about seventy-five pounds, and some guys get eighty, but sixty-five is OK. If you want to push for higher production you've got to beef a lot more of your cows. We say we 'beef 'em' when we sell 'em for beef."

Modern cows produce so much milk that they suffer intensely if they are not milked regularly, so the possibility of power outages in the milking barn is a constant concern of dairymen, and they all have standby diesel generators. "Just the other day a guy was out from the bank," Ron said, "and he was wondering if I had enough diesel fuel storage capacity to keep me going if I couldn't get any for a while. I told him that my tank holds 550 gallons, and that ought to be able to keep me going."

In 1998 Ron bought his feed concentrates from a dealer, and he bought alfalfa hay from a guy in the Imperial Valley. "We just leave it there," he said, "and he hauls it here as we need it. Twenty years ago you'd bring in all your hay and stack it, but it saves labor to put it in little stacks beside the corrals. In the Midwest you make two-wire rectangular bales that weigh around 80 pounds, but ours are around 130 or 135. You don't pick 'em up, you use your legs more and shove 'em, and we push 'em with a tractor."

Ron said you need shades in the corrals both winter and summer, and some shades have fans and misting machines for additional cooling. In hot weather dairy cows suffer severely, because they do not have sweat glands. They cannot perspire, so they must respire. They get rid of excess body heat by evaporating water from their lungs, so high temperatures make them breathe harder, eat less, and produce less milk. On a day when the temperature hits 100°F a cow standing out in the sun has to dissipate enough excess body heat to boil nine gallons of ice water.

The cows in the corrals of Chino produce an enormous total amount of manure, estimated at 490,000 tons a year. Dry-lot dairies have little place to spread it, and getting rid of it is an ever greater headache as urban growth gobbles up nearby farmland. Most Chino dairymen hire professional corral cleaners to haul their manure to distant farms or to one of ten local composting plants, where bacteria convert it into fertilizer.

Dairymen like to clean out their corrals twice a year, once when the manure has dried out after the winter rains have ended and again at the end of summer before the rains begin. The El Niño winter was a real mess, Ron said, "just slop all over. Our average rainfall here is thirteen inches a year, and that winter we got twenty inches in February alone. Manure was running down the streets ankle deep."

Ron pays a corral cleaner $20,000 to $25,000 a year to haul his manure to farmland near Riverside. Lew Aukeman said, "I am cleaning corrals right now. I haven't gotten the final bill yet, but for this year alone it will be about $50,000 just to haul the manure away. Up north, where there's farmers, they'll pay you two–three dollars a ton for it."

A dry-lot dairy needs one milker for each 250 cows, a relief milker, an outside ranch hand who feeds the cows and moves them to and from the milking barn, and a herdsman who checks the cows each day and supervises the entire operation. On smaller places the dairyman does some or all of these jobs himself. "As you get bigger," Ron said, "you lose personal contact with the cows, because you have to delegate authority to somebody else, and you start dealing with people rather than cows. Cows are a lot easier to deal with. They may kick at you, but they don't talk back."

Martin said, "It was about fifty/fifty Dutchmen and Portuguese when I started in the dairy business, but it looks like the Dutchmen have just about run the Portuguese out. Maybe they were smarter than us, they just made their pile and retired. There aren't too many of 'em left around here anymore, but there's quite a few up north in the Central Valley. They are basically Catholic. They have their own schools and social facilities, and these Holy Ghost kind of fraternities. They stick together socially. Some of the younger ones have married Dutch girls, but I don't know any Dutch boys that married Portuguese girls."

Lew said, "Twenty years ago I had only one Mexican working for me. It was all Dutch and Portuguese. They were hard-working frugal people, they put a little money together, and pretty soon they had a place of their own. There's no new immigrants from Europe anymore, and now most of our workers are Mexicans. They haven't started their own dairies yet. A lot of them never had much education, and I don't think their hopes and goals were that high. They were just after a whole loaf of bread instead of just three slices like they got in Mexico.

"The second generation is setting goals, like the guy cleaning my corrals. He's got five trucks running, and he's the boss. I had a Mexican boy work for me for twelve years, but he left just this past summer to manage a 500-cow dairy in South Carolina. He came here as a wetback, but he had a lot of ability. He just carried authority. He was always the boss. He had good judgment, and acted as our foreman when we weren't around. He was good at whatever he did. He was a good mechanic. He was a good cow man, and he bred cows for us.

"Before he went to South Carolina he went to Nebraska and worked in a slaughter plant for a while, but he said it was too dangerous. He worked there about three months, and not a day passed that somebody didn't get taken to the hospital because of injuries. He told me, 'I like what I've got, that's why I quit.'"

Proficient experienced workers and entrepreneurial owners were essential to the success of the Chino Valley dairy area, which epitomized the model of modern, efficient, large-scale dairying that had gestated at Artesia. The Chino area also had and needed a full panoply of dairy-related service businesses, such as feed and milk haulers, feed dealers, hay lots, equipment supply and repair companies, veterinarians, livestock auctioneers, calf nurseries, corral cleaners and manure haulers, and composting plants.

Despite all its assets, the Chino dairy area is doomed by urban encroachment. The escalating price of land is an incentive to sell out and relocate, but the difficulty of efficient dairying at the urban edge in an age of escalating environmental sensitivity probably has been an even stronger push factor. Wastewater spread on pastures can percolate down to the water table, and disposal of manure gets ever more expensive. Neighbors complain mostly about the flies, but some believe that gases and dust from corrals can cause respiratory and other ailments.

Concerns such as these have triggered a whole suite of new environmental regulations, and the end is not yet in sight. The average Chino dairy will have to invest $1 million or more to comply with them, and environmentalists keep identifying new causes for concern. It makes more sense to flee than to fight. Before too many years have passed the Chino Valley dairy area will have gone the way of Artesia. It will live on only in fanciful subdivision names, such as Cloverdale Farms and Archibald Ranch, and in some extraordinarily fertile lawns and flower beds.

Paradoxical though it may seem, the loss of farmland to urban encroachment in Chino has actually been a tremendous boon to the dairy business, because farmers who sell their land at handsome prices have to pay heavy capital gains taxes on their windfall profits if they do not reinvest them in another agricultural enterprise. High urban land prices have given relocating Chino dairymen the capital they need to build larger and more efficient state-of-the-art facilities in distant places where they do not have hordes of urban environmentalists scrutinizing their every action.

They have disseminated the model of the modern large-scale dairy farm to other parts of the United States, and other dairymen have adopted the Chino model. Some of the large new dairy farms are clustered, especially in the irrigated oases of the West, but in most of the East their geographic distribution is entrepreneurial. Many areas in the East have only a single large-scale dairy farm where a visionary entrepreneur has seen fit to invest in developing it.

5
Dairying in Other Areas

Most of the large dairies in Artesia and in Chino are owned and operated by Dutch or Portuguese immigrants or their offspring, but as Joe Pires observed, "Milking a lot of cows is not a Dutch thing or a Portuguese thing. It's a California thing." Dairymen from Chino have carried the idea of milking lots of cows to other parts of the West, and this idea has been adopted by local dairymen throughout the United States. The West has clusters of dairies with 500 cows or more, but in the East they are mostly one of a kind in the counties that have them (fig. 5.1). This distribution is essentially entrepreneurial. One enterprising person in the county has been willing to take the risk of investing several millions of dollars to develop a modern large-scale dairy.

The number of dairy farms in the United States has been dropping steadily since World War II, because only the larger and more efficient farms have been able to stay competitive. In 1949 a total of 2,006,800 farms had milk cows. The number had plummeted to only 117,000 farms in 1997, but the number of farms

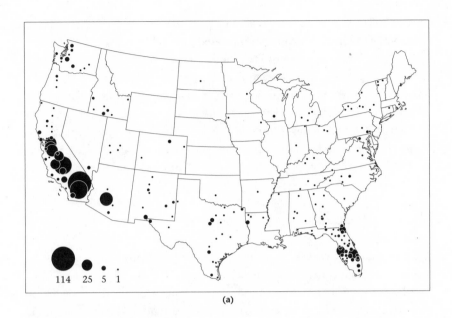

(a)

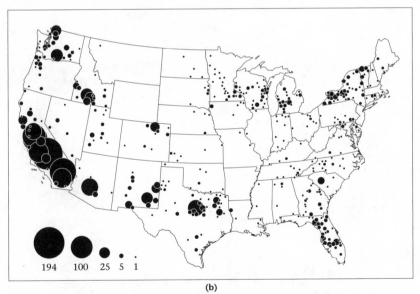

(b)

Figure 5.1. Number of farms with 500 or more milk cows, 1978 (a) and 1997 (b). Between 1978 and 1997 the idea of dairy farms with 500 cows or more diffused from California to other parts of the United States, but the traditional dairy areas in the Midwest lagged noticeably. (Data from relevant censuses of agriculture.)

milking 500 cows or more increased from 844 in 1978 to 2,257 in 1997, and their share of the nation's dairy cows had increased from 7.1 percent to 27.6 percent.[1] They are the future of dairying in the United States.

The large new dairies have modified the dry-lot system in two major ways. They house the cows in free-stall barns rather than in open corrals, and they chop alfalfa hay instead of baling it. Free-stall barns are long structures with open sides that can be closed with canvas curtains in severe weather. Chopping hay and storing it in huge mounds is cheaper than baling and unbaling it. The mounds are covered with sheets of white plastic, which are held in place by old automobile tires.

The San Joaquin Valley

Large new dairies have been popping up all over the San Joaquin Valley of California, with major clusters near Tulare and near Turlock (fig. 5.2). You can identify the dairies from a distance by their enormous white plastic-covered hay mounds speckled with black circles. Long low free-stall barns dwarf the parlors where the cows are milked and the metal-roofed commodity sheds where the concentrated feed is stored. Commodity sheds look like handball courts, with five or six open bays separated by concrete walls. Each bay is wide enough for trucks to back in and dump their loads of whichever concentrate is cheapest at the moment.

Farmers in the San Joaquin Valley started dairying in the late 1920s. Those in

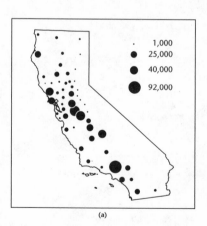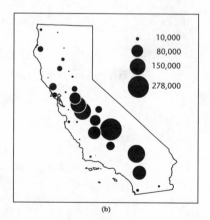

Figure 5.2. Number of dairy cows in California in 1950 (a) and 1997 (b). (Data from relevant censuses of agriculture.)

the northern cluster near Turlock looked to San Francisco, and those in the slightly smaller southern cluster near Tulare looked to Los Angeles.[2] They shipped fluid milk to meet peak weekend and seasonal demand in the cities, but most of their milk was made into butter, cheese, ice cream, and other manufactured products.

Before World War II dairies in the Valley were small, and dairying was only part of a general farm operation. Most farmers also grew their own feed, raised their own replacement cows, and produced crops that were not dairy-related. After the war they began to enlarge their dairies and to specialize in producing milk, because urban expansion was obliterating dairies near the cities, and the demand for fluid milk from the Valley was increasing, although even now much Valley milk still goes into manufactured products. Thanks in no small part to dairymen who relocated from Los Angeles, the Tulare cluster has become slightly larger; in 1997 the two clusters boasted more than one-quarter of all the nation's farms with 500 dairy cows or more (fig. 5.2).

Joe Pires grew up on a dairy farm near Tulare. His parents had immigrated to the United States through Ellis Island, and they came to Tulare, where they had relatives in the dairy business. In 1929 his father bought forty acres, started a twenty-cow dairy farm, and gradually added more cows when he could afford it. He had built up to sixty cows in 1947, when Joe graduated from high school, and he bought eighty more acres to keep Joe on the farm with him.

They kept adding cows gradually, and in 1957 they remodeled their barn to hold 300 cows, "which was real big in those days," Joe remembers. "The bank kept pushing us to enlarge our herd to improve our cash flow, because the price of milk in California is low. We kept adding cows. It was just a slow evolution." In 1983 they built a complete new barn for 1,300 cows, and they covered all forty acres of the original farm with corrals.

Joe helped his son, Larry, and his son-in-law, Gary, to get started in the dairy business, and in 1994 Joe was milking 1,300 cows, Larry was milking 700, and Gary was milking 1,000. That was the year the boys decided to sell their California dairies and develop new dairies in South Dakota, so Joe figured it was time for him to retire. He sold his cows and rented his facilities to Frank Garcia. Joe said a reasonable rent in the area would be $10 per cow per month.

Frank Garcia immigrated to the United States from the Azores in 1975. For my benefit he politely spoke English, but he obviously was far more comfortable in Portuguese when he and Joe got down to business. When he first arrived, Frank worked as a herdsman, and for six years he never took a single day off. By 1984 he had saved enough money to rent a small farm with 30 cows, and he has added around 100 cows a year. "Every penny goes back into his operation," Joe said with admiration, and he told me that Frank has helped to set up Frank Jr. on his own 1,300-cow dairy.

Edwin Koetsier was 25 years old in 1990 when his father bought a 215-acre farm near Tulare and they moved north from Chino. His father had started dairy-ing near Artesia in 1954 and had moved to Chino in 1962. "People were kind of crowding up fairly close," Edwin said, "and we wanted to get out of Chino. There was already a big dairy base here that had a lot of the necessary dairy services, and another big thing was there's a fairly good-sized Dutch community."

The Koetsiers buy their feed from the same company from which they bought feed in Chino. The company saw the dairies moving north, and it estab-lished a branch in Tulare to serve its former customers who have moved. The Koetsiers started with 450 cows, and they had built up to 950 in 1998. They had 40 acres of dairy and buildings and 175 acres of cropland. "We didn't know any-thing about farming," Edwin said, "and we didn't want to get into it, so we lease out the cropland to one of the best farmers in the area, who alternates cotton and corn on it. We call it nutrient management land, because that's where we spread our manure."

Tulare once had 450 dairymen. In 1998 the number was down to around 250 and still dropping, but Edwin thought the dairies that remain will continue to get larger, if they can find the land they need. "Land here costs $3,000 to $5,000 an acre," he said, "if you can find any for sale. You are allowed eight cows an acre, but if you get over that they'll get on your case. I can't expand until I can find some more land to buy, that's the key.

"The big problem that's facing the dairy industry here is water quality regu-lations, making sure you contain 100 percent of your runoff, making sure no wastewater gets off your property. I don't know what the magic number is going to be, where the size is going to stop, but I do know that there's a lot of people here that are doubling their milking pits."

Southwestern Kansas

During the 1990s a modest new dairy area developed in southwestern Kansas, which already boasted one of the nation's greatest concentrations of feedyards for beef cattle. In 1992 this area had fewer than 100 milk cows, but by 1998 it had more than 16,000 on nine new dairies, two of which were so new that they were not even included in the *1997 Census of Agriculture*.[3]

Local businesses, chambers of commerce, and city and county officials have cooperated with economic development agencies in actively encouraging and recruiting dairies. They hope to diversify away from heavy dependence on beef cattle and have a goal of 20,000 milk cows, which they believe is the critical mass necessary to support a local milk-processing plant. They advertise that their area has abundant feed, a mild dry climate, banks and a labor force that know cattle, and low land prices, low taxes, low utility rates, and low labor costs.

The new dairies are widely scattered. Some have been started by local entrepreneurs and some by dairymen who have relocated from other areas. Pete and Todd Tul have come from Chino, where their father runs a 3,600-cow dairy that was started by their grandfather when he immigrated from Holland. They have 40 acres of shaded corrals and a double-30 milking parlor for 2,000 cows on the 640-acre farm they bought near Liberal. They had to buy water rights and design a special wastewater lagoon to satisfy state and federal requirements, but they are pleased with the large quantities of high-quality low-cost feed the area has to offer.

Jay Houtsma and Dan Senestraro are partners in a 3,000-cow dairy with a double-35 milking parlor south of Syracuse, Kansas. Jay's grandfather came from Holland in the 1920s to start a dairy in southern California, and Jay worked on the dairy for his father for eight years before he and Dan decided to escape the Southern California smog and move to Kansas. He said he also was attracted by the cheap and abundant high-quality feed in Kansas.

Larry Fallwell is a local go-getter who has been deeply involved in starting a large new dairy a few miles east of Coolidge, Kansas. Coolidge was a throbbing center that claimed a population of 3,500 people back in the days when it had the Santa Fe Railroad yards. Then the city fathers decided to tax the yards, and the railroad decided to move them to another town; Coolidge has been slipping downhill ever since. A sad string of derelict one-story stores lines the north side of U.S. 50. On the south side the grain elevator beside the railroad tracks that parallel the highway is the only business left in town, and the population has shriveled to fewer than 100 people.

Larry grew up on the Texas Panhandle, worked in the grain business for ten years, and then came to Coolidge to run the grain elevator. Soon he decided to branch out into farming. "I just rented a farm, bought a tractor, and took out!" he said. In 1998 he was row-cropping 2,200 acres, corn silage mainly, a little bit of sorghum silage, and he custom-farmed 8,500 acres of alfalfa. "Other farmers irrigate it and take care of the crop, and all I do is swath it, bale it, stack it, and market it."

He hauled the hay to dairies in Texas and picked up cottonseed and cotton hulls to bring back to local feed yards and dairies. "It makes my trucking operation work real well," he said, "being loaded both ways." He operated six big hay balers, five 18-foot swathers, two trucks, and eight flatbed semis, employing twenty-six people in his hay business, eight in his trucking business, and nine at the elevator.

Larry told me that Texas started large-scale dairying in the 1960s. Some of the Texas dairymen came straight from Holland. "We call 'em wooden-shoe Dutch," he said. He had been selling hay to dairy farmers in Texas for a number of years when he realized that in Kansas the cost of feed was good, the climate was good, and the area already had a lot of large beef feed yards. Why not start a dairy here? he wondered.

He knew that the area had had four to eight small mom-and-pop dairies up through the 1950s, and he tried to find out why they had closed. He learned that they had been too small, and sanitary regulations had shut them down. They had to scale up or get out, and the kids were not interested in taking them over and developing them, so they simply stopped milking.

Larry found three other local farmers to join him in trying to start a dairy. The local banks were helpful, local people were supportive, and they were able to raise $1 million of seed money. In 1993 they went to California to find a dairyman to run it. They hired Dale Senestraro, gave him a 30 percent interest in the dairy, and agreed to pay him a salary in addition. Larry said that it would probably take $17 million to start from scratch and build what they had in 1998, and he added that they are extremely highly leveraged.

"We built our dairy and started milking in a hundred days," said Larry, "which was unheard of for a double-fifty parlor. We opened July 18, 1996, and we haven't turned out the lights in the parlor since we opened. We milked 1,550 cows on the third day of opening, and in thirty to forty days we were up to over 3,000. We originally put in our plans to go to 5,000, but we had to bring the cows along gradually, and it has taken us two and a half years to get to where we're at now. We milk 520 to 540 cows an hour, and would like to be at 75 pounds of milk per cow per day."

The Coolidge Dairy sits on the crest of the dusty tan stream breaks that overlook the green irrigated fields of the Arkansas River valley. Many beef feed yards have similar sites on dry rangeland not suitable for cultivation. Near the bottom of the hill is a dry lot with 1,800 to 2,000 black-and-white replacement heifers. The dairy raises its own replacement cows but sells the bull calves immediately for whatever it can get for them. Larry said that a lot of small farmers and a few large feed yards in the area will buy and feed them for beef, even though they are not good for much except hamburger.

The two-story white 74' × 456' milking barn has "Coolidge Dairy" in black letters emblazoned above the entrance to the offices in the west end. The roof has a small belvedere with a splendid view of the pens and the valley beyond. Seven 300' × 920' pens hold 450 milk cows each, and separate pens of similar size hold dry cows and fresh cows (fig. 5.3). Oversized bales of corn stover are stacked two or three bales high along the west side of the pens as a windbreak.

Initially they thought that dry lots with windbreaks and bedding probably would be good enough shelter, Larry said, "but last October 25th a blizzard killed 550 cows. It was a terrible blizzard that probably killed 10 percent of all the beef cattle in this part of the country. We have changed our minds, because in summer the heat and no air movement hurt our milk production, so we are constructing a 1,920-foot free-stall barn right now, and we're looking at doing another next year.

"We feed the cows four to six times a day. All my crops go into our dairy.

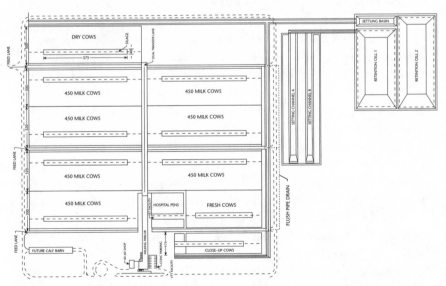

Figure 5.3. Site plan of the Coolidge Dairy in 1998. (Based on a plan provided by Larry Fall-well; used by permission.)

Everything I raise is value added, because I don't sell my crops, we just turn them into milk, and we sell the milk. Last year we fed around 70,000 tons of alfalfa." Trucks automatically unload the feed on the paved lanes that run beside each pen, and the cows stick their heads through the stanchions to eat it.

The area inside the pen where the cows stand while eating is slightly depressed, and it is flushed regularly into a composting system at the bottom of the hill. "We have a certified composting operation," Larry said. "We are composting the manure for lawn and garden sale, and we hope to turn the waste portion of the dairy into a profit center. I guess you could say that I am an elevator operator/farmer/trucker/dairyman/compost merchant."

Tim Dewey is a local farmer who has moved laterally into dairying. His new dairy is about fifteen miles north of Cimarron. Tim cherishes his privacy and his independence. "The county commissioners tried to get me to build the dairy up on the oil [road]," he said. "They wanted to have easy access. I would love to have easy access, but the reason I built it two miles back off the oil is not to upset people. Nobody can see it unless they come out here looking for it."

Tim would not even let me take his picture. "You can take a picture of anything else around here," he said, "but you can't take a picture of me. I really don't want to be that public. I get stopped in Wal-Mart and every place I go anyway. I don't mind people like you that call and make an appointment to come out here and talk to me, but I don't like people that make surveys and send me forms to fill out. Them people don't realize how much time it takes to do that stuff, and besides, it works against us every time. There's already too much information out there. If they figure we're gonna have a ten-bushel bigger corn crop, they cut the price. We can't even hold it off the market, because they already know what we've got in the bins, and they price it accordingly. Let them guys speculate about what we're gonna have out here."

Tim started farming with his father in 1973. I asked him how much land he had, and he replied, "I don't like to send that out." He did tell me that he had something like 62 center-pivot sprinkler irrigation systems, which water 125 acres each, "but I also have a lot of dry land and grass and that kind of stuff. When I started it was ditch irrigation, with a siphon tube for each row, then we went to pipe, and then to sprinkler. We have gone from three-row equipment to six, then eight, and now it's all sixteen."

He used to have 1,000-, 1,200-, 1,500-gallon wells that tapped the Ogallala aquifer. In 1998 those same wells had dropped to 600 or 700, "so the water is depleting to some extent, although over the last ten years it's more holding its own.

It's still depleting pretty fast when we run 1,200 gallons through them sprinklers out there."

He grew alfalfa, milo (sorghum), corn, and wheat. Milo is for grain, which heads out three or four feet above the ground. For silage Tim planted another variety of sorghum that grows six feet high or higher. Alfalfa takes a little more water than corn, milo a little less, and wheat the least of all. "If you had a field that didn't have very good water, you would probably plant it in wheat or maybe milo." Tim expected five tons of alfalfa to the acre, 175 to 200 bushels of corn, and 105 bushels of milo if it is irrigated, 75 if it is not.

In 1983 Tim built a feed yard for 5,000 beef cattle, but he was not happy with it. "In the cattle-feeding business you had to get a lot larger and you had to deal with customers," he said, and in 1995 the price of cattle was so low that he decided to quit feeding and build a dairy. "It was just simpler to work within our own organization," he said. "We own our own cows, we do our own thing, and we don't have to solicit any customers."

In 1995 Tim converted the eighty-acre feed yard into dry-lot pens for dry cows, replacement heifers, and calves. Looming over the lots are the four towering cylindrical concrete silos and two squat corrugated metal grain bins of the feed mill. Across the road is the eighty-acre dairy, where the cows are housed in four open-sided one-story metal sheds that seem to go on forever, although the longest one really is only 2,300 feet long, slightly less than half a mile.

Two double-50 milking parlors connect each pair of free-stall barns. Tim started milking 2,700 cows three times a day in 1995, but in 2001 he expanded to 8,000 and milked them only twice a day. He said he ought to get 85 pounds of milk per cow per day, "and we're not there yet, but we're getting there." He feeds his own silage, milo, corn, and some of his own hay, but he looks for the best hay he can find to buy.

A couple of times Tim has brought in managers to run the dairy, but it just didn't work out, and now "I run the dairy myself," he said, "but I've got a lot of good help. You know what you expect, and the only way to get it like you expect it is to do it yourself, but I couldn't possibly do it without the quality help I've got. That's the whole key to everything. I'd be pretty helpless without 'em, I'll tell you for sure. Dairying is about as big as farming for me now. It's just a big diversified company with eighty to a hundred employees."

Tim uses his irrigation rights at the dairy to wash and clean it, and then he sprinkles the washwater on his fields for irrigation. He hauls and spreads the manure from the dry-lot pens but flushes the manure from the barns through a line of rectangular earthen basins. "The first settlement basin takes out about 70 percent of it and aerobic action in the second basin takes care of the rest. Then it goes to the pond that the flushwater and irrigation water comes out of, either to the fields or back to flush the alleys in the barn." Periodically he drains the first basin and lets it dry down to 18 percent for fertilizer, or he composts it for bedding for the cows in the barn.

Tim said, "I had a government environmental man out here about a month ago, and he couldn't find nothing wrong except he thought maybe I had too many weeds around my ponds. He didn't even know that they stop erosion. Them people just don't have any idea, really, about what they are doing, or about what we are doing and need to do. Some people do abuse the environment, and them kind of people need to be attended to, but we want a good clean country even more than anyone else does, because after all, we live here.

"Western Kansas is agriculture," Tim said, "and it's highly successful agriculture. Anybody that comes to western Kansas should know that they're going to have to deal with hogs and cattle and irrigation and dairies and them kinds of things. Anybody that don't wanna deal with them kinds of things, why in the world they'd even wanna live here I don't know. I'd rather live in the mountains."

Florida

Florida is the only area outside California that had a significant concentration of large dairies in 1978, when the census of agriculture first began publishing information about them, and in 1997 the state still had more large dairies than Wisconsin and Minnesota combined (fig. 5.1). The influx of affluent and retired people from the North has created a steadily increasing demand for milk, and the state has no ingrained tradition about the "proper" size of a dairy that might have dissuaded farmers from adopting new technology for large-scale production when it became available.

Fifteen miles north of Lake Okeechobee on U.S. 441 a large white billboard heralds "McArthur Farms" in white letters on a red medallion, with "Dairy Beef Citrus" in smaller black letters above it. The dairies are parallel clusters of long, one-story, open-sided structures whose white metal roofs shimmer in the subtropical sunshine. They are set a quarter of a mile back from the highway, with a sign at the entrance of each dairy saying, "Keep Out. No Trespassing. No Visitors."

Nonetheless, Bob Rydzewski, 49, the manager, greeted me cordially, and he laughed when I reminded him that the farm once had welcomed visitors with handsome white-painted board fences along the highway. "We used to be completely open door," he said, "but we had so many problems with inconsiderate visitors that we have had to clamp down. Once a big old Rolls-Royce with New York license plates drove right down through the middle of one of our barns when we were feeding the cows."

Bob told me that in 1921 James N. McArthur came from Mississippi to teach vocational agriculture in a Miami high school. He realized that the whole southern part of Florida suffered from a serious shortage of milk, so in 1929 he bought four Jersey cows and started a dairy north of Miami, in Broward County. He gradually kept adding to his herd, buying more land, and buying out other dairies until by 1939 he was milking more than 1,000 cows and selling milk in the entire area south of Orlando. In the late 1950s he moved his dairy from the rapidly urbanizing area near Miami to its present isolated site north of Lake Okeechobee.

"Mr. McArthur believed you could never own enough land," Bob said, "and he bought a 10,000-acre ranch west of here on the Kissimmee River, where we have a cow-calf herd of 4,000 Braford beef cows." Each year McArthur Farms sells 3,500 beef calves at a weight of 400 to 500 pounds to feedlot operators by video auction. The auction company publishes a sales guide that describes the calves, videotapes load lots on the farm, and sells 30,000 to 40,000 head a year on rented television channels.

In the early 1980s McArthur Farms decided to diversify into citrus production and planted 600 acres in St. Lucie County, on the east coast. "Timing is everything," Bob said, "and we were lucky, because we started before the big freezes of the mid-eighties wiped out 200,000 acres of citrus groves on the Citrus Ridge, near Orlando." They have expanded to 1,700 acres in four groves and sell mostly fresh fruit, but some is processed into frozen concentrate.

Before he died, in the early 1980s, Mr. McArthur incorporated his entire business, which has gross annual sales of around $25 million, as McArthur Farms, and he gave the stock to his grandchildren. They all are on the board of directors, but the only one who is somewhat active in the company is the president, and he expects Bob to make all of the day-to-day decisions.

McArthur Farms employs forty people in the dairies, fifteen in the citrus groves, and seven on the beef ranch. Forty percent of the workers are Hispanic, and their number is steadily increasing. The farm must provide housing for them, and it has sixty-five houses for workers, although only thirty-four were actually occupied in 1997. "We have profit sharing, pensions, and group insurance for the workers," Bob said, "because it is just the right thing to do."

In 1998 the McArthur Farms dairy operation had 6,300 milking cows, 2,000 to 2,500 dry cows, and 4,500 to 5,000 replacement heifers, for a total herd of 13,000 dairy cattle. It kept its own heifer calves for replacements, Bob said, "but the market for bull calves is so soft we just knock 'em in the head and haul the carcasses to the rendering plant." The dry cows and replacement heifers ran free on vast flat pastures, where they were worked by cowboys on horses. During the heat of the day they often huddled beneath the flat metal shades or waded in one of the shallow ponds that dot the pastures.

The dairy operation had 10,000 acres of pasture. Around 1,000 acres of Bermuda grass were irrigated with center-pivot sprinkler systems on fields that were ditched and diked for water control, and another 2,000 acres were also harvested when the heifers were not on them. The grass was cut for haylage and stored in pits or in large plastic tubes, but Bob said that it is so lush that harvesting it is a headache, and it is only low- to medium-quality forage.

The milking cows were in four units of 1,500 to 1,600 each in four or five parallel barns. The two older units had flat barns and the other two had free-stall barns. All of the barns had large fans and sprinkler systems to keep the cows cool. The cows never left the free-stall barns except to be milked, but the flat barns had a couple of hundred acres of exercise lots on which the cows were free to roam.

"We put double-twenty herringbone milking parlors on the flat barns about five years ago," Bob said, "and the newer free-stall units have three double-eight herringbone milking parlors, which is kind of a contradiction to what is done all over the country, but it seems to work well for us. Those double-eights were designed for reliability and maximum flexibility. You can still keep operating the other two when one goes down, and that's important when you're milking 1,600 cows and milking around the clock."

They milked each cow twice a day. They would like 20,000 pounds of milk per cow per year, but averaged only 16,000 to 17,000. Mr. McArthur started with Jersey cows, which produce milk that is rich in butterfat, but not a lot of it. Health-conscious consumers have turned away from rich whole milk and processors refuse to pay a premium for it, so McArthur Farms has switched to Holstein cows; it sold its last Jerseys in 1991. "We sell volume," Bob said, "and that means Holstein cows, but there's still a place in the cheese business for Jersey and Guernsey cows.

"We feed the cows everything they get," Bob said. In cooperation with another large dairy McArthur Farms owned feed mills on two railroad lines, in order to get competitive freight rates. The two dairies were the only customers of the two mills and bought all their feed and ingredients, 140,000 tons a year, from them. Feed came from all over the country, wherever the price was best: alfalfa hay from Idaho, corn and soybeans from the Midwest, cottonseed from the Southeast, citrus pulp and pellets from Florida.

Bob said they reached for feed as far as the price of transportation would permit. Some low-value by-products, such as wet brewers' grains, waste from bakeries and potato chip factories, and citrus pulp, must be fed fairly close to the plant. "Of course a lot of these milling companies don't even call it a by-product anymore," he laughed. "That's a dirty word to them now, and they call it a co-product instead of a by-product." He said that the cost of moving things is not as great as it used to be, and they even shipped some fresh citrus by air freight to England, but the cost of transportation is still the driving force in what they feed.

Manure flushed from the barns with recycled water was pumped to a solids separator. The liquid was sprayed onto the fields from which haylage was harvested, and the solids were also used for fertilizer. The farm has an elaborate system of lagoons to collect and recycle all runoff water from the heavy subtropical rainfall, and to keep it from flowing toward and polluting Lake Okeechobee. The principal problem is phosphorus, which stays in the water until it is taken up by plants. Bob said they have already had to close down one barn because environmental considerations made it too costly to operate, and several local dairies have actually been forced out of business by environmental regulations.

The lagoons are popular with alligators. They became so numerous that the farm was allowed to shoot some of them in 1997, and it sold 110 hides for $20 to $40 a foot. Bob said they only shot about 10 percent, "so there's probably a thousand more of 'em still out there in that pond."

McArthur Farms sold all of its milk in bulk through the Florida Dairy Farmers Co-op. Mr. McArthur had his own milk-processing plant, because he believed firmly in vertical integration, but paradoxically, he was also a founding member of the co-op. He sold milk through the co-op, and then he bought milk from the co-op for his milk plant, apparently as a way of figuring how to set his prices. He sold his plant in 1981 because the chain food stores had become so large that they had started their own plants, and he realized that independent brands could not compete with the store brands for shelf space in grocery stores.

Fred Gore also sold milk through the Florida Dairy Farmers Co-op, to the tune of $6–7 million worth a year. His 1,900-cow dairy is at the northern edge of the town of Zephyrhills, twenty-seven miles northeast of Tampa, and in 1998 he was already wondering when the growth of Zephyrhills was going to force him to relocate farther out. Fred's father, Lee, started milking eighteen cows by hand in 1943, and he developed his own home delivery sales route.

By 1948 Lee had built his herd up to 100 cows, and he sold his milk route. He had grown to 175 cows by 1955, when Fred came back to join him. In 1956 they grew to 450, and in 1957 they built a milking parlor. Fred has continued to enlarge his herd, and he expected to add 200 more cows soon, because 1,900 are not enough to keep his milkers busy for a full shift. "Florida is a tough place to be in the dairy business," he said, "and I have to produce milk at the lowest possible cost."

Fred Gore employed thirty people. His herdsman was Eric Diepersloot, who was born in California and came to Florida with his parents. Eric grouped the cows by how fast they milk, so he could move them in and out of the milking parlors at the same time. They were milked three times a day, in two double-twelve and one double-ten parlors. Eric liked small parlors with only one milker in each pit, because he said it cuts down on the time wasted in chit-chat. The cows averaged 65 to 70 pounds of milk a day in winter but only 58 to 60 in summer, because their ideal temperature is 45°F, and they do not like the hot, muggy Florida summers.

Fred bought all his replacement heifers when they were sixty days from coming fresh. He bought them from contract growers in New York, because they grow better in cool weather, and he sold his calves to New York growers, who like them because the lush Florida pastures give them good rumen size. He had 100 bulls, because he does not like artificial insemination. He bought bulls that weighed 900 pounds and did not keep them long. He ran five or six bulls with each herd of 175 to 200 milking cows. He worked them for two weeks and then rested them for two weeks.

Fred bought all his feed, 80 tons a day. His principal feed was top-quality alfalfa hay from Idaho, which cost him $150 a ton delivered to the farm. I wondered about the cost of shipping a bulky commodity 2,600 miles, more than one-tenth of the way around the world, and Fred said that the railroad gave him a very favorable backhaul freight rate in the cars that carried cottonseed from the South to dairy farms in Idaho.

I also wondered how he disposed of his manure, because he had only 300 acres of land and he ran dry cows on most of it. He chuckled and said, "We have a magic wand that just makes it disappear." In fact, he recycled, flushed, and digested it and stored it in six manure ponds, from which he irrigated 85 acres of

Bermuda grass hay with a center-pivot sprinkler system. "We are doing our best," he said, "but the environmentalists are really trying to shut us down."

The Gore dairy, McArthur Farms, the new dairies in southwestern Kansas, the new dairies in the San Joaquin Valley, and other large new dairies in other parts of the United States all are manifestations of the idea of efficient modern large-scale dairies. Producers who have brought their capital gains from the Los Angeles area have started some of the new dairies, but local entrepreneurs have also started some.

Modern dairy farmers are managers who are no longer "tied to the cow's tail," as their grandparents were. When necessary they can do any job that has to be done on the farm, but they hire workers to do these jobs on a day-to-day basis. They are free to get away to visit other dairy areas, which they do regularly, so they are keenly aware of the latest developments elsewhere.

Good modern large-scale dairy producers also are sensitive to the environmental impact of their operations and they strive to keep it to the minimum, but they claim that environmentalists have criticized them unfairly because the environmentalists do not really understand how modern dairies operate.

6

Can Midwest Dairying Thrive?

The traditional dairy farming areas in the Midwest have missed the boat. Their farmers have been too conservative and too complacent, and time has passed them by. They have been tied to the cow's tail and their horizons have been too restricted. Their imagination has been dulled by the drudgery of milking every twelve hours, seven days a week, fifty-two weeks a year. Willingness to work hard has been their lodestone to success, and they have felt little need for new ideas and innovations. The regular arrival of the monthly milk check has assured them of their righteousness.

Now they have lost their competitive edge, and they are paying the price for their failure to invest in up-to-date technology and to develop large-scale modern operations. In 1997 half the dairy farms in Wisconsin and Minnesota were milking fewer than 50 cows, and only one in ten was milking 100 or more.[1] In 1997 no fewer than six counties in California *each* had more 500-or-more-cow dairies than the two states of Wisconsin and Minnesota combined, and Tulare County alone had twice as many (fig. 5.1).

The undersized dairy farms of Wisconsin and Minnesota cannot provide an acceptable standard of living. A farm couple might be able to hang on, if the farm is bought and paid for, by living frugally on their capital, but their children will not come home to work on a 50-cow dairy farm. Even a 100-cow dairy farm is a last-generation farm, and it will go out of business when ma and pa stop milking.

The farmstead that once was the pride and joy of the family is starting to look tired and threadbare. The house is overdue for a paint job, shingles are missing from the barn roof, the lawn is overgrown and shaggy, and weeds are popping up along the fence lines. Some barnyards still have little herds of black-and-white dairy cows, but some have only weeds. Many of the occupied farmsteads have become decrepit homes for old folks who cannot manage to maintain them properly, and they will be abandoned when the old folks go on to their reward.

Politicians like to blame the problems of dairy farming areas in the Midwest on a milk pricing system that is a relic of the horse-and-buggy and railroad era, and has been rendered obsolete by tanker truck transport, whereas in fact the problem of the Midwest is too many undersized high-cost milk producers who cannot compete with lower-cost producers in other parts of the country.

Well-intentioned populist laws against corporate farms also have been a significant barrier to the development of competitive large-scale dairies in the Midwest, because they prevent farmers from recruiting outside investors. For example, a new 500-cow dairy would cost around $2.25 million, and even the most benevolent bank will not lend a farmer more than 80 percent of the cost. Few farmers have $450,000 of their own to invest. The hope for the future seems to depend on the formation of alliances of independent farmers who can pool their resources to develop cooperative ventures of the size necessary.

The future of dairy farming in the Midwest may be even more parlous than it seems, because many of the milk-processing plants in the area are getting old, and they must be modernized. A modern milk-processing plant needs a steady supply of 40 million pounds of milk a day, which would require 400 1,400-cow farms producing an average of 70 pounds of milk per cow per day, or more than 11,000 50-cow farms.

Where should the milk-processing company place its bet? Should it invest its capital in updating an old plant in an area of small farms where milk production may be dwindling, or should it build a brand-new plant in an area of large farms where production is increasing? If milk-processing plants in the Midwest are not modernized, and especially if they are closed, will milk production spiral downward because producers have no place to sell their milk?

In 1996 the secretaries of agriculture in North Dakota, South Dakota, and Minnesota were so concerned about the future of dairying in their states that they developed a tristate initiative to retain and enhance the industry. This initiative makes development loans to farms of all sizes, but it strongly encourages small farmers to form alliances to achieve the scale necessary for success.

"You can't dairy today with less than 700 cows, which is the absolute minimum," said Harold Stanislawski, agricultural development specialist with the Minnesota Department of Agriculture, in 2001. "Freight, labor, forage, and manure all affect the optimum size, which is probably around 1,400 cows. To feed a 1,400-cow dairy you would need around 1,000 acres of alfalfa for hay, 1,000 acres of silage corn, and 700–800 acres of dry corn. You would need to own or hold easements for spreading manure on about 3,500 acres, or about two and a half acres per cow.

"The ideal site would be on a ten-ton road at least a mile from any lakes, rivers, or streams and with few neighbors. You would need three-phase electric power and a well that produces 100 gallons of water a minute. You would need a 16-million-gallon manure lagoon for 1,400 cows, and heavy clay loam soil would save you the cost of lining it. You would need a full-time labor force of twenty-two dependable people."

The good news is that the traditional dairy farming areas of the Midwest are gradually modernizing. A few entrepreneurs, albeit far too few thus far, have introduced the technology of large-scale dairying. In 1997 Wisconsin had fifty-four 500-or-more-cow dairy farms, and Minnesota had twenty-nine (fig. 5.1). Three large-scale dairies illustrate three distinctive strategies of development. Joe Pires has transplanted his dairy operation from California to eastern South Dakota. Ron Tobkin has developed Little Pine Dairy from scratch. Gary Allen has built Gar-Lin Dairy entirely by internal growth.

Joe Pires

In 1996, on my annual trek to talk at the South Dakota State Geography Convention in Brookings, I spotted a large new construction site on a bleak wind-swept hillside just west of the Minnesota state line. I stopped to find out what was going on, and that was when I first met Joe Pires, whom I later visited in California. He told me he had a 1,200-cow dairy in Tulare and was helping his son, Larry, and his son-in-law, Gary, set up a 1,400-cow dairy in South Dakota.

"Why would anyone want to move from California to South Dakota?" I asked him.

He thought a moment, shrugged, and said, "They're crazy."

Then he got serious. He told me that Larry had been coming to South Dakota to buy replacement heifers for several years, ever since he had started developing his own 700-cow dairy, and eventually he decided that he was moving the cows in the wrong direction. "They should stay right here," he told Joe, "where there are very good markets and ample feed supplies. Everything is actually more conducive to producing dairy here than it is in California, and it is also a better atmosphere in which to raise a family."

Joe assured me that southeastern South Dakota is the best place in North America to milk cows. "The dairy animal produces best at a temperature of 40 to 45 degrees," he said, "and the average annual temperature here is 40 degrees. This area has only ten stress days a year. A stress day is colder than 20 below or hotter than 90. South Dakota also has a lot better tax structure than California. South Dakota has no income tax, and in California it's 12 percent. My real estate tax in California was $75 an acre, but here it's only $15."

Joe was already semiretired and the boys were pretty much running the business in California when they decided to sell their dairies and move to South Dakota. "I was not going to stay there and milk cows," Joe said, "so I sold my own cows and rented out the facilities. Now I spend summers in South Dakota and winters in California. I did help them finance it, but this is their dairy. There's $4.2 million in the facility with the land, another $2.1 million in cattle."

Two 700' × 100' green metal loafing barns with white-curtained sides are perched on the hillside. Each barn has four pens that can hold 175 cows each. Covered walkways connect the barns with a central 95' × 60' double-24 herringbone milking parlor, with a 160' × 60' holding pen in the north end for the cows waiting to be milked. The parlor can milk 48 cows, the equivalent of an entire average Wisconsin or Minnesota dairy herd, at one time. To the west are the shop, the commodity barn, and the hay barn. The house trailer in front of the milking barn is for winter emergencies, such as blizzards. One bad storm last winter trapped a milking crew on the farm for four days.

The boys bought new cows when they moved to South Dakota. In 1998 they were milking 1,200 twice a day, and planned to add 200 bred heifers in 1999.

Eventually they plan to milk three times a day and to start raising their own replacement heifers, but they were reluctant to try too many new things at once. "You know you are going to make mistakes when you start something new," Joe said. "They are trying to break in slowly and get used to the area and not make too many."

They were averaging 65 pounds of milk per cow per day, and had been pushing 70 before the weather got hot. They pumped the milk directly into tank trucks, which hauled it to the creamery, so they have not had to spend $100,000 on stainless steel milk storage tanks, and they were spared the chore of washing the tanks.

The creamery is one of six milk-processing plants in the area to which they might have sold milk, but some of them could be in serious trouble because they are having difficulty finding enough milk to buy. The creamery manager told Joe that forty to fifty local farmers have stopped milking in the last year or two, and the industry will die without large new dairies such as his to sustain it.

The boys have made a special effort to support the economy by buying as much locally as they possibly can, but they have had to go outside the area for some of the technical expertise they have needed. They employed sixteen to eighteen people, sometimes twenty in the wintertime. Initially they hired local people, but they gradually have been switching to Hispanics, who seem willing to work harder.

After we had visited for a while I started to give Joe a hard time about building barns that look as though they were in danger of slipping off the hillside, but he cut me off short. "I did it on purpose," he said. "Both barns have automatic flushing systems to clean out the manure, and if we hadn't built on the slope, the flushwater couldn't get down to the lower end without freezing. We can flush down to zero with no problem. Anything below zero is a problem, but even on a day below zero we can still flush if the afternoon gets above zero. Maybe two weeks out of the year you shouldn't be able to flush here, but last winter was so bad we had forty-five days."

They flush the manure into a little house with two large circular sieves that filter out the solids, and they recirculate the liquid by pumping it back up into the flush tank at the top of each barn. The only new fresh water that enters the system is used to flush the milk parlor, where sanitary regulations forbid the use of recirculated water.

They let the solids dry and then recirculate them for bedding in the barns. My body language must have suggested that I was less than enthusiastic about the idea of using manure, even separated manure, for bedding, because Joe scooped up some of the stuff, handed it to me, and said, "Here, smell it!" Now what do you do when your friend gives you a handful of separated cow manure? You force a smile, try to thank him as politely as you can, sniff it very gingerly, and discover to your surprise that it has no more odor than chopped straw, which it closely resembles.

Joe told me that they spread surplus manure on corn for fertilizer when they have more than they need for bedding. They own 1,200 acres but can grow corn on only about 800; the rest is pasture and wetlands. They grow their own corn silage, "because it would be awfully tough to put together the 10,000 tons a year we need from guys who have only twenty or thirty acres to sell," Joe said, "and none of them want to grow silage anyhow; they would rather grow grain."

A neighbor farms the land for them. They buy all the materials and pay him by the hour for his equipment. Eventually the boys expect to start farming the land themselves, but Joe said that's another project they were not quite ready to tackle in 1998.

Ron Tobkin

Ron Tobkin has developed the 1,400-cow Little Pine Dairy from scratch. He was born on April 5, 1948, and grew up on a diversified 450-acre farm on the sandy glacial outwash plains near Perham, Minnesota, with ten brothers and sisters. His father had forty-five milk cows, raised his own young stock, and also had hogs and chickens, but when Ron left for college in 1967, his father sold off the livestock and concentrated on growing cash crops—corn, kidney beans, a small acreage of potatoes.

Ron said his father always thought of himself first and foremost as a farmer, but on the side he had a variety of interests, including a seed-cleaning plant, a feed business, an animal health business, hardware and furniture stores, and a fertilizer and farm chemical business. In the late 1960s he was the first farmer in the area to invest in a center-pivot sprinkler irrigation system. He got the idea from talking to farmers from Nebraska who were vacationing at one of the local lakes. It worked well on the sandy loam soil of the outwash plain, which is highly productive but droughty, and has an abundant supply of groundwater.

Ron took a degree in agronomy. In 1972 he was working as a soil scientist at the agricultural experiment station and thinking about graduate school when his father asked him to come home to run the fertilizer business, because it was taking too much of his time. Two years later his father helped Ron buy his first farm, 320 acres, and they have steadily increased until in 1999 they were farming 4,000 acres of cash crops, all irrigated.

In their early days they did not have the equipment they needed to grow potatoes, so they swapped land with a potato grower in the off year of their three-year rotation of kidney beans, corn, and potatoes. The potato farmer got virgin land for potatoes and they got virgin land for beans. By 1982 they had gone from 240 acres of beans to more than 2,000, and they started the first kidney bean processing plant in Minnesota to save the cost of shipping beans to Wisconsin for processing. The plant opened an opportunity for other local farmers to grow a good cash crop, and in ten years it expanded from 300,000 pounds to more than 25 million.

"By the late eighties," Ron said, "we had a pretty intense rotation of kidney beans, potatoes, and corn. Dry beans and potatoes are very good cash crops, but they take a lot out of the soil and don't put much back in. We keep very good records, and we saw that our costs were going up and our yields were going down, because our rotation was not putting enough organic matter back in the soil. This area was like the Dust Bowl, because our soil structure had been depleted of organic matter and there was nothing to hold the soil and keep it from blowing. These past four years, with manure and alfalfa, our land hasn't hardly blown at all."

They realized that strictly cash-crop farming was taking a financial toll on their farm operations and an environmental toll on the health and productivity of their soil. They had to be better stewards of the land, and the only way they could really and honestly do so was to get back into some kind of livestock enterprise. "Even back in the old days," Ron said, "the best-producing land was the land right around the barn, because that's where most of the manure went."

They looked at pork, they looked at poultry, they looked at dairy. Dairy was the best fit, because cows consume the largest amounts of forage. They did a lot of work to find the minimum size necessary to pay for the technologies they needed to be successful. "Back in 1995 we found we had to milk at least 500 cows starting from scratch to make this thing cash flow, retire our debt, and still make a profit," Ron said. "In 2000 it's probably around 700 if you are going to start from scratch, because there's some expensive new technology out there."

Ron admits that he knew little about large-scale dairy when he started, "but you can always hire experts. Back in those days nobody in Minnesota really knew much about large dairies. The land-grant colleges still don't. They can't afford to put up $6 million experiment stations just for dairy, and they are learning a lot from us. I went out and solicited advice from experts in feed companies and processing companies about cash flows, nutrition, and large herd management and development. I took in some meetings and visited other areas of the country that were in large dairy production."

He knew that they needed to grow 1,400 acres of alfalfa to build up their soil. A dairy cow needs about an acre of alfalfa hay and an acre of corn silage, so a 1,400-cow dairy looked about the right size for them. "We designed our scale of production around the amount of land we are farming," said Ron. In November 1995 Little Pine Dairy opened with a 528' × 109' 700-cow barn and a 477' × 54' double-24 milking parlor, and in 1998 it added a second 480' × 106' 700-cow barn. The milking parlor cost $2.2 million and the complete 1,400-cow setup cost $6.3 million (fig. 6.1).

Teams of two workers on eight-hour shifts milked the cows three times a day. The daily average per cow was 73 pounds of milk, which was cooled and stored in a stainless steel tank until the truck came to pick it up and haul it to the processing plant. Ron contracted milk nine months ahead. He sold the steer calves to local farmers, who fed them for beef, and sent his heifer calves to a specialist custom heifer raiser, who prepared them to be herd replacements.

In 2000 Ron was pumping the manure into an earthen lagoon with a capacity of 16 million gallons and storing it until he could spread it on cropland. He told me that he was spending $60,000 a year to monitor the groundwater around it, to be sure he was not polluting it. The lagoon was crusted over and its odor did not seem particularly strong, but I asked Ron how close he could live to it in reasonable comfort.

"I wouldn't have any problem with a quarter of a mile," he said. "In fact, I've got a brand-new neighbor that's put up a brand-new house less than a quarter of a mile southeast of the dairy, and the prevailing winds are from the northwest. He's doing that after we have been in operation for five years, so I guess odor is not a problem for him."

Ron handled manure just like commercial fertilizer. He had it analyzed twice a year, so he knew the nutrients it contained. He tested the soil in each field each year and applied enough manure to supply the nutrients necessary to get a normal yield of the crop he planned to grow on it. For each field each year he has a complete record of the crop, the gallons of manure applied, and the date when it was applied.

Ron was looking at new technologies for improving the way he was handling manure, and he hoped to turn it into a source of profit. He was studying the feasibility of a methane digestion system that could produce 1,000 gallons of methanol a day, which could generate enough electricity to supply the entire dairy plus some for sale.

He had also spent $250,000 for a manure micronization system that separates and composts the solids. Then it centrifuges the liquid to remove the sus-

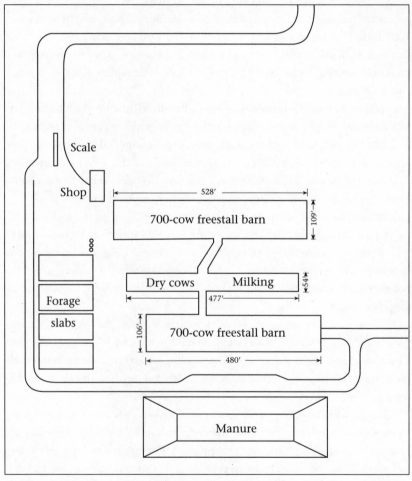

Figure 6.1. Site plan of the Little Pine Dairy in Perham, Minnesota, in 2000. (Based on a plan provided by Ron Tobkin; used by permission.)

pended solids and adds them to the compost. "Eventually you wind up with plain water," Ron said. "You probably wouldn't want to drink it, but we can use it to irrigate our cropland."

Ron's brother was in charge of the entire cropping operation: 1,500 acres of corn, 1,200 of alfalfa, 1,000 of potatoes, and 300 of kidney beans. In 1999 they farmed 32 separate parcels of land strung out over a distance of 25 miles (fig. 6.2). They rented some of their land, but Ron said they greatly prefer lease-purchase, because they want to own the land after they have built it up by putting a lot of manure on it.

Another brother runs the fertilizer and agricultural chemical company, but they all work together and help each other when they need help. Ron's oldest son graduated from college as a dairy specialist. He was working for a feed company to learn the ropes of nutrition, and got involved in farm operations on weekends. "He's still young and single," Ron said, "but someday he will probably replace me. My younger son starts college next year and hopes to partner with his brother. This really is a family operation. Seven of us own the company, which has thirty-five employees and an annual payroll of $650,000. We pay our top management people $50,000 to $90,000 a year.

"It takes a lot of money to run this operation. A while ago I was asked to be on a bank board, and my brother is on the board of another bank. I always understood the economics behind business, but now I've got an insight into how banks work and how examiners work. One of the partners in the bank lives in

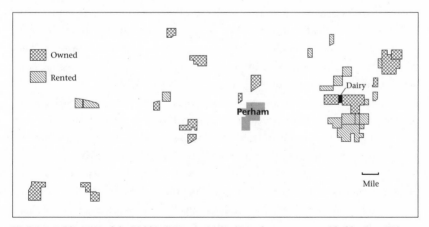

Figure 6.2. Plat map of the Tobkin Farms in 2000. (Based on a map provided by Ron Tobkin; used by permission.)

Naples, Florida, and he has gotten us involved in some business investments down there, because he's there to watch out what's going on for us."

Normally I am reluctant to ask farmers about their finances, but Ron was so open about his business that I decided to take a chance and ask him about the gross annual sales of the Tobkin Farms. "You're a smart fellow," he said, "you can do the arithmetic for yourself."

13,000 tons of corn silage @ $22/ton	$ 286,000
11,000 tons of alfalfa hay @ $49/ton	539,000
150,000 bushels of dry corn @ $2.55/bushel	382,500
800,000 pounds of kidney beans @ 27¢/pound	216,000
120,000 cwt. of potatoes @ $4.35/cwt	522,000
2.7 million pounds milk/month @ $14.60/cwt	4,730,400

"That looks like a total of nearly $6.7 million a year."

Then he filled me in on the role he has played in fostering dairy farming in the Midwest. One of the men who worked for him had a Ph.D. in animal nutrition, and Ron knew the agronomic end of the business, growing forages. He also knew personnel management, so in 1997 they formed a dairy management services company that helped start two large new dairies in Iowa, one in South Dakota, and two in Minnesota. Each of these new dairies has the same layout as the Little Pine model (fig. 6.1).

Ron takes an ownership position in new dairies and works with groups of farmers to help develop them. He was managing a new 1,600-cow dairy at Lancaster, in the very far northwestern corner of Minnesota, expected to put another 2,500-cow dairy next to it, and hoped to get into processing. The prime mover for this project has been a local developer, who has involved ten owners. They have invested a total of $7.2 million, although they have not invested equal amounts and do not own equal shares.

Ron was not bothered by the remoteness of the location, because he hoped to build a reverse-osmosis processing plant that would take the lactose and protein and butterfat out of the milk, leaving just pure water. They would save transport costs by shipping only the components to cheese plants, and they would also save by recycling the water, because water costs them $1.50 per 1,000 gallons. The new dairies will employ seventy-five people and the processing plant will employ five in an area that is economically challenged, but Ron did admit that it is difficult to recruit top management people to the remote northwestern corner of Minnesota, because there are few jobs for their wives.

Gary Allen

Gary Allen has shown how good management can build a traditional dairy farm up to viable size by internal growth. His grandfather immigrated from Denmark to North Dakota, where he tried to farm, but in the Depression he lost everything. He moved to Minnesota with six horses, rented a farm near Eyota, east of Rochester, and got a few milk cows. He raised six children. The boys all worked on farms for $1 a day and board, but in the winter months they often worked only for room and board, nothing else.

When Gary's father got out of the Army after World War II, his father gave him ten cows and ten sows, and he rented a farm north of Eyota. The banker loaned him the money to buy feed. They nearly froze to death in the farmhouse that winter, so he rented another place for five years, and then in 1951 he bought the farm where Gary now lives. He had $9,000 in the bank, which was a lot of money back in those days.

Gary said his father worked like a horse. "He was not a good adopter of technology, and he wasn't too good with the business side, but boy, could he work! He probably did twice as much as the average guy, but technology caught up with him in the early sixties, feeding practices, breeding, herbicides, things like that, and he was starting to slide backwards."

Gary started farming with his father in 1970, when he was 24. His parents, his mother mainly, said he had to go to college, because there's no money in farming. He worked in engineering for six years but was frustrated by all the politics, and deep down he had always liked farming, so he quit and came home. "Linda, the wife," he said, "was going to school that fall, and we had a young child. She said, 'You've gotta be crazy,' but I said, 'We'll be OK. We're young.'"

That winter Gary straightened out some problems, and the more he dug into it, the more intrigued he got, so he took over the management completely the following year. "I've got to give Dad a lot of credit for stepping aside," he said, "because I don't step aside that easily with my boys, but I do have a lot of experience to bring. He could see that he didn't understand a lot of these things, but they were getting better, and he didn't have to worry about them. He would just come in and say, 'Well, what are we going to do today?'"

By 1976 Gary was thinking about leaving and starting on his own, because he and Linda were still living in a trailer on the farm, he was working for $300 a month, and he was not sharing any of the growth. His father decided to keep him by retiring and setting up a partnership that gave Gary half of the increase, but he had to pay market price for everything. "When I came here in 1970 there were forty cows," he said, "and they sold me forty cows when I bought the first half, because I had already grown the herd to eighty. I had to buy another sixty when I bought the second half, because by then we had a hundred cows."

Gary started the growth process right away, but he grew in steps, depending on economic conditions. He believes that adversity creates opportunity. "Tough times stretch your management ability," he said. "We get sloppy and lax if it's too easy, and I have learned more about business and how to handle costs of production during times of adversity."

He took control of the farm during a period of adversity, and there were days during the middle '80s when he had a net worth of zero dollars, but he was able to stay in farming because he had performance, was profitable, paid income tax, and had lenders that stayed with him. "The eighties took out a lot of good farmers," he said, "but they sifted out a lot of chaff, too, and we're going to sift out some more chaff pretty soon. You can already hear 'em squealing. Everybody's comfortable with the way things were twenty years ago, but things have spun so fast that it just smokes a lot of these guys."

He said you could make vast leaps ahead when feed prices were low or milk prices were high. "When we had $19 milk I didn't go out and buy new tractors or new land. I paid down my debts and put money away for when we had another time of low prices. I have been through three of those. I just sustained through the first two, but now I am on the right side to take advantage of opportunity."

Gary has never bought many cows, and has gone from 40 to 600 by raising his own replacement heifers. Linda has taken care of the calves. For three or four years at a time she never lost a single calf, and of course Gary has always figured that he could save every cow. He said, "You almost have to think like a cow to be a good dairyman, because cow comfort equals production. What does that cow want to do?" He has had no formal agricultural training; he has taught himself through the extension service, getting hooked up with the right people at the university, reading a lot, and bringing in good consultants who know what they are doing in specific areas.

In 1999 Gary needed three-quarters of an acre of alfalfa hay and three-quarters of an acre of corn to feed a cow and her replacement, and he expected her to produce 30,000 pounds of milk. He also bought concentrates. "The ration is very complicated," he said, "it's not just plain old corn, oats, and hay anymore, and we are constantly adjusting it for where the cows are in the reproductive cycle, for the season of the year, and for the quality of the forage." Most large dairies hire Ph.D.'s as nutritional consultants, and Gary's daughter, Dana, was taking her Ph.D. in animal nutrition.

Gary owned 900 acres and farmed 2,010: 1,050 of corn, 530 of alfalfa, 200 of soybeans, 190 of peas, and 40 of sweet corn. All of his land was within five miles. The canning crops, peas and sweet corn, were very profitable, and they were also integral to his scrape-and-haul manure management system. He does not have pits to hold manure, so he has to scrape the barns and spread it every five days, and he needs open ground all year round where he can spread it. He establishes alfalfa after peas in the fall.

Gary has to enlarge his operation to keep his family in the dairy business. His cow numbers are going up, fifty to seventy-five a year, and he needs a place to put them. He has made feasibility studies, but he was not sure if this was the right time to expand, because his older son, Dean, 35, went through a divorce this spring, and his younger son, Tim, is only 22. His only question is when, not if.

Gary is constantly positioning himself, and in 1999 he added 400 acres. Two or three years earlier he visited one of his neighbors and said, "I hear you're thinking of quitting. I am not going to bother you again, but see me if you would like me to run it for you." Last winter the neighbor called and asked Gary to rent his farm. Gary said it's some of the best dirt in southeastern Minnesota, so that was a good feeling, and usually if someone is renting to you, at some point he is going to sell it to you.

"Usually farmland is not a good investment," Gary said, "but there's something about it. There's only so much, and it does hold against inflation. What's a fair price? Fair means cash flow, so I suppose you're talking $1,000 to $1,200 an acre, but you won't be able to buy much of anything for less than $2,000."

Gary incorporated as Gar-Lin Dairy Farms in 1996, when he took Dean in. Gar-Lin is for Gary and Linda. "The boys wanted to change the name," Gary said, "but I told them that's one thing you will never change." Gary and Linda each owned 45 percent of the stock and Dean owned 10. Gary said he incorporated for asset transfer reasons, because it's easy to give shares or to sell shares.

He said he needs a business-type structure for legal protection. He does all of his own internal accounting and cost of production analyses, and his annual depreciation is close to $250,000. He uses four computers on a daily basis, and he even has one in his feed truck, in addition to the four obsolete computers up in the attic. "We like to see 50 to 60 percent asset turnover," he said. "Asset turnover is the percentage of your total equity you can gross in a year. Small farms do 20 to 30 percent, larger farms get toward 50 to 60. Right now I am close to 85 percent equity, and last year we saw 30 percent return on equity."

In 1999 Gary employed seventeen full-time people and six part-time. He had a full 401(k), a good health insurance plan, and very little turnover. This spring they went to wearing uniforms. The boys wanted to do it. "I don't like to walk around town boasting I'm Gar-Lin Dairy Farms and I'm a better farmer than everybody else when I'm not," Gary said, "but we put the question to the hired help, and they all wanted uniforms."

Gary works on holidays to give the help time off, and he has a strong sense of community responsibility. He told me that he spends $15,000 a year at the local hardware store to help keep it in business, even though he could get things cheaper elsewhere. He and Linda get away three or four times a year for four- or five-day vacations, but he is always happy to get back.

"There are some things that make a good farmer," Gary said. "One of them is the excitement of a new calf born every day. Or a nice two-year-old heifer that comes in with a beautiful udder of milk. Or cutting a good hay crop that is just as thick as can be. Or when the corn comes up in the spring, the rows are straight and the color is good and it looks better than the neighbor's does across the road. He's planting three days too early, but it's too wet and I know it's going to bother him. I will be there when it's right, and I will work as hard as I can to get as much done as I can when it's just right.

"Or when you get the first hay crop, 530 acres in four days, with no rain on any of it, and it's all covered and put away. Half the guys got rain because they didn't do it in time, but I got super-good feed and lower cost of production. Each one of these little things, you inch out a little bit each time. It comes in just little bitty steps. That heifer calf that didn't die and didn't get sick. That hay crop is ten points better in relative feed value because I didn't have any weeds in my alfalfa, I cut it when it was supposed to be, I didn't get any rain on it, I covered it and protected it. My corn was put in at optimum soil moisture. All those little advantages are huge in the end, they are almost exponential.

"Each one of these little areas is an excitement, and you get a high off it. I really love my job. The successful ones in agriculture are the ones that really love their job. I guess that's true in every business."

Loving the job is necessary, but of course it is not sufficient. Gary Allen, like Rob Tobkin and Joe Pires, is also a superlative manager, and all three have demonstrated that large modern dairies can flourish in the traditional dairy belt of the

Midwest. The two big questions facing the region at the end of the twentieth century were whether traditional small dairy farms, which have lagged in adopting modern technology to secure economies of scale, can successfully make the leap to large-scale production, and whether enough will make the leap to produce the volume of milk that large modern processing plants must have in order to operate profitably, remain in business, and justify the investment necessary to keep them in business.

7
Broilers

Broilers are meat-type chickens six to twelve weeks old. In 1954, when the census of agriculture first reported separate data on broilers, American farmers produced and sold 792 million.[1] Nearly 800 million broilers sounds like an awful lot until you realize that in 1997 our farmers produced and sold 6,742 million, or roughly 24 for every man, woman, and child in the United States.[2] This phenomenal increase is important in its own right, but it is equally important because the transformation of broiler production served as a model for the subsequent transformation of turkey, egg, and hog production.[3]

Before World War II farmers kept chickens mainly to lay eggs, and the meat was a treat reserved for special occasions. In 1934 Americans ate 67 million pounds of chicken; today we eat that much in only two days. Chicken was such a delicacy that in 1932 the Republican Party campaigned on the slogan "A chicken in every pot," which it deemed the ultimate symbol of the good life.

Most farm families kept flocks of fifty to one hundred heavy laying hens, and baked them for Sunday dinner when their laying days were done. Some farmers housed their birds in small coops inside fenced pens, where the farm wife fed them, but many flocks had free run of the barnyard and even the house yard, where they were left to scratch for themselves. They pecked for worms and insects, scrambled for kitchen scraps and grain tossed to them occasionally, and found secret places to lay their eggs and hatch their chicks.

The farm wife hunted for eggs until she had collected a basketful, and she took them to the local general store, where she bartered them for goods the farm could not produce. The storekeeper then sold these "farm fresh" eggs to his customers. Cracking an egg back in those days was a real adventure, because some had gone too long undiscovered, and some had already been fertilized. You never knew when the egg you cracked would greet you with the revolting stench of hydrogen sulfide or the stomach-wrenching sight of a chick embryo. Early on I learned the habit, which I have never been able to break, of cracking each egg into a separate bowl rather than directly into the frying pan or dish, because you did not want to add a bad egg to those you had already cracked.

In the fall, as the days grew shorter, the hens began to molt and stopped laying eggs. They began to lay once again in the spring, and the farmer set a dozen eggs or so under an old broody hen to hatch out. He kept the pullets for laying hens, but fed out the cockerels for ten weeks or so and sold them as "frying size" broilers. Some farmers hatched out their own eggs, but after World War I commercial hatcheries with large incubators had become common, and many farmers bought day-old chicks by mail, even though the animal rights activists of the day complained that shipping live chicks by mail was cruel and inhumane.

Preparing chicken for dinner was not a pleasant task. I can remember my grandmother wading into the squawking flock of barnyard chickens in search of likely-looking birds. When she spotted one, she grabbed it by the head, snapped its neck with a quick flick of her wrist, and left it flopping around in the dust until she had enough for the meal. Then she scalded the birds with hot water to ease the task of pulling out the feathers, and eviscerated them. She saved the giblets, the edible internal organs, and cooked them as special delicacies or used them to season gravy. Preparing chickens for your own table was such a chore that few people were willing to do the job for anyone else.

The demands of city folk for chicken were met by men known as chicken haulers, or assemblers, who roamed the countryside buying any birds that farmers were willing to sell. Once they had assembled a load, they shipped it by train or truck to brokers in the city, who sold the birds to processors and butcher shops. The birds were shipped live, because refrigeration was too expensive. They were sold "live weight," and unscrupulous haulers and brokers were not above feeding them salt to increase their water consumption, or even lacing their feed with lead shot or gravel.

The production and marketing of surplus farm chickens was a fairly casual, hit-or-miss affair. By all accounts, the first person to start a commercial broiler operation was Mrs. Wilmer Steele, the wife of a Coast Guardsman stationed at Ocean View, in far southeastern Delaware. In 1923 Mrs. Steele started a flock of 500 chicks and sold them when they weighed two pounds. The next year she started 1,000 chicks, and by 1926 she had built a house that held 10,000 birds, a truly astonishing size at that time.

Her neighbors began to imitate her, because they needed a more reliable source of income, and they turned the Delmarva Peninsula (Delaware, Maryland, and Virginia) into the nation's first major commercial broiler-producing area. The Delmarva Peninsula lies between Chesapeake and Delaware bays. The flat sandy land is suitable for growing truck crops, but truck crops are always a gamble, and fishing is equally unpredictable.

Some fishermen and others in Delmarva already were supplementing their income by keeping flocks of laying hens to produce eggs for sale, but in 1926 a disease called "range paralysis" put them out of the egg business. This disease did not attack chickens until they were twelve weeks old, so the egg producers switched to selling their birds for meat before they reached that age. The number of broilers produced in Delmarva skyrocketed to 3.6 million in 1929 and then to 25.3 million in 1939.

The first broiler houses were 16' × 16' coops with straight shed roofs. The birds could run outside in yards fenced with chicken wire. Growers merely added more houses of the same size when they enlarged their flocks. A few early growers confined their birds in long, low, narrow broiler houses, which eventually became the norm and replaced colonies of small coops and fenced yards. By the early 1950s one-story broiler houses that measured 28' × 200' and housed 8,000 birds had become standard features on the rural landscapes of broiler-producing areas.

The growth of broiler production increased sales opportunities for feed dealers. Local flour millers began mixing and selling special feed for broilers, and regional and national companies sold feed through local dealers or directly to farmers. The feed companies hired knowledgeable salesmen, whom they called "servicemen." Each serviceman regularly visited the farmers in his territory, and they came to depend on him for expert advice, veterinary assistance, and suggestions for improvements in management.

Feed dealers enhanced their sales by encouraging farmers to grow broilers. Some sold chicks and feed to farmers on 90- to 120-day credit, long enough for the farmer to feed the birds to market weight, and then they bought and marketed the finished birds. Some contracted with farmers to feed birds for them. They paid a flat fee per bird plus a bonus for efficient feed conversion. The feed dealer was like an insurance policy for the farmer who was reluctant to take a chance on the mercurial fluctuations of the broiler market. The dealer could spread the risk over many farms, and could cover losses one week by profits the next.

The marketing of broilers remained loosely organized. The principal markets were New York City, where live birds were essential for the important kosher trade, Philadelphia, and other large eastern cities. Some feed dealers hauled the live birds to the city themselves, or hired local truckers. Some broiler growers sold their birds to live poultry buyers and haulers who bought farm flocks. A grower notified several buyers when the flock was ready, and the buyers came to the farm to bid on it.

Some buyers had the idea of processing the birds before hauling them to market. In 1938 the first broiler-processing plant in Delmarva was opened in an abandoned canning factory, of which the peninsula had a plethora. The birds were hung by their feet from steel shackles attached to a conveyor belt that carried them slowly through the plant. Their throats were slit, they were bled, and their bodies were scalded in tanks of hot water to loosen their feathers. All jobs were done by hand, and each worker performed the same monotonous task, over and over and over. The wages were low, the hours were long, and a processing plant was a vile and nasty place to work.

The term "New York dressed" was applied to birds that had been slaughtered, bled, and plucked but still had their heads, feet, and all their innards. Often the head and feet were tucked neatly under a wing. It is hard to realize that 83 percent of the chickens sold in the United States as late as 1962 were "New York dressed," because few modern Americans would know what to do with such a bird.

The 1930s were a period of research and solidification that laid a sound foundation for the future growth of the broiler business. Developing effective health measures was essential, because cramming thousands of chickens so close together under a single roof was simply asking for trouble with parasites and diseases.

University experiment stations worked closely with federal and state agencies to learn how to control diseases, and their efforts were enthusiastically supported by drug companies, because broiler producers were some of their best customers. They learned to lace feed with medications and to put vaccines in drinking water to control pullorum, coccidiosis, rickets, perosis, leukosis, synovitis, and other poultry diseases of which most of us have never even heard.

Breeders developed birds that grew faster with less feed and put on more weight in all the right places. Nutritionists developed high-energy feeds for these better birds, and they calculated the precise mix that was ideal for each week of their growth. They added vitamin D to the feed to substitute for natural sunlight, so growers could raise their birds indoors. They identified forty specific nutrients that all broilers must have, and they boasted that we know more about the nutrition of chickens than about that of any other animals, including people. If people grew as fast as broilers, they said, an eight-week-old baby would weigh 350 pounds.

By 1940 the stage was set for the rapid growth of the broiler business, but first there was a war that had to be taken care of.

World War II stimulated the rapid development of new broiler-producing areas in northeastern Georgia and northwestern Arkansas. In 1942 the War Food Administration commandeered all Delmarva broiler production for the armed forces, and producers in Georgia and Arkansas were able to invade markets that Delmarva had dominated. Red meat was rationed but chicken was not, the wartime price of chicken was high, and producing food was a patriotic duty.

Gordon Sawyer says that the government chose Delmarva because it was easy to control. There were only three ways off the peninsula, and two of them crossed large bodies of water. He says that the government despaired of controlling production in the broiler areas of Georgia and Arkansas, which had a long tradition of illegal production of moonshine whiskey.

After broiler production had become well established in northeastern Georgia, they liked to tell the story of the old boy who was hauled before the judge for the umpteenth time for making moonshine. When the judge handed him a stiff fine and a jail sentence, he protested vehemently that the judge had never treated him this way before. "I know," said the judge, "but now a man can make an honest living in these parts by raising broilers, so he doesn't need to break the law by moonshining any longer."

Jesse D. Jewell, of Gainesville, Georgia, was the pioneering entrepreneur who developed the first modern, vertically integrated broiler-producing company, and some say that he merely stumbled into it. In 1930, when he was 28 years old, he took over the failing family feed and fertilizer business. To build sales he gave farmers day-old baby chicks, and he sold them feed on credit to raise the chicks. When the birds were full grown he loaded them live into an old Reo truck and hauled them to Miami to sell. He was a supersalesman, and he talked local banks and major feed companies into financing his business.

By the late 1930s Jewell was having so much trouble getting enough chicks from distant hatcheries that he built his own hatchery, and in 1940 he decided to build a processing plant and start marketing his own birds. He knew that customers in the South had no particular preference for live or New York–dressed birds, so he removed the heads, feet, and entrails and advertised that his broilers were "pan ready." He packed them on ice in wooden barrels and shipped them by rail to stores all over the South.

Jewell was sensitive to the importance of promotion marketing. He created brand names for advertising his birds, because he realized that customers prefer to buy brand-name products they can trust, and they like products that are easy to prepare. In 1951 Jewell converted completely to frozen packaged products, which were well suited to self-service supermarkets, because the customer could take them out of the case and they did not require an in-store butcher.

In 1954 Jesse Jewell completed the vertical integration of his company when he built a feed mill to use grain shipped in cheaply from the Midwest by barge on the Tennessee River waterway that had been developed by the Tennessee Valley Authority (TVA). He owned the hatchery and feed mill, and he contracted with farmers to grow the birds that he processed and marketed. He developed an effective management structure, hired good people, and paid them well. His operation served as a model for the development of other broiler-producing companies.

A company is vertically integrated when it controls successive phases of production, processing, and distribution, either by direct ownership or under contract. In the broiler business a vertically integrated company might have started with a hatchery, a feed mill, or a processing plant; it became vertically integrated when it acquired all three stages of production and contracted with farmers to raise the birds.

Before the broiler business became vertically integrated, it was too fragmented, with too many individual profit points. The hatchery, the feed mill, the feed dealer, the grower, the processor, the marketer, each had to make a profit, and there was hardly enough for any one of them. The profit could be a lot smaller if all of these activities were integrated in a single company, and the company could use creative bookkeeping to reduce its taxes by internal reallocation of funds.

The vertically integrated company contracted with farmer/growers to feed baby chicks to market weight, although some companies had a few grow-out houses of their own and hired the workers they needed. The grow-out houses had to be within twenty to thirty miles of the company's feed mill and processing plant to control the expense of transporting feed and live birds. The company furnished chicks, feed, and supervision, and assumed the financial risk. The grower furnished the houses, equipment, and labor, and was paid a set fee per bird plus a bonus for efficient feed conversion.

Converted school buses delivered day-old chicks from the company hatchery and company trucks kept the feed bins full. Company servicemen had "routes" of twenty to thirty-five grower farms, and they visited each one at least once a week, usually more often, to supervise the operation and offer advice.

The company could cope with the volatile fluctuations of broiler prices because it contracted with many growers, and it could schedule their birds to come to market in a steady flow. Individual growers could not afford to take a chance on the market, and they had to sacrifice some of their cherished independence for the reliable income the company gave them. Some companies were easy to deal with, but Bill Goodwin, the county agent in Scott County, Mississippi, said, "Some of these broiler companies have such strict rules and controls that I don't even want to set foot in one of their houses when I visit a farm."

Over the years broiler houses have steadily become larger and more efficient. In 1940 a 1,500-bird house was considered large, but 5,000-bird houses were common in the 1950s, and by 1990 companies would not even deal with growers whose houses held fewer than 20,000 birds. The rule of thumb was 0.72 square feet per bird. In 1997 a standard broiler house was 40 feet wide, 400 feet long, and 10 feet high, with a capacity of 22,000 birds.

The lower walls of a broiler house are solid, but the upper half is a wire mesh screen with canvas curtains that can be raised or lowered for light and ventilation. Most growers have at least four houses, which require an area of around twenty acres. Next to each house is a pair of tall, cylindrical metal feed bins with funnel-shaped bottoms that lead to the automatic feeding system inside the house. One bin is always kept full to ensure a steady supply of feed.

A metal feed trough runs the length of the floor and circles back to the feed bin. An endless flat link chain carries feed through the trough at a slow set speed, and it is automatically filled when it passes the feed bin. Down the side and across the center are pipelines with drinking nipples or metal watering troughs that are also filled automatically. Above them are lines of circular heaters, and the ceiling is studded with rows of bright white lights that stay on all night to encourage the birds to eat as much as possible.

The interior of a broiler house is a piano-wire jungle, because all of the equipment is suspended by wires that can winch it up to the ceiling to get it out of the way when the birds are full grown and the catchers come to collect them. The grower replaces the white light bulbs with blue bulbs to make the birds think it is night so they will settle down and be easier to catch. The catchers are rough old boys who grab birds by the handful and stuff them into cages, fourteen to a cage, to be trucked off to the processing plant.

When the birds are gone, it takes about a week to clean up the house and get it ready for the next batch of chicks. The floor has to be covered with six inches to a foot of clean straw to absorb their droppings. Growers spread the litter on cropland or pasture when they clean out their houses, because it is exceptionally rich fertilizer. It is almost too rich. "We used to say that you used all the litter you could get whenever you could get it," said Bill Goodwin, "but now we have to be more careful. We test the soil to find how much litter it can safely take, and a grower must have an approved litter disposal plan before he is allowed to put up a new broiler house."

Many broiler growers also have herds of cattle to graze their litter-enriched pastures. They know that cattle like to munch on the chunks of litter, which is rich in protein, and some actually treat it with molasses, mix it with grain, and feed it directly to the cattle.

The South was ripe for broilers at the end of World War II. The boll weevil had devoured King Cotton, which had been the economic mainstay of the region, and many former cotton farmers were desperate. They needed and welcomed a new source of reliable farm income that would keep their family farms alive and viable. The broiler business was so good that almost anyone could borrow the money to build a broiler house. Fuel and building costs were lower in the South than in other parts of the country and labor was cheaper, both on the farm and in the feed mills and processing plants.

Broilers supplemented meager farm income, and they also meshed well with off-farm employment, because women and children could handle most of the work in a broiler house. Erstwhile cotton farmers were perfectly willing to contract with broiler companies, because farming with other folks' money had been their way of life. Country stores had sold them seed, fertilizer, and even groceries on credit and collected after the cotton crop had been harvested and sold.

The farmers could not have done it alone, but the South also had entrepreneurs who were eager to emulate the Jesse Jewell model of vertical integration by developing their own broiler companies. They were young men in a hurry who felt that the war had cost them a lot of time from their lives, and they wanted to make it up fast. Broilers were a high-risk business with an enticingly high payoff. The local bankers were willing to help them because they already were familiar with crop loans, and they had fewer options for lending their money than banks in other parts of the country.

Some entrepreneurs made tremendous profits, and they plowed their profits back into expanding their businesses. They were strong-minded people, and few have ever been accused of suffering from excessive modesty. An entrepreneur has to be fairly confident to begin with, and there's nothing quite like making a large amount of money to give a businessman a smug sense of sublime confidence in his own wisdom and good judgment. Entrepreneurs have assiduously cultivated politicians, who make the laws that regulate their businesses, and politicians have assiduously cultivated entrepreneurs, because they are influential citizens and potential major contributors to their campaign funds.

The entrepreneurs were a hard-charging lot who were constantly looking for new ideas and better ways of doing things. They picked the brains of technical experts at agricultural colleges and experiment stations, and they flew all over the country to find out what others were doing. They were almost fanatical about cutting production costs. They mechanized and automated broiler houses, feed mills, and processing plants. They pushed breeders to develop birds that would produce more meat in less time with less feed.

The A&P food stores helped. They spurred breeders to develop "meat type" birds with larger breasts, thicker thighs, and smaller bones, They gained widespread national publicity for broilers by sponsoring a "Chicken of Tomorrow" contest with lavish cash prizes. In 1951 10,000 people showed up in Fayetteville, Arkansas, for the final judging, a week-long extravaganza with street dances, a rodeo, a queen's ball, and speeches by all manner of eminent dignitaries, including Alben W. Barkley, vice president of the United States, who was affectionately know as the Veep.

The development of large-scale integrated broiler operations reduced production costs and consumer prices, and they made chicken our most affordable meat. The price of chicken in real 1967 dollars peaked at close to 50 cents a pound in 1945, then plummeted to a mere 5 cents a pound in 1980, and it has remained consistently low ever since.[4]

The cascading price of chicken stimulated demand. In the early 1960s

Colonel Harlan Sanders introduced his famous Kentucky Fried Chicken, and other fast-food chains have also kept the processors busy. These chains wanted cut pieces, breasts, thighs, and wings, rather than whole birds, and further processing added to the profits of the broiler companies.

Health-conscious Americans discovered that chicken is low in cholesterol, and per capita consumption has increased steadily, while per capita consumption of beef has dropped and per capita consumption of pork has not changed much. In the 1990s chicken passed beef to become our most popular meat (fig. 7.1). Consumers want ready-to-use products in convenient packages, and processors have been happy to add to their profits by producing a wider variety of such value-added products.

Processors have also actively developed export markets, because the foreign preference for dark meat meshes well with the American preference for white meat. (Some foreigners complain that American meat has no taste. I have spent enough time in barnyards to know what I am tasting when I eat meat in foreign countries, and I don't like it!) Exports were so successful, in fact, that they led to the "chicken war" of the early 1960s, when the European Economic Community tried to discriminate against American broilers, and some processors became so incensed that they refused to allow Volkswagens to be parked on their premises.

The major national feed companies recognized the huge potential of the broiler business, which offered the largest new market for their products in many

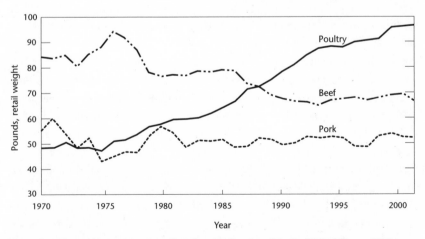

Figure 7.1. Per capita consumption of poultry, beef, and pork in the United States, 1970–2002. (Used by permission of *Economic Review,* Federal Reserve Bank of Kansas City.)

years, and they targeted the South, which was a feed-deficit area. The entire state of Georgia, for example, never produced enough corn and soybeans to feed all of its broilers even for a single week, and the feed had to be shipped in from the cash-grain farming areas of the Midwest.

In the early days the feed came in hundred-pound sacks that had to be man-handled at the feed mill and on the farm. The sacks were made of colorful "dress print" fabrics, and companies competed with each other for the most attractive patterns, because farm wives used the emptied sacks to make dresses and other articles of clothing. Presumably the men were happier than the women with the shift in the early 1950s to bulk feed trucks that were filled automatically at the mill and unloaded automatically into farm feed bins with no more human effort than merely pushing a button.

The early feed mixes had to contain grit, granules of hard sharp rock, because chickens have no teeth. The grit went to their gizzards, where it ground up the feed that the birds had eaten. In the barnyard chickens could scratch up their own grit, but in a broiler house the grower had to include it in the feed mix. Nowadays grit is no longer necessary, because manufacturers pelletize feed into crumbles that are hard enough to do the same job.

In 1960, 10 million tons of chicken feed were shipped from the Midwest to the South, mainly by barge or truck, but in the early 1960s the Southern Railway began to compete effectively by introducing "Big John," a covered aluminum hopper car that could haul 100 tons of grain, twice the payload of a conventional steel car. The railroad was able to reduce its terminal switching costs by moving groups of five, ten, or even twenty cars, precursors of today's unit trains, at one time to a single destination.

As their companies grew and prospered, the freewheeling entrepreneurs began to realize that starting a business and running it successfully required different talents, and they had to supplement their production skills with management skills. For example, they had to schedule the orderly flow of thousands of birds a day, from hatchery to supermarket, with no wasteful shortages or surpluses at any stage of production. They had to guess what they could sell on each day in the future, then arrange to deliver enough eggs to the hatchery to produce enough chicks for enough growers to deliver enough birds to the processing plant on just the right day, and they had to schedule the flow of birds consistently, day after day after day.

In 1957 the University of Georgia offered the first of a series of short courses in poultry business management, and they attracted a veritable who's who of the leaders of the rapidly growing broiler business. The participants studied management, organization, personnel, and finances, but they might well have learned as much from their discussions with their fellow students as they learned from their instructors, and they developed close ties across the industry.

The growth of the broiler business was plagued by the same kind of livestock cycle that bedevils all forms of livestock production. Producers increase their production when prices are high, and new producers are attracted into the business. Eventually they produce more than anyone wants to buy, and the surplus depresses prices. Low prices force some producers out of business, and others have to tighten their belts. Eventually they produce too little to satisfy the market, the price begins to rise, and the cycle starts all over again.

The broiler business made millionaires, but its rapid growth often outstripped demand, and it suffered many periods of depressed prices, when some millionaires went broke. During such periods various groups and individuals proposed some kind of government production control program in an attempt to stabilize prices, but the industry adamantly and consistently opposed any kind of government program except health inspection.

The broiler industry did welcome the 1957 Poultry Products Inspection Act, which required that all poultry products shipped in interstate commerce had to be inspected for wholesomeness by the U.S. Department of Agriculture. In 1968 this act was amended to include all poultry shipments, intrastate as well as interstate. The magnitude of the task, and of the poultry industry, is indicated by the fact that in 1995 the inspection program required 9,700 staff years of work and had a budget of $517 million, more than half a billion dollars.[5]

Table 7.1
Average weight of broiler, feed required per pound of bird, and market age, 1935–1994

Year	Weight (pounds)	Feed per pound (pounds)	Market age (weeks)
1935	2.80	4.4	16.0
1950	3.00	3.5	11.0
1975	3.75	2.0	8.0
1994	4.65	1.9	6.5

Source: *Poultry Tribune*, September 1995, 16.

The history of the broiler business since the early 1960s has been a story of consolidation and concentration, a labyrinthine tale of buyouts and mergers. The names have kept changing as companies small and not so small have been acquired by a few giants, such as Tyson, Gold Kist, Perdue, and ConAgra. In 1972 the four largest companies processed only 17 percent of all broilers, but in 1994 the four largest companies processed 42 percent, and the top twenty processed 80 percent.[6]

Size brings problems. Many layers of management now separate the top executives from the farmers who produce broilers for them, and many managers are MBAs who speak the language of the boardroom more comfortably than they speak the language of the barnyard. The companies boast waiting lists of eager would-be growers, but they have become large and impersonal, and many growers long for the old days of small paternalistic companies, when they knew the owners as their friends.

In summary, during the latter half of the twentieth century the United States has gone from a few chickens on every farm to a few farms with tens of thousands of chickens, and the vertical integration of broiler production has been the model for the organization of a modern livestock economy. Large-scale operations have standardized inputs and products, and they have reduced production costs and consumer prices.

Broiler production is more and more concentrated on larger farms and in larger firms. Centralized control of production has facilitated the rapid adoption of new labor-saving technologies, and mechanization and automation have made broiler houses and processing plants more efficient. The farmers who grow broilers have had to trade some of their cherished independence for greater financial security, and some feel that they have become mere pawns of the integrator companies.

In 1950 the average broiler house needed ten pounds of feed to produce a three-pound bird in eleven weeks, and put through four batches of 5,000 birds a year. In 1994 the average house used nine pounds of feed to produce a five-pound bird in seven weeks, and put through six batches of 22,000 birds a year (table 7.1).

The average processing plant handled 2,000 birds a day in 1950, 200,000 birds a day in 1990. Machines now perform many of the unpleasant tasks that once had to be done by hand, but they have increased stress by speeding up the line, and the plants that process our cheapest and most popular meat still are nasty places to work.

8
Broiler Areas and
Broiler People

By the early 1960s the broiler business had pretty well matured, and it had stabilized geographically. It has continued to grow and to grow quite rapidly, but most of its growth has been concentrated in the existing producing areas, and few new producing areas have developed. The *1997 Census of Agriculture* shows that the arc of states from Arkansas and Texas to Delaware produced 81 percent of the nation's broilers in 1964, and this area has never since dropped below that share, while the national total has increased from 1.9 billion in 1964 to 6.7 billion in 1997 (fig. 8.1).

The patterns on the map suggest that most broiler production is clustered within a thirty-mile radius of a complex consisting of a processing plant, a feed mill, and possibly a hatchery. Most clusters have more than one of these complexes, which entrepreneurs developed in the heady days of the broiler business in the late 1940s and early 1950s. The traditional producing areas in Delmarva were slow to recover from World War II, but the new producing areas in Georgia and Arkansas grew rapidly, and entrepreneurs were developing new producing areas in other parts of the South.

Northern Alabama

Broiler production in northern Alabama started on Sand Mountain after World War II. In Alabama they call it Sand Mountain, but it really is a rolling upland that is the southern part of the Appalachian Plateau. It has never been an especially good crop-farming area, because its sandy soils are too droughty and most farms are undersized.

Toward the end of World War II Dr. P. O. Davis, director of the Alabama Agricultural Extension Service, realized that farmers in Alabama could no longer depend on only cotton and corn, that they needed something else to increase their farm income. He got the state to commit the money to build two poultry-processing plants, one in the north and one in the south. The one in the south, near Montgomery, was political, and in a month's time it was flat broke.

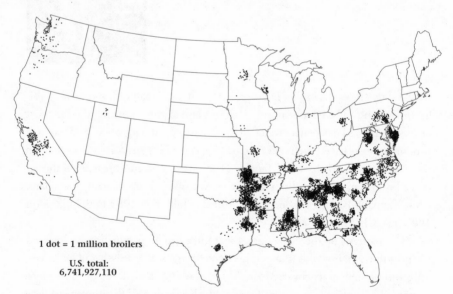

1 dot = 1 million broilers

U.S. total:
6,741,927,110

Figure 8.1. Broilers and other meat-type chickens sold, 1997. (Source: *1997 Census of Agriculture,* vol. 2, pt. 1 [Washington, D.C.: U.S. Department of Agriculture, National Agricultural Statistics Service, 1999].)

The plant in northern Alabama was to be either in Cullman or in Albertville, and the town that raised the operating money first would get it. Hogan Jackson, then 75 years old, president of the Albertville National Bank, was especially eager to get the plant. He personally raised $23,500 of operating capital by selling stock at $10 a share, and the plant was built in Albertville.

John Livingston had graduated from Auburn in 1941 with a degree in agriculture. He got a job as assistant county agent in Morgan County, but he was called into service by the Navy, which gave him a commission and sent him to the South Pacific for four years. He wound up as the executive officer of an attack transport ship with a crew of 523 officers and enlisted men when he was only 26 years old. When the war ended he returned to his former job, but he wanted to get into some kind of business. The directors of the poultry-processing plant in Albertville asked the extension service to find them a manager, and he was one of three people who were nominated.

The directors hired John as manager of the North Alabama Poultry Cooperative in Albertville in November 1947. "At the time I knew nothing about processing chickens," John said, "but I thought I might as well take a stab at it." The building was almost complete by that time. The directors turned over to him the $23,500 they had raised and said, "Now, you make it work." He had to spend all of that money just to buy the equipment to process the chickens, but he started up the plant in February 1948, when it actually processed its first chickens.

"We had a problem," John said. "We had no commercial broiler production. Here we had a plant all ready to go and we didn't have any chickens to process." John remembered a small hatchery owner named Daniel in Morgan County who put out about 600 baby chicks to a few farmers in his area. They grew those chicks to about thirteen weeks old, when they weighed about two and three-quarters to three pounds dressed. John bought those chickens from Mr. Daniel. "They were old Barred Rock chickens," he said, "the hardest chickens to process I ever saw. We really had a hard time getting the feathers off of those things."

"After I processed the first 600 chickens, it really hit me: to whom could I sell them? I knew nothing about how to sell chickens." He started out store to store trying to peddle them. In one store he met a man he knew who was selling meat, and this man gave him the name of his company's district produce manager in Atlanta. His name was M. D. Norton.

John went straight back to the plant and called Mr. Norton. He told him that he was trying to start a broiler business. "Well," Mr. Norton said, "I'm not interested in broilers, but I remember being in that area back in the 1920s, and we would have hen-buying days. We loaded a freight car in Boaz, Alabama, and shipped them live to New York City.

"That area has a lot of small farms, and nearly every one of those farms has one or two hundred hens. The women take care of the hens, and they sell the eggs to peddlers who come through the country and buy the eggs and maybe some butter from the farm women. I am interested in buying those spent hens. Do you suppose you could buy them for me?"

John said, "Mr. Norton, we are trying to get a broiler business going."

He said, "I believe I am going to come over there and talk to you." The next day he drove to Albertville. John remembers that "he was as old as my father. He had a coat and tie and a big Buick automobile. I was impressed with him. He was a nice man and spent half a day with me."

Mr. Norton told John, "Here's how to buy the hens. Here's what you pay for them. Here's what to charge for them when you get them processed. I will buy all the spent hens you process. I'll ship those hens to our branches in Birmingham, New Orleans, Jacksonville, Miami. We want those hens."

At that time a new radio station had just been built in Albertville, so John went out to the radio station and put out an ad saying that he would buy spent hens at certain times on certain days. "Well, they just covered us up with hens!" he said.

John processed the hens and shipped them in 50-gallon wooden barrels. He put a 25-pound block of ice on the bottom of each barrel, then a layer of hen and a layer of ice until he filled it and covered it with an old croaker sack. He shipped the barrels by railway express, and the railroad would re-ice them en route. "We made money on those old hens," John said. "They gave us the operating money we needed to keep going."

In the meantime John was going to every farmer who would listen to him, trying to talk someone into building a broiler house. The Ralston Purina feed company also was eager to get the broiler business going, because they hoped to sell more feed. Jimmy Garvin was the manager of the local store. Eventually they got a man named J. Q. Ham to build a 2,000-capacity broiler house. Jimmy got 2,000 baby chicks for J. Q. and furnished the feed. John bought the birds that J. Q. grew out, and paid him 45 cents a pound live, which was a tremendously high price at that time.

J. Q. made enough money on that one batch of broilers to buy his wife a new stove and a new refrigerator. "That word spread around real quick," John said, "and it wasn't long before we had Sand Mountain covered up with broiler houses. The early houses were, say, 4,000 capacity, but pretty soon they started building

6,000-capacity houses, a little after that 10,000, and later 20,000. They just kept growing and growing and growing."

Albertville is in Marshall County. In Cullman County one of the early promoters of the broiler business was Ray Fechtel, who had a hatchery in Georgia. He and Forrest Ingram built a little peckerwood feed mill in Cullman and started putting out chickens. "In the early days," John said, "I bought chickens from Forrest, and he is one of my good friends to this day, but he produced terrible quality. They were just awful chickens."

John told me he finally called Forrest and said, "Forrest, you have got to do a better job of growing chickens. If you can't do better than this, I'm not going to buy any more of these sorry old chickens."

Forrest said, "Well, John, don't worry about it. I can sell them someplace else."

John said, "Well, I'm going to quit, then."

Then a month hadn't passed before John found himself in a bad spot. He had sold chickens he didn't have, he couldn't cover them, and he couldn't find any anywhere. In desperation he called Forrest and said, "Forrest, I told you I wasn't going to buy any more of your sorry old chickens, but I have gotten myself in a bad tight. I sold chickens I can't deliver. I have got to have some chickens. Can you, will you send me a truckload of chickens?"

"Oh, sure, John, I'll be glad to," he said, and he sent them right over.

"Now that is the kind of fellow he is," said John. "He is the nicest fellow I have ever done business with."

Meantime, John was struggling trying to sell chickens. One day he got a call from a man in Memphis who wanted to buy some broilers. John's old Chevrolet had 110,000 miles on it, and he wasn't sure it could make the trip to Memphis and back, so he borrowed his father-in-law's new car.

He had been shipping chickens in wooden barrels or in used wire-bound orange crates lined with waxed paper, but a new company in Decatur had started to make wire-bound boxes specially for chickens. John put some of those nice clean white wire-bound boxes in the trunk of the car and went proudly to Memphis. When he got there the man drove too hard a deal. He wanted John to do things he simply could not do and make any money.

"I left his office feeling down in the dumps something awful," John said. "Here I had wasted a whole day driving to Memphis, and I couldn't do any business. I was driving up River Street when I saw a sign, Wilson Packing Company, so I went in and asked to see the produce manager."

"Do you sell broilers?" John asked him.

"No," he said.

"Have you ever sold broilers?"

"Yes."

"Would you be interested in selling broilers again?"

"No."

"Would you tell me why?"

"Yes. Our company has a plant over in Georgia, and they would never send me what I ordered, so I just quit."

"Well, try me," John said. "I will send what you order."

"I'll think about it," the man said.

So John called him twice a week trying to get an order, and he finally got an order to ship ten boxes by railway express, which he did.

John called him and asked, "Was that all right?"

"That was fine," he said.

The next week he ordered twenty boxes, next week forty boxes, then he was ordering truckloads, and soon John was shipping a truckload of broilers to Memphis every other day. "That was a big plus to get started," John said. Later he met a buyer from the A&P Company in Louisville, and made a deal to ship broilers to Louisville. First he had a small truck that hauled 150 boxes twice a week, but later he sent two trailers twice a week.

Things went so well from 1951 to 1953 that the Ralston Purina feed company decided to build a competing processing plant in Albertville in 1954. "When they opened, we didn't have enough chickens to run two plants," John said, "so we had a little war going on trying to buy the chickens, and that was a hard time for both plants, but it wasn't too long before we had enough chicken houses to run both of them.

"Then about a year later Gold Kist built a plant just down the road in Boaz. We had a little tight supply for a while, but it wasn't long before we had enough chickens to run all three plants. Two years later a fellow named Harold Green built a plant in Guntersville. He went broke, but Gold Kist bought it and modernized it, so by 1958 we had four major processing plants in Marshall County, and we still do.

"That's how I started," John said. "I was the manager of a processing plant, and I had to get out and sell chickens. Of course we had to have a hatchery and a feed warehouse. We built a small hatchery in the early days, hatched out a few chickens, and put those out with farmers. Eventually we got up to producing maybe 150,000 to 180,000 a week of our own."

Allied Mills had a large feed mill in Memphis. John would send a truckload of chickens to Memphis, and then the truck would go to the feed mill and pick up a load of feed to bring back. In 1957 a feed company built a mill at Guntersville, on the Tennessee River, where it was cheap to barge in grain from the Midwest, and it grew 200,000 broilers. John bought those. He also bought broilers from Allied Mills, which had no processing plant "until they bought ours in 1964," said John, "but that's getting ahead of the story.

"We went through a terrible period of overproduction in 1961. We produced more broilers than we could sell, and we were selling broilers at less than the cost of producing them. Everyone was losing money and there was a big upheaval in the business. Those of us that survived got bigger, and it's been getting bigger ever since.

"In 1961 Ralston Purina bought ten poultry plants, from Maine all the way to Texas. It wasn't because they wanted those plants. The plants and their producers all owed Ralston so much money that Ralston was doing a self-defense thing. Then Ralston decided to get out of the business completely because of the price fluctuations. They didn't like the ups and downs of the prices, so they decided to sell all ten plants to their managers."

In 1964 Allied Mills bought the Co-op plant and asked John to stay on as manager. Then about three years later the Continental Grain Company bought Allied Mills, and it still operates the plant. Allied Mills also owned a plant in Union Springs, Alabama, and it was losing money while John's plant was making a good profit.

Just before Christmas his boss called him and said, "I've just fired the manager at Union Springs. Will you please go down there and see what you can do about things?" That was the year Auburn was playing Nebraska in the Orange Bowl, and John and a group of his friends had chartered a plane to fly to Miami to see the game. John did not want to back out, so his boss said, "Well, it won't be any worse off with no manager at all than it was with that guy I fired, but will you please go down there when you get back?"

John straightened out the situation in Union Springs, and then he was asked to help out in Georgia, where Allied Mills had a little feed mill operation and was growing about 200,000 broilers a week. He told his boss, Mr. Lynn, "You can never make any money doing that. You've got to have your own processing plant. You've got to have your own hatchery. Why don't we just close down this feed mill in Georgia? I'd rather be in Arkansas, where we could ship to the West Coast."

John told me that he was the first one who shipped processed chickens to the

West Coast, and he wanted to get closer to the West Coast market. He also figured that he could get to Chicago from Arkansas just as easily as he could get there from Alabama.

Mr. Lynn just shook his finger at John, and he said, "Young man, if other people can do it in Georgia, then we can too. I am not going to close down that feed mill. If you say we need a hatchery and a processing plant, then you build us one. You are in charge!"

After John had gotten them going, Mr. Lynn said to him, "Now, if you say we need to be in Arkansas, you go out there and find a processing plant for us, and we'll buy it." So John did. Later he also found one in Mississippi that Allied bought, and when he retired, the company had four processing plants in Alabama, one in Georgia, one in Arkansas, one in Mississippi, and one in North Carolina.

South-Central Mississippi

In 1931 Bennie Clyde Rogers ran a hardware store in Morton, Mississippi, about thirty miles east of Jackson. His sister, Lola, like most farm wives, kept a few hens and sold the eggs. She bought a sack of feed in Jackson and was so impressed by the way it increased her egg production that she asked "B. C." to get some more for her. He took the name and address off the empty sack and wrote Ralston Purina in St. Louis to order thirty sacks.

B. C. sold out the entire lot in two days and realized he had stumbled onto a good thing, but few farm families had enough cash to pay for feed during the Depression. He hit on the idea of trading chicken feed for eggs, and he hauled the eggs to Jackson, Memphis, and New Orleans, where he sold them to restaurants. In New Orleans he realized that he could make even more money selling live chickens, and he built up a network of independent farmers with whom he traded chicken feed for eggs and live birds. He became one of the leading feed dealers in Mississippi.

World War II put a crimp in his business because tires and gas were rationed, and hauling eggs and chickens to New Orleans was just too difficult. He decided that he could make powdered eggs and sell them to the military, so he built one of the first egg-dehydrating plants in the United States. He found the equipment he needed in Dallas and moved it to Morton.

In 1942 his plant was all set up and ready to go, but some bureaucrat denied him a permit to operate it because he had moved the equipment across state lines, which was against wartime regulations, and the plant had not been inspected. B. C. did what came naturally. He immediately got on a plane to Washington and explained his predicament to his friend Senator James Eastland of Mississippi. Within three days Eastland was able to get him a permit signed by President Roosevelt himself.

Bennie Clyde Rogers made a fortune selling powdered eggs to the government on a cost-plus basis during World War II. Then in 1946 a fire completely destroyed his dehydrating plant, but it was not the disaster it might have seemed, because people were tired of eating wartime food and the demand for powdered eggs was evaporating. B. C. was already planning to move into the broiler business, and he built a broiler-processing plant virtually on the ashes of this dehydrating plant. Initially he bought about half of his birds from independent farmers, but he quickly moved to complete contracting.

He did so well that in 1963 *Time* magazine wrote:

> The richest and one of the biggest independent broiler producers in the U.S. is balding Bennie Clyde Rogers, 58, of Morton, Miss., who has 6,000,000 birds under his wing. They are delivered around the U.S. in 144 Rogers trucks that are gassed up by the Rogers Oil Co. "Most everything in town I've got my mark on," says Bennie Rogers, who also chairs Morton's only bank, owns its main stores, and has 1,000 head of cattle grazing on 3,500 Mississippi acres that are enriched by fertilizer from his chickens. Rogers lives in a 25-room house and trades in his white, air-conditioned Cadillac for a new model every year.

Despite his wealth, B. C. Rogers was notorious for his frugality. He believed firmly in paying cash for everything, even his new plants, for which he needed no financing. He also recognized the importance of good public relations, and each year between 1947 and 1957 he splurged with a mammoth chicken barbecue on the last Friday in May. It featured well-known entertainers and attracted hundreds of people, including growers, plant employees, poultry buyers, grocery and feed company executives, and important political figures.

In 1964 he finally built his own feed mill. For years he had loyally been hauling Purina feed concentrate from Memphis, 120 tons 200 miles five days a week, but he decided he had to save time and money by producing his own feed. He spent most of his time in grow-out, because he enjoyed working with his 220 contract farmers.

Fred Garner remembers that he stopped B. C. on the street one day in 1964 and asked him for a loan of $13,500 to buy a broiler farm. "He told me to go to the bank and tell Mr. Bird to draw a check for the amount I needed," said Fred, "and I have been growing broilers for him ever since. I raise 150,000 a year in three houses, and I also run a few beef cattle on my sixty-five-acre farm."

Fred had a full-time job as a night-shift maintenance electrician and took care of the chickens during the day. Juanita, his wife, took over when she came home from her full-time day job. "I was working in Jackson when Fred and I got married," she said, "and I knew I would have to find a job here, so I called B. C. and asked if he had anything. I didn't know him personally, just by name. He asked me who I was marrying, and when I told him, he asked me when I wanted to start work."

B. C. Rogers died in 1972, and his son, John, took over the company. In 1973 he built a hatchery, and in 1978 he bought a processing plant in Macomb. His big breakthrough came in 1980, when he contracted with McDonald's to produce Chicken McNuggets on a cost-plus basis. McDonald's needed volume production, and Rogers seized the chance to become proficient at deboning and producing portion-controlled pieces.

In 1985 the company opened its third processing plant and in 1988 it opened its second hatchery. In 1997 it employed 3,600 people to process 1.4 million chickens per week. It specializes in producing boneless and value-added products for the food-service, restaurant and hotel, institutional, and export markets. The export market is important because the preference of the Pacific Rim and Eastern European countries for dark meat meshes nicely with the American preference for white meat.

Fred Gaddis took a different tack. He grew up on a small cotton farm near Forest, ten miles east of Morton. Before World War II his father raised about 500 chickens a year in an old smokehouse that was heated in winter by a wood-burning furnace. He sold them live to a trucker who hauled them live to a restaurant in Jackson.

When he came back from the military in 1947, Fred and his brother Ed borrowed $12,000 from the bank to buy a small feed and seed store in Forest from a man who was already raising 3,000 or 4,000 chickens a week and selling them to truckers who hauled them to New Orleans or Houston. They sold the chickens to farmers on credit and contracted with them to supply the feed. The farmers paid them when they sold the chickens after feeding them for fifteen or sixteen weeks.

In 1950 they were buying complete feed in hundred-pound sacks when they got the idea of buying only the concentrate, vitamins and minerals, and cotton-seed meal. They bought a corn grinder, mixed in the concentrate, and sacked up the feed themselves. Then they hired a nutritionist to tell them how to add amino acids, soybean meal, fish meal, and alfalfa, and in the early 1960s they built their own feed mill because they could buy the ingredients more cheaply than they could buy concentrate.

At times chicken sold for less than the cost of the baby chicks and feed, and farmers refused to deal with them. Fred says that he and Ed invented contract growing around 1955. If a grower would let them give him the baby chicks and feed, they guaranteed him $50 a thousand when they sold the birds. Other dealers said they were crazy, and Fred said, "Of course we were. It was like shooting craps, and by golly, we hit!" The price went way up before their first contract chickens came to market, and they made a very nice profit on them.

"A lot of people in town were envious," said Fred. "They figured that if we could make it, maybe they could too, but most of them went broke."

The Gaddises started processing in the late 1950s. Before that they had hauled chickens live to Birmingham, New Orleans, Houston. They did not have the money themselves, but the banks were pushing industrial development, and they found enough local investors to raise around $200,000 to build a processing plant. "We did pretty good," said Fred, "considering that this was during a transition stage from marketing through live truck haulers to marketing through processing. There were times when we would have done better selling our chickens to a trucker rather than to our own plant, but then what would our labor have done that week?"

At that time the city allowed them to dump the feathers and entrails from the processing plant into the municipal sewage system. It was perfectly legal, because it was before the EPA, but Fred realized that they were wasting money. He got six of his competitors together and talked them into starting a by-products company and rendering plant, which has been quite successful. "We were at each other's throats any time anybody bought a chicken," he said, "but we worked together if all of us could make a profit, and we were good friends."

Some people put all the money they made back into the poultry business, but Fred was reluctant to risk everything he had on broilers. Once he had reached a certain size he began to invest in other things: shopping centers, apartment complexes, banks, a motel in Biloxi, stocks and bonds, 5,000 acres of land, more than 1,000 head of beef cattle.

He was hit hard in 1974 when he had to destroy $1,037,000 worth of chickens because they showed traces of dieldrin, a pesticide that had been used on their feed. His good friend H. F. McCarty Jr. offered him a very favorable price for his broiler business, and he decided to sell it and retire from poultry. He sold the entire business: the hatchery, the feed mill and all the feed trucks, the entire inventory of broilers and breeding hens, the processing plant, and an interest in the by-products company.

Fred remembers well the day of their last business transaction. "Don't feel sorry for me," he said to McCarty. "You just got done telling me that everything you own and possess except your marriage license is in the chicken business, but I don't care to gamble all of mine on broilers.

"I got out my little book with a summary of what he owed me and what else I owned, and he said, 'My God, Fred, you should have bought me out!'"

H. F. "Mac" McCarty is one of the nicest people I have ever met. His mother died when he was 3. His father remarried, and Mac was adopted and raised by two aunts. He always wanted to be a lawyer. After serving as an Air Force navigator/instructor during World War II, he attended the University of South Carolina, in his wife's home state, on the GI Bill, and received his master's degree in history. In the fall of 1947 he took a job teaching history at the University of Mississippi, because it allowed him to attend law school.

Mary Ann, his wife, said that their living conditions in Oxford were horrible. "We didn't have a bathtub," she said, "and we cooked on a hot plate. We had two rooms, but we had to share a bath. Mac had to walk two miles back and forth to school. I had a year-old baby. I needed a bathtub and a washing machine and a couch, so after one semester we moved to Magee."

Mac's father had a feed, seed, and fertilizer store in Collins. He was opening a branch in Magee and offered Mac a partnership. "He and I didn't get along," Mac said. "I didn't think we would. That's the reason I hadn't gone into business with him sooner. A couple times I got disgusted with him up to here and was ready to toss him the key, but my stepmother talked me out of it, that's what it amounts to.

"Then almost a year to the day after I came here he died unexpectedly, and I bought the business from my stepmother. Dad had a little commercial hatchery behind the house in Collins, and the banker talked me into assuming an obligation of $3,200 on that hatchery as part of settling the estate."

Fred Gaddis told me, "Mac won't tell you this, but I will. His father had a bunch of accounts payable when he died. Mac told the creditors, 'If you want to push me, then I'll have to declare bankruptcy and you won't be any better off, but if you give me time, I'll pay you back every last penny my father owed you,' and he did!"

At first Mac sold baby chicks to farmers, but in 1949 he started contracting with them. Many farmers were interested, because cotton was a failing crop. They needed something else they could grow, and they needed someone to show them how. "B. C. Rogers started broilers in Mississippi," Mac said, "and we copied producers in Georgia. In the early 1950s there were more than twenty broiler firms in Forest alone, but most of them went broke or were bought out."

Mac and Fred Gaddis flew to Shreveport, rented a car, and studied how broiler houses were built in east Texas. Mac also went to North Carolina to visit Marvin Johnson, who tried to talk him into producing turkeys. At that time Marvin was still growing turkeys on range, and he was just beginning to grow some in houses. Mac was also an eager and enthusiastic participant in the poultry management workshops at the University of Georgia in the 1960s.

"We just grew," Mac said. He installed a hammer mill and feed mixer in 1951, and in 1953 he built better milling and storage facilities. In 1957 he built a new hatchery in Magee and created separate corporations for the hatchery, the feed mill, and the grow-out operation.

Until 1967 he supplied birds to a processing plant in Jackson and split the profits right down the middle, but then he realized that growing was the biggest part of the business, so he told the owner to sell him an interest or he would build his own plant. He bought a 27 percent interest in the plant and incorporated it in the names of his four children, and it paid their way through college.

In 1973 McCarty had an exceptionally profitable year, so he increased his contract payments to growers from 2.25 to 2.76 cents a pound and made the increase retroactive for the preceding ten months. Then he had to destroy 2.25 million chickens during the dieldrin crisis of 1974, but still was able to buy out Fred Gaddis in 1975. Through the years he survived low chicken prices and high corn prices, fires and high winds, a tornado in 1980, and some overly ambitious expansions. In 1991 he decided it was time to sell the company, but then he was plagued by a series of bad years.

Mac was chairman of the board, and his son, John, and all three daughters were active in the company. He made John CEO in 1992. John chided him for not having done it sooner, but Mac said, "I hated for him to come aboard as CEO in a bad year, a loss year. We finally made a little money in 1994, but the handwriting was on the wall. Don Tyson had been trying to buy us for six or seven years, and we decided to sell to him in 1995.

"John and Marsha did an excellent job of selling the business," said Mac. "They sold it for $50 million more than I thought it was worth, a whole lot more than I would have asked for, but I was looking at financial statements and they were looking at the potential of people and facilities. We had good facilities and good people. A lot of them got good jobs with Tyson, but there was no place for some of them in Tyson's organization."

The company McCarty sold to Tyson in 1995 had seven processing plants, two feed mills, three hatcheries, 4,000 employees, and annual sales of $300 million. It had grown from 35 contract growers in 1958 to 85 in 1963 and more than 400 in 1995, from 1 million birds in 1958 to 7 million in 1963 and 120 million in 1995.

"We couldn't compete," Mac said. "Tyson could run circles around us on cost of feed ingredients, and they could afford expensive new equipment that cut labor costs. We only had an in-house computer system, and they were a whole lot more computerized. They take the business to heart, and they're doing a magnificent job. I think they're doing the same job with 3,000 people that we were doing with 4,000."

Mac told me that he ran into one of his former contractors in the post office the other day and asked him if he was still growing chickens. "No," he said, "they cut us off. You made a fortune on those old chicken houses, but the new ones cost too much money."

Mac said, "I told him that the name of the game in business is you've got to stay competitive, and what was good twenty years ago is not good enough now. When I started, a house had 2,200 chicks, but now houses hold 20–25,000 birds. Growers have up to seven houses, and they put through five or six batches a year. It's no longer a part-time job.

"Two and a half was the average weight when I started, but now they're selling birds over five pounds. A good conversion in those days was three pounds of feed to a pound of meat, but now they've gotten it down to one-eighty-five. Our first chickens we grew in eleven-twelve weeks, but we were selling an eight-week-old bird when we sold the business, and now they probably are growing a five-pound bird in seven weeks."

Mac was active in poultry industry organizations, and he has enjoyed philanthropy. He has set up the H. F. McCarty Jr. Family Foundation, which has zeroed in on higher education, because neither he nor Mary Ann could have gone to college without financial help. They have endowed chairs in five colleges and universities, and they have established scholarship funds in no fewer than eleven.

As I was leaving, Mac gave me a funny little look and said, "You know, I've got a confession to make to you. I was flattered when you called yesterday and said you wanted to talk to me, but then I fretted because I realized that I really didn't know anything about you or who you might be. I've got a phobia about some member of my family being kidnapped. The wife of one of my best friends was kidnapped, and she has never been found.

"Or you might be a representative of the contract growers' association they're promoting right now. It's just a unionization deal and it isn't going anywhere. But just as soon as I got a good look at you I felt better, because you obviously are nothing but a harmless college professor."

Dennis Ramsey of Duplin County

The *Census of Agriculture* says that Duplin County, North Carolina, produced 42,000 broilers in 1954, 10,317,000 in 1959, and 22,294,000 in 1964. Blame this phenomenal increase on television and on Dennis Ramsey.

When he was discharged from the army at the end of World War II, Dennis Ramsey was invited to Rose Hill, a small town in southern Duplin County, to open a movie theater. He liked to talk to his customers as they were leaving, and he knew that the local farmers were worried because the government had cut the tobacco program, and tobacco was the only money crop they had.

Dennis also was worried. "The farmers came in to town to watch the cowboys and Indians on the silver screen," he said, "but I knew that television was right around the corner, and before long they would be able to stay home and watch the cowboys and Indians. I knew that I had to find some new means of livelihood."

His wife was from north Georgia, and she gave him the idea of looking into broilers. He went to consult the poultry experts at the North Carolina Department of Agriculture, where some bureaucrat told him, "They've never grown a good broiler in Duplin County and they never will. Go home, boy, and don't bother me." Later Dennis learned this bureaucrat had his own pet poultry project that he was promoting.

The poultry experts at North Carolina State University, Dennis said, actually were very helpful. "The state already had a lot of little old log poultry houses in Wilkes and Chatham Counties," he said, but he wanted to build modern houses, so he went to Georgia, where his wife's cousin was in the chicken business, and he spent a couple of weeks learning how to take care of chickens.

In 1954 Dennis founded the Ramsey Feed Company and began contracting with farmers to grow broilers. Allied Mills, a feed company, financed him. "They advanced me operating money," he said, "and they sold me feed on credit. How much is between me and Allied Mills and the good Lord, and I certainly am not going to tell you how much. At first I sold bag feed in dress material that the farm wives used to make dresses and even underwear, or so I was told, but I can't prove it because I never saw any of it.

"I took a sheet of paper and across the top I wrote what I wanted the farmer to do. He had to build a barn and to furnish utilities and labor. Then lower down I wrote what we would do for him. We would furnish the chicks and feed and we would provide a serviceman. We would load the birds and take them to a processor. I would guarantee him a certain amount of money per thousand birds. Later, when I began to get competition in the broiler business, I developed an incentive pay plan, with a set floor and a bonus for above-average feed conversion."

His first year Dennis had ten 40' × 400' broiler houses that held 4,000 birds each. One of them was his own as a demonstration unit. He had six or seven full-time employees, none with any poultry experience, and he had to develop an on-the-job training program for them. He strongly encouraged each one of them to contract to raise a batch of chickens in the house he owned, because they learned the business, and they liked the additional income.

The county agent was trying to get farmers to produce eggs when Dennis was pushing broilers. Dennis was able to persuade a very influential farmer to grow broilers rather than eggs, and this farmer helped Dennis persuade other farmers to grow broilers, but Dennis said he was one of the worst growers he had. "I listen to the serviceman very intently," he told Dennis, "and then I go ahead and do what I damn well please."

Allied Mills helped Dennis find baby chicks and feed. He got chicks from Shelton Lewis, who had a 350,000-bird hatchery. At first he took birds to four processors, including a seasonal turkey plant that wanted to process broilers to keep it working year-round, but eventually he wound up with E. T. Watson in what he called "cooperative integration": Lewis hatched the birds, Dennis grew them, and Watson processed them.

He continued to operate the theater until 1956, when he built his own feed mill. He bought grain on contract and added corn, soy meal, and fish meal to concentrate he bought from Allied. "It was 'Big John' that made the broiler business possible," he said. "Those big new cars could carry 100 tons, and we got favorable freight rates by bringing them in fourteen at a time.

"Processing was not my business, and I stayed away from it. I stuck to grow-out. At my peak I was producing half a million birds a week. I had 250 growers in a forty-mile radius of Rose Hill, 200 employees, and 100 trucks and other pieces of highway equipment. I was in business, just trying to make a living, from 1954 until 1973, then I sold out and retired."

Perdue and Promotion

In 1920 Arthur Perdue was the Railway Express agent in Salisbury, Maryland. The company promoted him and wanted to transfer him, but he did not want to leave Salisbury, so he bought some land, built a 10' × 20' chicken house, stocked it with 200 laying hens, and started selling eggs. He made enough money his first year to build a second house, and he continued to use his profits to add another new house each year. Before long he built his first "big house," which measured 25' × 50'.

In the late 1930s Perdue shifted from table eggs to the production of live broilers. Some he grew on his own, some he contracted with local farmers, and he sold them all live to processors. His only son, Franklin P. Perdue, joined him in the family business in 1939. They steadily expanded their feed business and had developed into one of the largest broiler producers in Delmarva when Frank took over the company in 1950.

"Our biggest point of growth," said Frank, "was the feed mill we built in 1960. It uses 15 to 16 million bushels of corn and soybeans a year. Dad is pretty conservative. He was proud that he had never borrowed money. I can see how he felt, signing notes for hundreds of thousands at the age of 75, but he didn't argue about it.

"In 1968 the economics of losses forced us to go into poultry processing, which I really didn't want to do." They bought and renovated a processing plant in Salisbury that processed 14,000 birds an hour, and they tried to develop brand-name loyalty by attaching a distinctive red-and-yellow tag to the wing of each processed chicken.

Up until this point the story is unexceptional. What set Frank Perdue apart was his decision to invest heavily in advertising his brand-name chicken on television in New York City, the center of the national communications media. The intensity with which he set about selecting an advertising agency is the stuff of legend. He read everything he could find and asked questions of everyone who would talk to him.

He interviewed no fewer than fifty agencies and came up with a short list of nine. Toward the end of his search he invited the top brass of one prominent agency to lunch at the Plaza. They assumed that he was going to tell them that they had won the account, but he startled them by telling them that they had not even made his short list. Then he asked them to help him rank the nine agencies that had made his list.

The agency he selected decided to star Frank Perdue in his own ads, and they made him a celebrity. He has a shiny bald head, a large nose, and a high-pitched nasal voice, and more than one person has observed that he looks like a tough little bantam rooster himself. His ads boasted, "It takes a tough man to make a tender chicken," and they had a lighthearted folksy touch that was wondrously successful.

Perdue's ads increased public awareness of broilers throughout the nation. They were the talk of New York, and people in other parts of the country read about them and heard about them even though they had never seen them. They heard about them even more when the ads won prestigious awards and were written up in the national media.

Perdue demonstrated that consumers were willing to pay premium prices for the quality guaranteed by an advertised brand name. He insisted that his ads cost less than a penny per pound of chicken sold, and his higher prices more than covered their cost. His success encouraged other processors to develop their own brand names and to improve their marketing strategies.

"By 1971," he said, "we were doing so well that we had to have another plant, so we built a 28,000-bird-an-hour plant for $7 million in Accomac, Virginia, fifty miles south of Salisbury in an area that had more labor available. We still had more demand than we could supply, so in 1975 we opened a 7,000-an-hour plant in North Carolina, and in a year we had to double its output."

By 1982 the Perdue company had grown to become the nation's third largest broiler producer, and it has held that rank ever since, with production of more than 12 million birds a week in 1996. Perdue specializes in the retail trade. It sells only fresh (never frozen) chicken and limits its market to the area that can be served overnight by truck from one of its processing plants.

Perdue is aware that public recognition of good work is a better motivation than punishment for poor. Around 1995 it instituted a program of rewarding outstanding workers with certificates that were good for a free lunch in the company cafeteria, but it discovered that employees were framing the certificates instead of cashing them in for their lunches, so it amended the program to include both a certificate and a lunch ticket.

Tyson the Titan

John Tyson grew up on a farm near Kansas City. He had a truck, hauled hay from his father's farm to farms in northwest Arkansas, and hauled their fruit back to Kansas City. He remembered one trip when he arrived in Springdale, Arkansas, with half a load of hay and a nickel in his pocket. "That is everything I had," he said. "I wanted a cup of coffee, and I had the money to pay for it. I will never forget tossing that nickel down on the counter. I tried to make it look like I had a big bankroll in my pocket to back it up. Then I went out and started looking for a load to haul somewhere."

Fruit farmers in northwest Arkansas were having tough times. They had suffered a series of bad years, and some of them were beginning to grow chickens to supplement their farm income. In 1931 John Tyson moved to Springdale and developed a business hauling chickens to Kansas City and St. Louis.[1] In 1936 he read in a newspaper that chicken prices were better in Chicago, so he outfitted a truck with a trough for feed and water between the coops to enable the birds to stand the 700-mile trip, and he hauled 500 live spring chickens to Chicago. He did so well that soon he was hauling live birds to Detroit, Cleveland, Houston, and other distant cities.

John Tyson realized that local farmers were having trouble getting enough baby chicks, so he started his own small hatchery. He became a feed dealer for Ralston Purina, but they could not supply him with as much feed as he needed, so he built his own feed mill and bought corn, wheat bran, and soybean meal to process in it. He built up his own fleet of trucks, and in 1943 he bought a forty-acre farm and put his own broiler houses on it.

After World War II John Tyson began contracting with farmers to grow broilers for him. By 1952 he employed fifty-two people, had annual sales of around $1 million, and sold 12,000 birds a week to the processing companies that were building new plants in the area, but competition was intense. Tyson was only one of nineteen broiler companies in Springdale, and he seriously considered selling his business to one of the processing companies until he realized that his son, Don, wanted to join him.

Don Tyson grew up in the broiler business. He started catching chickens, shoveling litter out of broiler houses, and driving trucks when he was 14. He studied animal nutrition at the University of Arkansas and joined the company when he graduated in 1952. John's father had lost his farm during the Depression, and John was conservative financially, but Don is a freewheeling swashbuckler who has built Tyson Foods into the nation's largest poultry company. Every day he wore the company uniform of an open-neck khaki shirt with the red-and-orange Tyson logo on the left chest and his first name stitched in script on his right chest.

In 1957 the Tysons built a broiler-processing plant and in 1963 they made their first major acquisition when they bought a small neighboring broiler company. In 1964 Don Tyson decided that buying other processing plants at bargain-basement prices was a faster and cheaper way to grow than building his own plants from scratch, and he developed a company policy of buying rather than building.

He understood the cyclical nature of the broiler business, and he realized that many small companies were in financial straits and vulnerable to takeovers during periods of overproduction and high feed prices. He determined to build his cash reserves when times were good so that he would be able to pounce on other companies when times were bad.

Don Tyson had the cash and the courage to move against the market, and in 1966 he began the systematic acquisition of other broiler companies. In 1996 Tyson Foods, Inc., owned fifty-seven processing plants, but the company had built only two of them itself and had bought the rest. At first Tyson bought anything that came down the pike, but in time it has become more selective, and it has bought only companies that strengthen its existing operations, add market share, or introduce new product lines and customers.

In 1964 Don Tyson also made a strategic decision to emphasize production of further-processed and value-added products, which are far more profitable than fresh or iced broilers. Initially Tyson sold these products to fast-food chains and to the commercial and institutional food-service industry, but the company has developed similar products for retail sale and has tried to foster consumer awareness of its brand names.

In 1977 Tyson started producing hogs as well as broilers, and subsequently the company has branched out into production of seafood and Mexican foods. In 2000 Tyson Foods, Inc., produced 17.5 million hogs, had 7,038 contract poultry growers who produced 2.2 billion chickens, and had sales of $23.8 billion, a far cry indeed from John Tyson's nickel cup of coffee.[2]

Don Tyson is one of the entrepreneurs who have integrated and modernized the broiler business. They started small, with feed mills or processing plants, and were organizers rather than growers. They contracted with farmers in a thirty-mile radius to grow the birds. Contract broiler production has been most successful in the South, where farmers have a tradition of risk-sharing. Supplemental income from broilers has enabled many farmers to remain on their farms. Some people are critical of contract production, but the broiler companies merely shrug and point to the waiting lists of farmers who are eager to sign contracts with them.

The broiler business has become concentrated in fewer and fewer larger and larger companies as it has matured. Many early broiler companies have faltered in hard times, and other companies have bought their assets. As the surviving companies have grown, they have bought and sold feed mills, processing plants, and even entire companies, which seem to have become mere pawns on a gigantic corporate chessboard, where acquisitions and mergers are constantly shifting assets around.

9
Eggs

An explosive increase in the scale of egg production has been one of the best-kept secrets in American agriculture.[1] Of course the people in the business know about it, but few outsiders realize how greatly it has changed. The *Census of Agriculture* says that 5 million farms produced eggs in 1935, but even the largest operations had no more than 100 to 300 laying hens. In 2000 fewer than 500 operations produced 95 percent of our eggs, and most of them had 1 to 3 million hens.

As late as 1955 a diligent worker could feed, water, and collect the eggs from no more than about 5,000 laying hens, which had a lay of 40 percent (four eggs every ten days), and the few farms that had more than 15,000 birds were considered huge, as indeed they were.[2] In 2000 a single worker could easily take care of 100,000 hens or more. They had a lay of 70 percent or better, and egg-producing complexes of 1.5 million birds were standard.

Egg production has grown like Topsy. Everyone tells me that the scale of production just sort of increased gradually, and there seems to have been no magic moment, breakthrough, or innovator. Improvements in the automation of feeding, egg collection, processing, and manure management apparently were incremental, and they necessitated and reinforced each other. A technological innovation in one phase of production induced change in another, and producers borrowed ideas liberally from each other. The 100,000-bird house did not suddenly appear overnight; it is the logical product of an evolutionary process that still continues.

Before World War II most farms had barnyard flocks of chickens for eggs and Sunday dinner. The hens lived on waste grain, weed seed, insects, and anything else they could scavenge. Finding and collecting the eggs was women's work, and many farm wives used china eggs as nest eggs to encourage the hens to lay their eggs in nests where they would be easy to find. Some farm women bartered their eggs at the local store, but others sold them to hucksters who drove from farm to farm buying farmhouse butter and barnyard eggs. The huckster graded and packed the eggs from many farms and shipped them to major markets. The eggs were of highly uneven quality and uncertain age, and cracking them could be an adventure.

Progressive producers built houses for their hens, and they bypassed hucksters by forming cooperatives to process and market their eggs. Specialized clusters with large numbers of small egg farms produced high-quality table eggs for major cities. The cluster at Vineland, in southern New Jersey, served New York and Philadelphia, and the cluster at Petaluma, north of San Francisco Bay, once had more than 4,000 egg producers. Flocks of 500 to 2,000 hens ranged freely on farms of one to ten acres, and laid their eggs in shelters that the farmer periodically moved to clean ground.

During World War II egg producers near Los Angeles started housing their hens in wooden cages with wire floors, one bird to a cage. Cages improved sanitation and health, because the birds no longer had to live in their own waste, they made feed management easier, and they enabled producers to cull their flocks continuously. Cages made so much sense that the idea quickly spread to other parts of the country, and today virtually all egg producers keep their laying hens in cages.

Soaring real estate prices after World War II forced egg producers in Los Angeles to relocate inland to Riverside and San Bernardino counties. Producers sold their farms for such lucrative prices that they could afford to build large in-line complexes embodying state-of-the-art labor-saving equipment. These complexes could be far more profitable than the small old houses, but they demanded much greater managerial skill, and they could lose money just as fast as they could make it if they were not managed well. Some producers, especially the older ones, declined to take the risk, and they went out of business.

By the 1960s fully automated complexes with 100,000 hens or more were common in the inland counties in Southern California. Each complex had its own feed mill and automated feeding system. The hens were in stacked cages. Their manure was collected in a deep pit beneath the cages or removed to a stockpile by conveyor belt. Automatic egg collection by conveyor belts had completely replaced tedious gathering by hand. The conveyor belts gently carried the eggs to the processing plant, where they were washed, candled (inspected in front of a light to detect flaws and imperfections), graded by size, and packed in standard pulp cartons of one dozen for the retail trade or on industrial five-by-six egg "flats" that held two and a half dozen. Eggs in quantity are measured by "cases" of thirty dozen.

The large egg complexes in California were so successful that they emboldened entrepreneurs in broiler areas in the Southeast to branch out into egg production. They took full advantage of the excellent transport system that brought feed from the Midwest for broilers, and they copied the broiler model of contract production. They built egg-processing plants and contracted with local farmers to produce eggs and place them on flats for delivery to the plant.

At the processing plant a vacuum-lift machine transferred the eggs from flats to the processing line. This machine had an arm with thirty small rubber suction cups in five rows of six cups. One cup attached to each egg on the flat, the arm lifted them all together, swung around, and gently placed them in the processing line to be washed, candled, graded, and packaged. It all happens faster than you can describe it, and it's fun to watch.

The rapid growth of egg production in the early 1960s almost inevitably resulted in overproduction, and it kicked off a cycle of profits and losses that has bedeviled the egg business ever since. The problem was exacerbated by the growth of supermarket chains, whose size gave them greater bargaining power. They were able to force egg prices down, which was nice for their customers but tough on egg producers, and many producers have been forced right out of the business.

To make matters worse, Americans have been eating fewer eggs. In 1960 our standard breakfast was eggs and bacon, but we have become so busy that we have started to skip breakfast or to eat it on the run, and we have cut back from six eggs a week in 1960 to slightly more than four a week today.[3] A difference of two eggs per person per week does not sound like very much, but it adds up to around 29 billion fewer eggs a year.

We also reduced our egg consumption for health reasons. In the 1950s a renowned heart surgeon told the press that he spent much of his time scraping scrambled eggs from clogged arteries. Others took up the cry, and many people jumped to the conclusion that the cholesterol in eggs caused heart attacks. In time the egg industry was able to demonstrate that the cholesterol content of eggs was lower than had been thought, and in 1988 it convinced the American Heart Association to raise its recommendation from three eggs a week to four, but many people still are afraid of eggs.

Outbreaks of food poisoning from salmonella in the late 1980s, which were initially blamed on contaminated eggs, did nothing to still their fears. These outbreaks eventually were traced to infected food handlers and improperly handled food, but the damage had already been done. The egg industry must work hard to restore public confidence in eggs as food, and to break the traditional association of eggs only with breakfast.

The only part of the egg business that has continued to grow in recent years has been egg-breaking, which is the name given to the production of liquid, frozen, and dried eggs in bulk.[4] The consumption of broken-egg products in the United States more than doubled between 1960 and 2000, from the equivalent of thirty eggs per person per year in 1960 to more than sixty in 2000. Most of us are eating an egg a week more than we realize.

Once producers broke eggs only during the spring lay, as a sideline operation to salvage a bit of income from surplus shell eggs when their hens were laying more than they could sell. Most broken eggs were dried and exported, but our armed forces consumed large quantities, however reluctantly, during World War II. The increase in egg-breaking was facilitated by new machines that were developed during the 1950s. An experienced worker could break no more than about 900 eggs an hour by hand, but the machines could easily break 900 a minute, and they needed no rest breaks.

Most of us do not even realize that producers intentionally break billions of eggs each year. We see few egg products on the shelves of our grocery stores, because we still prefer to buy our eggs in the shell, the way the hen laid them. Most egg products are sold in bulk. Slightly more than half are shipped in tank trucks to bakeries and other food manufacturers to be made into pasta, pastries, dressings, ice cream, and other delicacies, and most of the rest are sold to restaurants, hospitals, fast-food chains, and other food-service establishments.

Some egg producers are building whole new complexes that are designed solely for breaking, and others have processing plants that can be shifted back and forth between breaking and packaging. Breaking is especially appropriate for older hens, which lay heavier eggs. The interiors of egg-breaking plants are all gleaming stainless steel, as antiseptic as hospital operating rooms. A steady stream of more than 1,650 eggs a minute flows into the machine, where sharp knives slit either side of the shell and the contents are emptied into a huge vat. The shells, which are sold for fertilizer, are carried to a pile where they accumulate at a rate of thirty-five pounds a minute, better than a ton an hour.

The percentage of our eggs that are broken has been increasing steadily. In 2000 the United States had around 320 million laying hens, which laid 83 billion eggs. Some 20 million went to hatcheries to produce more chickens. About half of the rest were packed in cartons and sold at retail, 20 percent or so were sold in the shell to food-service establishments, and about 30 percent were broken, but that figure is expected to rise to around 50 percent, because the demand for egg products is growing while the demand for shell eggs is stagnant.[5]

The egg business is intensely competitive, and it has had a massive shake-out in recent years. The average egg producer lost money in half of the years between 1985 and 1995, and for the decade profits exceeded losses by only 2 cents a dozen. The largest producers have expanded and become more efficient by achieving top performance from their flocks, by adopting technologies that have been profitable, by managing their finances wisely, by timing their expansion well, and by achieving economies of scale. Many smaller and less efficient producers have been bought out by larger companies or gone broke.

The egg business has become concentrated in fewer but larger companies. The United States had 10,000 egg producers in 1975, 3,000 in 1985, and fewer than 1,000 in 1995.[6] In 1997 two-thirds of the nation's eggs were laid in fewer than 600 in-line production complexes that had 100,000 hens or more each, and at least fifty of these complexes had more than a million hens. It is unfortunate that numbers like these, and most other statistics about egg production and laying hens in the United States, are no more than educated guesses, because egg production has become concentrated in such large operations, but so few of them, that official census data about it are extremely limited.

The census of agriculture does a superb job of collecting complete data about American agriculture, and it does an equally superb job of honoring its commitment to protect the privacy of individual operators. It publishes no more than the numbers of operations in counties that have three or fewer of anything and in counties in which a single operation produces 60 percent of the total or more. As a consequence, we have far less information than we would like about the distribution of laying hens and egg production in the United States.

Veteran users of census data are all too familiar with the irksome little symbol "(D)," which indicates that data are withheld to avoid disclosing information about individual farms. The disclosure problem is especially acute for eggs and hens. For example, the census reports that the state of Indiana had 22.7 million laying hens in 1997, but the county tables have only "(D)" for 22.2 million of these hens, and we can only guess where they are within the state. The scrupulous care with which the census protects the privacy of individuals is admirable, but sometimes it can be a pain in the clavicle for geographers.

The census does publish maps of laying hens, because its employees are allowed to compile them from data that no outsider is ever allowed to see or use. The map of laying hens in 1997 is quintessentially a map of entrepreneurs (fig. 9.1). The counties where entrepreneurs have invested in egg-production complexes have large numbers of laying hens, and most other counties have none at all, with almost no in-betweens.

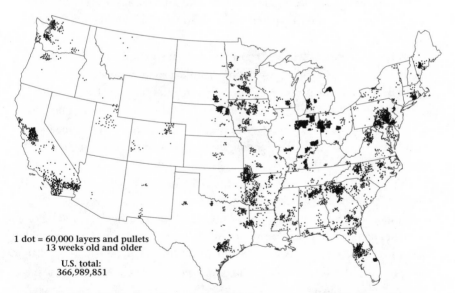

1 dot = 60,000 layers and pullets
        13 weeks old and older

U.S. total:
366,989,851

Figure 9.1. The distribution of laying hens in 1997 has an entrepreneurial pattern. (Source: *1997 Census of Agriculture*, vol. 2, pt. 1 [Washington, D.C.: U.S. Department of Agriculture, National Agricultural Statistics Service, 1999].)

The distribution of laying hens and egg production has changed considerably in the last quarter-century. California and the Southeast dominated the egg business in the early 1970s, but both areas had serious problems. An outbreak of Newcastle disease wiped out more than 10 million hens in California, and many producers were forced out of business. California and the Southeast both were too far from the source of their feed in the agricultural heartland in the Midwest and from the markets for their eggs in the cities of the Northeast, and many of their facilities were old and outdated.

Egg producers updated some old plants, but they simply abandoned others and built modern new complexes in more appropriate areas. In 1997 California was still the leading egg-producing state, and the traditional areas in the Southeast and near cities in the Northeast remained important, but entrepreneurs had transformed two dozen counties in the Midwest into major centers of egg production (fig. 9.1).

A modern in-line egg-production complex has eight or more parallel hen-houses, two stories high and up to 40 feet wide and 500 feet long, that hold 100,000 or more birds each. Looming above them at one end are the tall grain elevator and huge, squat metal grain bins that store corn and soybeans for the feed mill, from which specially prepared feed is delivered to and through the houses automatically.

Very small differences in feed consumption by huge numbers of hens can determine the profitability of the operation, and the producer must watch it carefully. The feed mill, like everything else in the complex, is controlled and monitored by computers. Nutritionists have identified the nutrient needs of birds of specific ages, species, and objectives, such as growth or egg production, and it is said that no other animal, including the human animal, enjoys such a well-balanced daily diet as the chicken.

By careful selection breeders have developed specific genetic strains of chickens for specific objectives. The egg producer, for example, needs birds that will lay more eggs with less feed, and the broiler strains bred for meat production would be completely out of place in a henhouse. Egg producers buy their day-old chicks from hatcheries, which maintain parent flocks of purebred stock. The hatchery must be able to deliver hundreds of thousands of chicks on the day the producer needs them.

A chicken is a pullet until she is eighteen to twenty weeks old, when she starts to lay eggs and becomes a hen. Producers often keep their pullets in a separate pullet house, and move them to one of the henhouses when they are ready to start laying. Hens lay for about fifty weeks and then the producer must sell or "force molt" them. Force molting is a procedure for resting hens so they can continue to lay eggs for another year, but it is a dreadfully poorly chosen name for a natural process.

In the barnyard hens laid eggs mainly during the spring and early summer. As the autumn days got shorter, they began to prepare for winter by laying fewer eggs and by shedding their feathers (molting), just as deciduous trees start to shed their leaves when the days get shorter. Back in the old days egg merchants needed massive cold storage facilities to keep stocks of eggs through the winter, when hens were not laying.

Artificial lighting enabled producers to extend the length of the laying cycle by keeping the apparent length of day constant in enclosed houses, and since 1970 hens have been laying eggs at the same steady rate throughout the year. Producers can induce them to molt at the end of a fifty-week laying cycle by reducing the light in the houses from twelve hours to eight, and by cutting back on their feed and water.

After a force molt of six to eight weeks the hens are raring to start laying eggs again. The second laying cycle usually is eight to ten weeks shorter than the first, and the hens lay heavier eggs, which are good for breaking. It is cheaper to recycle hens with a force molt than it is to buy new pullets that have to be fed for eighteen to twenty weeks before they are ready to start laying, and recycling by force molting has become standard in the egg business.

Producers carefully control the temperature inside their henhouses, because they want the birds to use feed to lay eggs, not to maintain their body heat. Batteries of exhaust fans along the side of the house remove stale air, moisture, and ammonia, and fresh air is sucked in through intakes to keep the temperature constant. Inside the house the birds are in wire cages stacked three, four, or five tiers high (fig. 9.2). The number of birds per cage varies with the size of the cage, but five birds per cage probably is most common.

The back of each cage is a "splatter board" that deflects the droppings from the tiers above into a nine-foot-deep manure pit beneath the row of cages. Another configuration has a manure collection belt beneath each tier of cages. This belt carries the manure to the end of the building, where it is scraped off and stockpiled. Each hen produces about a quarter of a pound per day, which does not sound like much, but 100,000 birds produce 12.5 tons a day, and that is quite a lot. Chicken manure is excellent fertilizer, because urine is mixed with solid matter inside the bird, and the droppings are a rich moist mixture. Producers spread it on cropland or sell it to other farmers, who are delighted to buy it.

The wire floor of each cage tilts down toward the front, and when a hen lays an egg it rolls gently onto a collection belt in front of the cage. This belt carries the eggs to the end of the house, where they join the larger stream of eggs from other houses that is flowing toward the processing plant. Hens generally lay their eggs in the morning, but the plant runs all day, so computers start and stop the individual belts to prevent traffic jams and maintain a steady flow of eggs.

The river of eggs that the conveyor belts bring into the processing plant is mesmerizing. It is up to a yard wide and moves at a rate of 2,500 eggs a minute. Just imagine a steady stream of 200 dozen eggs a minute. It flows through the washing machine, through the candling machine, where workers identify defective eggs for automatic removal by touching them with an electronic wand, and on to the packaging machine, which grades the eggs by size and places them gently in cartons or on flats.

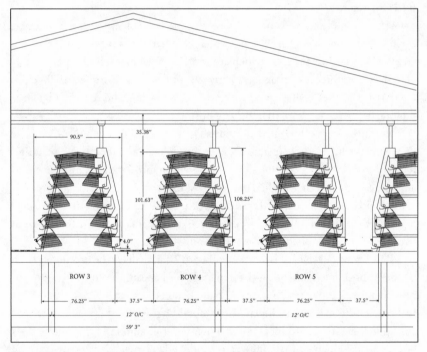

Figure 9.2. Cross section of cages for laying hens. The front of each cage has conveyor belts for distributing feed and collecting eggs. The back of each cage is a splatter board to deflect droppings from above into the pit beneath. (Reproduced from a building layout plan prepared by the Fort Recovery Equipment Company; used by permission.)

The packaged eggs are stored in a cool room at a temperature of 48°F until they are loaded onto delivery trucks. The warehouses of producers who sell mainly to retail chains are veritable rainbows of stacks of empty cartons waiting to be filled. Some are traditional gray pulp, but many are gaily colored foam, because each chain has its own distinctive trademark carton.

Egg producers have so many identical animals cooped up in such close proximity that they are understandably worried about disease. In the barnyard mortality ran as high as 20 to 30 percent a year, but it has been greatly reduced in modern henhouses by better sanitation, better medications, and better biosecurity. Many egg producers require you to put on disposable plastic coveralls and hair covers before you enter their houses, and they will not let you enter at all if you have been on another poultry farm recently.

Egg producers must also be concerned about animal welfare activists, who are maddened by the very idea of hundreds of thousands of hens cooped up in cages. They protest that it is not "natural" for birds to be in cages, but neither is it natural for people to live in houses, and producers say that laying hens in their environmentally controlled buildings are better sheltered from rain and snow, better fed, better protected from diseases and parasites, and safer from predators than their ancestors were in the barnyard.

Unfortunately, irresponsible activists have done millions of dollars' worth of damage by vandalizing livestock farms and animal research laboratories, and they have done their best to terrorize teachers and scare the wits out of schoolchildren by circulating lurid but totally erroneous descriptions of the way farmers treat their animals. As a consequence, many egg producers are understandably wary of strangers.

The good producers have nothing to hide, and they are proud of their operations, but they must guard their property and their livelihood against irresponsible vandals. They are also painfully aware that a few rotten producers have given all egg producers a black eye. Most are highly critical of Jack DeCoster of Turner, Maine, whose intransigent behavior has tarnished the image of the entire egg industry. DeCoster ignored my efforts to give him a chance to tell his side of the story, and I have had to glean what little I know of his operation from the public prints.

On August 29, 1996, the *New York Times* reported that DeCoster started out with 125 hens and had built an empire of 5 million hens producing 23 million eggs a week. He had egg operations in Maine, Iowa, and Ohio and hog farms in Iowa. The U.S. Occupational Safety and Health Administration had just fined his Maine operation $3.8 million after its inspectors had found unguarded machinery, electrical hazards, and workers handling manure and dead chickens with their bare hands in his plant.

Most of DeCoster's Maine workers were Hispanic, and some of them lived in his company's trailer park. Many of the trailers were old, with gaping holes in their floors and walls, and they were overrun by rats and cockroaches. Several grocery chains announced a boycott of his eggs, and he took out full-page ads in local newspapers apologizing to consumers "for the controversy," but his attorney quit his case, and so did the business advisory team he had hired to help him set things right.

On October 24, 1996, the *Des Moines Register* reported that the Iowa Division of Labor had fined DeCoster Farms of Iowa $489,950 for alleged violation of workplace safety laws and wage and hour laws. Furthermore, his hog operations in Iowa had been cited by the state Department of Natural Resources for numerous environmental violations.

On August 25, 1997, federal safety regulators proposed fines totaling more than $1 million for conditions at the Agri-General egg farm in Croton, Ohio, including high levels of ammonia and dust in the air, drinking water contaminated with insecticides and bacteria from chicken manure, and unsafe equipment. The president of Agri-General was Duke Goranites, who had worked for DeCoster until September 1996.

Operations such as these have been a source of intense embarrassment to the entire egg industry, but enough about the bad guys; let's visit some of the good guys.

The Boisterous Baer Boys

Amon Baer was born in 1953. His father, Allan, was a devoutly religious man who had grown up as a Mennonite and joined a Hutterite community in North Dakota. Hutterites have a tradition of challenging authority, and all members of the community are expected to share equally in all tasks. One day Allan wondered a bit too loudly why Heinie, the leader of the community, never helped to wash dishes, and he was told to leave.

Allan was absolutely penniless, with thirteen children and a pregnant wife. He borrowed $3,000 from his brother for the down payment on a rundown 240-acre farm in the choppy, lake-speckled, morainic hills east of Moorhead, Minnesota. The farmhouse had not been lived in for two or three years. He outfitted it with a cookstove, clothes wringer, and other necessities from the Salvation Army. The land was all buck brush and pasture but had no fences. Moraines are topographically picturesque, but they are difficult cropland, and Allan could not cultivate his land anyhow, because the entire farm was in the Soil Bank for several years after he bought it.

He put his boys to work to eke out a living. They had a huge garden, from which they sold tomatoes, and they cut down trees to make fence. Allan worked as a day laborer for $1.65 an hour, and would take any job that paid 10 cents an hour more than the one he had. Each Saturday he attended the local livestock auction and bought the animals no one else wanted, an old dairy cow one week, a flock of sheep the next. He removed the seats from the back of his old station wagon to make room to haul them to the farm. He sold cream and lambs, and butchered a ewe when the family needed meat.

In 1965, when he was 45 years old, Allan took a course to learn how to sell life insurance. He was an excellent salesman, but quit after he got stuck in a snowstorm in North Dakota. He wanted to develop something on the farm that would let him stay closer to his family. He had had some experience with the poultry business as a young man and had been in charge of the Hutterite poultry flock, so he sold a local banker on lending him $65,000 to build a house for 12,000 laying hens. He contracted with an egg company to provide the hens, with another company for the feed, and received a percentage of the egg checks.

Allan's first henhouse was so successful that in 1967 he built a second one. Everybody said that the first one was huge, and when he started making plans to build the second a friend asked him, "It's not going to be this big, is it?" "Oh, no," he said, "it's going to be twice this big, for 24,000 birds," and then in 1969 he built a third, for 80,000 birds. All of the feeding and egg gathering in these houses was done by hand.

In 1971 Amon graduated and went off to work on various construction jobs. Allan thought that the man who was selling him pullets was taking advantage of him, so he decided to build a pullet barn and produce his own. In 1973 he asked Amon to come home and build it for him. "I wasn't really sure that I wanted to keep on farming on a full-time basis," said Amon, "but it all just seemed to kind of all fall together, and I have stayed here ever since."

Allan's biggest cost of production after he had built the houses was feed, so in 1975 he built his own feed mill and bought grain from local farmers. A laying hen needs a bushel of corn a year, plus soybean meal and smaller amounts of other ingredients. By 1977 Amon's younger brothers Amos (born 1954), Joel (born 1956), and Jona (born 1957) had joined the operation, and they incorporated as Baer Brothers.

By the late 1970s the older buildings were starting to show their age, and egg prices were good, so they started to close down the old buildings and put up new ones: for 80,000 birds in 1975, another for 80,000 in 1977, and a third for 150,000 in 1979, all with fully automatic feeding and egg-collection systems. Then in 1980 egg prices dropped but inflation was rampant, interest rates went through the roof, they had built up a lot of debt, and they almost lost the farm, but fortunately egg prices recovered nicely in the early 1980s.

In 1982 Allan decided to retire and sell the farm to his sons, but the Baer boys are a boisterous bunch with strong opinions about everything and no qualms whatsoever about expressing them in loud and reverberating voices. "We were always at loggerheads," said Joel. "Where do you expand next and what do you buy and how much do you pay for it? The family corporation worked fine when Dad was head and everyone reported to him and he had final decision, but he realized that we are all strong-willed people, and he had to split up the farm among us as evenly as possible."

Working out a fair division took three full years. Amos got the pullet farm and Amon, Joel, and Jona each got an egg-laying operation and processing plant. They have added grading stations to enable them to sell their eggs to retail stores and institutions, because the liquid market is their only other outlet, and they realize they cannot compete with the new 2- and 3-million-bird in-line egg-breaking operations.

The division has worked out beautifully and the brothers work together well, if vociferously. In the early 1990s they coordinated an expansion to double the size of their operation so the members of the next generation could join it if they were interested. In 1999 Joel had 250,000 hens, Jona had 325,000, and Amon had 310,000. In 1994, when the owners retired, Amon bought the Mendelson Egg Company, a wholesaler to which they had been selling their eggs for thirty years, and he had to expand his carton storage space and cooler space.

The Baers have needed land on which they could spread manure from their henhouses, and they have expanded Allan's original 240-acre farm to 3,000 acres by buying neighboring land when it became available. They could pay more for land nearby, because it was cheaper to haul manure to it, but others know of their interest, and the price has gone up. "People complain that livestock farms depreciate the price of land," said Amon, "but land that borders ours sells for $800 to $1,000 an acre, while similar land five miles away sells for only $500 to $600."

In 1999 the Baers rented all of their land to crop farmers for $40 to $50 an acre, and charged them $15 an acre to cover the cost of hauling, spreading, and digging in manure on it. They like to clean out the manure pits under the houses and spread manure at least once a week, whenever the fields are dry, because they start to have fly problems if they let the pits go for a month.

They lost interest in buying land when they started making compost, but they are not ready to sell any, even though they are not cultivating it. "Land is not a great investment," said Joel, "but it's something I can sit in this pickup and drive over it, I can drive stakes in it, I can build a house on it, I can take my kids for a walk over it. I've got an attachment to land, not just this particular land but any land. I like to own land." Amon added, "Land does not depreciate like buildings and equipment, and I hope to have enough land to cash it out and have a good income when I decide to retire."

The Baers have received occasional complaints about the way they have been spreading manure on their land, and since 1996 they have been exploring more environmentally friendly ways of handling it. They thought about using heat to dry it, and Joel went to visit a manure-drying facility in Colorado. The first thing he saw when he got there was two gas wells, so he turned right around and came home. Jona visited an indoor composting operation in New York, but manure is so corrosive that the building was deteriorating rapidly, so they decided to try open-air composting.

In May 1998 they requested a compost permit from the state regulatory agency, which denied the request. Being Baers, they decided to go ahead and develop a facility anyhow. They complain that the agency bureaucrats do not understand the practicalities of farming, but I suspect that they may derive a certain small delight from rattling the cages of the bureaucrats. After many wrangles, the agency finally gave them a clean bill of health in August 1999, when their facility was already operating successfully.

They mix sunflower hulls with the manure and pile it in parallel rows 6 feet high, 10 feet wide, and 150 feet long. They bought a huge secondhand compost turning machine and fluff up each row two or three times a week. The compost heats up to around 140°F, which kills pathogens and weed seeds. After three months the compost is cured, and it is as odorless as dirt. They sell it to organic farmers up to sixty miles away, and have turned what was a waste into a source of profit.

Amon realizes that he still needs to broaden his agricultural base, and in 1997 he became involved with a group of twenty-two independent hog farmers who want to stay in the business but know that packing plants do not like to deal with small producers. They have formed a cooperative to develop a 5,000-sow farrowing farm that will produce 23 pigs per sow per year. Each member must take at least 3,000 pigs a year, feed them to market weight, and deliver them to the processing plant.

They expect to produce a minimum of 250,000 hogs a year, so they can go to a packing company and negotiate for the sale of a large number of hogs instead of trying to sell small lots of 3,000 to 5,000. They have even considered trying to buy their own packing plant so they can develop and market their own brand of pork products.

Amon's hogs are all on contract farms, where the farmer already has hog barns. Amon finances the hogs and feed, pays the farmer for his buildings and labor, and sells the hogs. He would like to build some hog barns on his own land, but getting a permit is so difficult that it is not worth the effort.

Nick Schimpf

Nick Schimpf, born in 1928, also composts and sells the manure from his henhouses. He had a friend in Milwaukee who was making good money with chickens in 1957, so Nick and his father-in-law decided to get into the business. They bought a farm thirty miles northwest of Milwaukee and started with 18,000 broilers. They thought their wives could take care of the birds and they could have other jobs, but Nick had to stay home so much that he decided the chickens were a full-time job.

After selling his first flock of broilers, Nick realized that there was more money in selling eggs to grocery stores. He has built up his business gradually, from 12,000 laying hens in a single building in 1958 to 1.35 million in twenty buildings in 2000. His big break came when the egg supplier for a major grocery chain was not able to deliver at Easter, of all times, and the chain turned to Nick. He ran his processing plant continuously for a week, with naps on the couch, and he has kept the account ever since.

His egg business is market-driven. "You've got to do whatever it takes to keep your customers happy," he said, "because they have customers they've got to keep happy. I have filled up my car with cartons of eggs and delivered them personally on weekends and holidays when a customer has needed them."

In 1976 Nick bought two larger farms west of Milwaukee to give him more land for spreading manure and more elbow room from neighbors. In 2000 he owned 1,000 acres, of which 800 were tillable, but they can produce only a three-week supply of corn and soybeans. He had a feed mill on each farm and bought twenty-six 27-ton loads of corn and nine 27-ton loads of soybeans from local farmers each week. He employed 110 workers, of whom about half were Hispanic, and their number was increasing, because they are more dependable and work harder than the Americans he can hire in the competitive Milwaukee labor market.

Each farm had long, parallel rows of henhouses of various sizes. A 40' × 400' building holds 63,000 birds and a 73' × 360' building holds 145,000, but the capacity of a house varies with the internal configuration of cages and the manure-handling system. A building with cages stacked six high and manure-removal belts can hold twice as many hens as one with cages three high and a deep-pit manure system.

The front ends of the buildings are connected by the enclosed passageway containing the principal conveyor belt that carries the eggs from each house to the processing plant. A slowly moving conveyor belt beneath each tier of cages carries manure to the back end of the building, where it is loaded onto trucks and hauled to the compost building. On the conveyor belt the manure dries and loses much of its weight.

Nick started composting in 1990, and in 1999 he built a special compost building to process 50 to 60 tons of manure a day. He bulks the manure with shredded wood or lawn clippings to increase aeration. After about a month he bags the compost and sells it to homeowners in the Milwaukee area, and he sells it in bulk to golf courses, nurseries, and organic farmers.

Bill Seifring

Bill Seifring was born in 1956 on a 190-acre dairy and hog farm in west-central Ohio, near the Indiana line. His father died when he was 11, and by the time he was 14 he had taken over the farm. In 1974 he sold the cows and hogs, which were not making much money, shifted completely to grain farming, and had a variety of jobs in town. He drove fifty miles each way and saved everything he made, except for the winter he got an apartment in town. He didn't save a thing that winter, he said, because after work he went out for a beer with the fellows.

In 1984 he bought the farm from his mother, who still lives with him. He has never gotten married and has put everything back in the farm. "I don't know how many girls I have broken up with when it came time to harvest," was his comment.

Between 1988 and 1993 he bought four more farms, totaling 345 acres, but still needs more land. He would be willing to pay extra for land right next door, even though farmland in the area is selling for $4,000 an acre. He farms all the cropland himself and is happy with 150-bushel corn yields and 40-bushel soybean yields.

In 1986 his brother wanted him to partner in an egg operation, but Bill decided to go it alone, because partnerships can be trouble. He started with an 80,000-bird house in 1986 and added houses in 1987, 1990, 1993, 1994, and 1995 for a total capacity of 888,000 laying hens. In 1995 he also built a processing plant, where the eggs are graded, placed on flats, and stored in a cold room at a constant temperature of 45°F until the truck comes to pick them up.

Bill does not own the hens. They belong to the Fort Recovery Equity Exchange, which pays him a set price per dozen eggs plus a feed conversion premium. In 1919 a group of farmers formed the Equity Exchange in Fort Recovery, Ohio, as a cooperative feed mill. It needed to expand, and in 1960 it began contracting with farmer-members in a thirty-mile radius to produce eggs. It has become the nation's sixth largest egg producer, with more than 7 million laying hens, but has never gotten around to changing its name.[7] Equity owns the hens and the farmer provides the houses and labor. The first houses held 3,000 birds, but in 1997 houses with a capacity of 120,000 to 180,000 hens were standard.

West-central Ohio has too many small undersized farms, and the farmers must supplement their crop income by taking off-farm jobs and by producing livestock. Contract egg production has helped the area tremendously, but unlike Bill, most contracting farms have only one henhouse. The farm wife spends three or four hours a day placing the eggs on flats and the husband does heavy jobs after he gets home from work. The flats are stored in a cooler room that holds a semitrailer load of eggs, and a truck comes to pick them up when it is full.

A henhouse 35 feet high, 70 feet wide, and 600 feet long holds 180,000 birds on the upper level, with a manure pit 9 feet deep below. The front end of the house has a small platform and door on the upper level for moving hens into and out of the house. The sides of the house have large ventilating fans on the lower level, and the back end has doors on the ground floor for hauling out the manure.

Bill made me don a disposable white plastic jumpsuit that covered everything but my face before he let me enter his henhouses. Each house has ten long rows of stepped cages, six birds to a cage, in back-to-back stacks, with narrow wooden walkways between the sets of stacks. In front of each row of cages are the feed trough, egg belt, and water nipples. The back of each cage is the splatter board that steers droppings into the manure pit below.

"Our computers tell us everything we need to know about the house," Bill said, "number of eggs per line, temperature, feed and water consumption. You feed young birds more, to make them grow, and older birds less, to avoid wasting feed. You keep the temperature between 72 and 80 degrees, warmer for the older birds that are getting less feed. You know something is wrong if they're not drinking enough water, or if they're drinking when the lights are off and they should be sleeping. The lights are out from 7 P.M. till 3 A.M., but of course we don't go to daylight saving. Most hens lay eggs when they get up in the morning, but a few lay during the day."

In 1997 Bill employed seven people in his six houses. A worker made a daily run through each house to look for water leaks, dead birds, and any other problems. His mortality rate is 10 percent a year, less than it would be on free range. He puts the dead birds in a freezer and takes them to a rendering plant, where they are made into protein concentrate for dog food.

A worker also walks each manure pit each day. The task is not so bad as it may sound. The piles in the pit are three to four feet high, but between them are aisles beneath the walkways between the stacks of cages above. The fans in the side walls suck fresh air in through the ceiling of the house and down through the cages, and they expel ammonia fumes and dust from the pit.

Poultry manure is splendid fertilizer, so Bill surprised me when he told me that he sells it instead of spreading it on his own cropland. "I need to get my rates down," he explained. "My phosphorus and calcium rates are high and my potassium and trace minerals are OK, so I use the manure money to buy nitrogen, which is the only nutrient I need."

He cleans out his manure pits each August, when farmers are ready to plow manure in on their wheat land to get ready for corn, and he sells the manure at a public auction. He started in 1994 and issued invitations the first year, but in 1997 he simply advertised and drew fifty to seventy-five farmers from a twenty-mile radius. He contracted seven trucks to haul the manure to the buyers' farms, because he did not want a lot of strange trucks messing up his own farm. He sold 7,500 tons for $3 to $4 a ton.

Dave Staples

Dave Staples has perfected and patented a process for pelletizing the manure from his henhouses, and manure has been his major profit-maker when egg prices have been low. Dave was born in Utah in 1941, grew up on a dairy farm, and went to Brigham Young University to become a veterinarian, but a poultry science professor took a keen personal interest in him and guided him into the poultry industry. Between 1967 and 1976 he worked for large egg producers in Illinois, California, Hawaii, and Utah before he joined Aaron Johnson.

Aaron Johnson's background was in manufacturing, but he liked having a farm. In 1969 he bought one with a 16,000-bird laying house east of Madison, Wisconsin. By 1976 he had built it up to 90,000 hens, but he realized that he needed a partner with poultry experience, and he invited Dave to buy in with him. "Partnerships are high risks," Dave said, "but fortunately he and I clicked, and we worked well together until I bought him out when he decided to retire in 1991."

In 1977 they built their own processing plant and sold shell eggs to retail stores and institutions in southern Wisconsin and northeastern Illinois. They contracted with other producers for 40 percent of their eggs. That procedure was inefficient, because the eggs had to be handled twice, which meant more labor and greater chance of breakage. They decided to produce all their own eggs, and had expanded to 665,000 hens by 1981 (fig. 9.3).

Dave was concerned that they were only producing a commodity, eggs, and he thought they were going to have to get into value-added production by breaking eggs. He even designed the processing plant for easy conversion to breaking. "On the shell side we loved it when they started to break eggs," he said, "because they took eggs we couldn't sell and kept our prices up. Then it shifted the other way, because the breakers could shift eggs to the shell side when the price was good. We used to love 'em, now we hate 'em."

In 2000, as he neared retirement age, Dave was selling his complex to an egg-breaking company, which was financing the reconfiguration of his houses and the replacement of all the old equipment with new German equipment that is better designed. Dave wanted a belt beneath each tier of cages to carry away the manure, because he wanted to get it out and dried quickly. He had traditional high-rise houses with three tiers of cages above a manure pit in the basement, but with belts he did not need the manure pit, so he put three tiers of cages in it, and his buildings now are all six cages high rather than three high.

Adding three new tiers of cages doubled the capacity of the nine 42' × 500' buildings, which in 2000 held 110,000 to 140,000 hens instead of 50,000 to 60,000. Under the old system one worker could take care of three houses. Now he can handle only two, but Dave had to hire only one new person to take care of double the number of birds. The new cages hold eight birds, but Dave said,

"Hens don't care how many sisters they have as long as they have enough room in the cage, and the new German cages are well designed. Feed, lights, air, and water, that old hen knows what she needs, and she'll lay more eggs if she's happy."

Dave replaced the hens in his laying houses on a 10-week cycle. He bought 110,000 to 140,000 chicks every 10 weeks and kept them in three pullet houses for 17 weeks. Then he sold a house of layers and moved in new pullets, which were in the laying house for 103 weeks. He had hoped for 500 eggs per hen in the 103-week laying cycle, but he got only around 490.

In the old days Dave scraped out the manure pits with a bobcat and spread manure on the 1,800 acres of land he has bought to buffer his complex. He spread manure just to get rid of it, but he believed it was a product that could have value

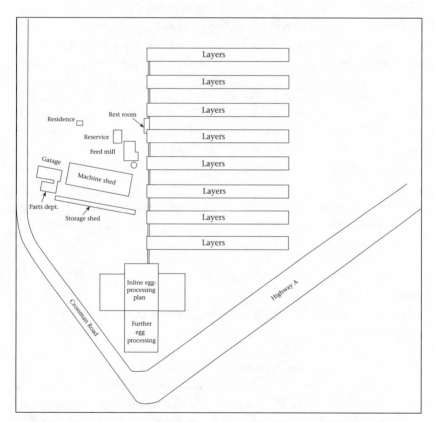

Figure 9.3. Ground plan of Creekwood Farms, Lake Mills, Wisconsin, 1990. (Based on a plan provided by Dave Staples; used by permission of Dale Siebenbruner.)

if he processed it properly. First he tried compost, but he said, "I realized that I was competing with every municipality in the United States, and compost doesn't have a whole lot of value."

He worked for several years to develop a process for drying and pelletizing the manure, and was pleasantly surprised to realize that he could patent his process, which he now sells to other producers. "Capturing the nitrogen is the hard part," he said. "You lose nitrogen in the buildings when the manure is wet, and I want to get it out and dry it as fast as possible. If I can smell it, I'm losing money." Dave emphasized that he is making pellets of dried chicken manure, not compost. Compost takes twelve weeks, and he can produce dry pellets in two. Compost is only 2 percent nitrogen and he is shooting for 5, but in 2000 he could guarantee only 4.

Dave's hens excrete 140 tons of manure a day at 70 to 80 percent moisture. He dried it down to 30 percent, stacked it for two weeks, put it through a screener, and compressed it into pellets that look like pipe tobacco. He sold the pellets for $80 a ton in 2000. They are 4-5-5 organic fertilizer, have almost no odor, and will not "burn" plants or turf, as raw manure does. The details of the process are proprietary, and Dave said with a smile, "If I told you any more about it, I'd have to shoot you."

Bob Sparboe

Bob Sparboe has built a chicken hatchery into a major corporation with a number of constituent companies that included one of the nation's top twenty egg producers and one of its top ten egg-breaking companies in 1996.[8] He was born in Iowa in 1930, the son of a hatcheryman. His father did not want him to get into the business, but in 1954 a poultry company offered him a chance to distribute its chicks either in Minnesota or in Missouri.

He chose Minnesota. He came to Litchfield, even though he had never seen the city or even been in this part of the state before, and founded the Sparboe Chick Company to hatch eggs and sell day-old chicks to farmers. He soon realized, however, that farmers were either getting out of the chicken business or becoming specialist producers, and the farmer market for chicks was vanishing, so he shifted to commercial pullet production. In 1960 he sold 75,000 20-week-old pullets to farm flock operators. In 1963 he expanded his business by lending money to farmers to build cage production units for 3,300 to 3,600 laying hens, and he developed joint-venture production contracts to market their eggs.

In the 1960s rising feed costs were a problem. "Five dollars for a ton of feed was equivalent to one cent a dozen," Bob said, "and back in those days the most money you could make was two and a half, maybe three cents a dozen." The Sparboe Agricultural Corporation began to formulate its own feed, and in 1970 Bob formed a separate feed company. At first it supplied feed for his own operation, but it has grown into a nutrition service that provides feed and technical services for egg producers all over the United States.

Egg sales continued to grow, and in 1974 Sparboe Summit Farms built one of Minnesota's first in-line egg-production complexes, a few miles east of Litchfield. This complex was gradually expanded until 1991, when it reached its 2002 capacity of 960,000 hens in twelve houses. It also processes eggs from contract producers who have 540,000 hens.

Bob realized that the rising costs of egg production were forcing contract producers out of the egg business, and in 1978 Sparboe Summit Farms began lending farmers money to build 60,000-hen laying houses. In 1987 the Sparboe Companies bought a bank in Litchfield and reoriented it to serve the special needs of the national poultry and food industries as well as the local area.

In 1988 Bob formed the Sparboe Iowa Corporation to buy two 80,000-hen houses and to build a processing plant in Iowa. By 1996 he had expanded his Iowa shell egg operation to ten houses with 1.12 million hens, and he had contract producers with 530,000 more hens. He had also seen the handwriting on the wall, and in 1996 he formed Sparboe Foods Corporation to buy an egg-breaking plant in Calmar, Iowa, which breaks 9 million eggs a week and sells tanker loads of liquid eggs for further processing. In 2000 the Sparboe Companies had more than 3 million hens that laid more than 756 million eggs, and they marketed another 156 million eggs from contract producers.

Bob Sparboe is a keen student of management, and I suspect he has kept his units small to encourage entrepreneurship, which cannot flourish in a large organization because it is stifled by the structure and function and policies and systems and rules and constraints that a large organization must have. "Entrepreneurs are not in business for the money," he said, "but they need money to reinvest in the business. They derive their satisfaction from the challenge of taking risks and the thrill of accomplishment.

"Animal agriculture is a tough, management-intensive business," he continued, "and it needs managers who are good entrepreneurs. It's hard to attract them, and especially their spouses, because it requires the commitment of 7 days a week, 365 days a year. Agriculture is constantly changing, and a successful farmer must constantly transform his operation to accommodate to change, to adapt to it, to adjust to it, even to bring it about, or he'll be swept away by it."

Entrepreneurs like Bob Sparboe have quietly but persistently increased the scale of egg production in the United States. In 2000 egg-production complexes with several million laying hens had become the norm, and egg production was tightly concentrated in areas where entrepreneurs have developed such complexes. Egg production is one of the lesser-known forms of large-scale animal agriculture in the United States, but it has drawn the ire of animal rights activists because producers keep their hens in cages and because they use the unfortunate term "force molting" to describe the hen's six-to-eight-week rest period between two fifty-week egg-laying cycles.

10
Turkeys

A whole roast turkey once was the centerpiece of a traditional Thanksgiving dinner, but a whole roast turkey is an awful lot of meat. We moaned about having to eat leftover turkey for days and days and days after Thanksgiving, and few Americans ate turkey more than once a year. Production was highly seasonal, and farmers who kept a gobbler and a few hens could easily satisfy local demand.

Today many people eat turkey every week, although they may not even realize it. Turkey processors market a bewildering variety of turkey products for year-round consumption. The meat is remarkably malleable, and processors have learned how to mold, compress, color, and season it into turkey ham, turkey frankfurters, turkey salami, even turkey bacon. They give helpful hints on how to substitute it for other meats in everything from veal picante to pork pies. Turkey is the cheapest meat in the supermarket. It is high in protein and low in fat and cholesterol, and many consumers see it as a healthy alternative to red meat.

Turkey producers have followed the trail blazed by broiler producers, but turkey production has become even more concentrated in the hands of a small number of large-scale producers. The U.S. *Census of Agriculture* says that more than 600,000 American farmers raised turkeys in 1929, and they produced an average of only 26 birds. By 1997 the number of turkey farmers had dwindled to a mere 6,000, but they produced an average of 51,000 birds each, and the 868 farms that sold 100,000 or more turkeys produced 63 percent of the national total. Turkey processing is equally concentrated. In 1997 the five largest companies processed 47 percent of the nation's turkeys, and the twenty largest processed 96 percent.[1]

The U.S. *Census of Agriculture* says that 160,000 farmers raised 36 million turkeys, one for each American family, in 1949. The average flock was only 225 birds, but flocks of 5,000 to 10,000, small by today's standards, were not unusual in the areas where entrepreneurs had started to specialize and were producing on a larger scale. The principal producing areas in 1949 were the Shenandoah Valley of Virginia, scattered counties in Minnesota and Iowa, and irrigated valleys in the West, especially the Central Valley of California.

Up until the mid-1960s most turkey production in the United States was seasonal and "on range."[2] From June until early November the birds ran free on pastures fenced with heavy-gauge woven chicken wire six feet high. Small 10' × 12' shelter sheds protected them against rain, strong winds, and extreme temperatures. Each thousand birds needed two to five acres of good range.

Growers seeded the range to alfalfa, bluegrass, rape, or similar plants. They divided it into lots and moved the birds to a new lot each week to control disease. The shelters, feeding troughs, and watering pans were on skids, and within the lot the grower moved them every day or two to get the birds to use clean ground.

Growers moved the turkey range around on their farms. They used a given piece of ground only once every two to four years, to prevent the buildup of disease. In the intervening years it produced a fine crop, because the turkeys had fertilized it so richly with their droppings.

Range production of turkeys was not efficient, because the birds ran off energy that increased their feed bills. Growers lost birds to soil-borne diseases and parasites, to insects, to adverse weather, to thieves, and to predatory animals, such as hawks, horned owls, foxes, coyotes, and neighbors' dogs. Predators caused heavy losses both by direct attack and by stampeding the birds, which are easily frightened.

Before around 1965 turkey processing, like turkey production, was seasonal, and the processing facilities were primitive by modern standards. Some growers sold their birds to chicken processors, who temporarily converted their plants to dress, pack, and ship whole slaughtered turkeys, but many plucked their birds in their own barns and sold them directly to consumers.

The modern turkey business in the United States was born during the 1960s. It sprang from four closely related changes: a shift to better breeds of birds of more uniform quality; a shift from seasonal production on free range to more efficient year-round production in specialized houses; a shift to more sophisticated processing and marketing; and a shift to greater concentration of production and processing in vertically integrated companies, with attendant economies of scale.

The U.S. *Census of Agriculture* shows that in 1959 the United States had 86,838 turkey farmers who produced an average of 985 birds; in 1969 it had only 5,425 turkey farmers, but they averaged 19,070 birds. In 1969 the broiler areas of North Carolina and Arkansas-Missouri had begun to move into large-scale turkey production, and by 1980 North Carolina had become the nation's leading turkey state; it has held that rank ever since. In 1997 six states (North Carolina, Minnesota, Virginia, Arkansas, California, and Missouri) produced two-thirds of our turkeys (fig. 10.1).

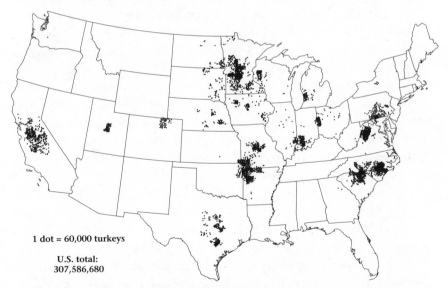

1 dot = 60,000 turkeys

U.S. total:
307,586,680

Figure 10.1. Number of turkeys sold, 1997. Clusters on the map are associated with the activities of Max Foster, Earl B. Olson, Wally Jerome, Sam Wampler, Bruce Cuddy, Ottis Carroll, and Marvin Johnson, among others. (Source: *1997 Census of Agriculture,* vol. 2, pt. 1 [Washington, D.C.: U.S. Department of Agriculture, National Agricultural Statistics Service, 1999].)

Before 1960 the common domestic turkey in the United States was the Broad Breasted Bronze (BBB) variety, which had black feathers tinged with white and copper. BBB birds had black pinfeathers, small feathers just emerging through the skin that look like human blackheads. Consumers disliked these black pinfeathers on their roast turkeys, so BBB birds have been replaced by white varieties. Breeders have fine-tuned their ability to develop specific types of birds for specific market products. Some birds have such enormous breasts that they cannot mate naturally, and they require artificial insemination.

During the late 1960s turkey growers began to move their birds indoors. Instead of letting the birds run free on range they started to raise them in grow-out houses that look for all the world like broiler houses, and nowadays few if any commercial turkeys are produced on free range. Houses require less labor than range grow-out, they facilitate and encourage year-round production, and they enable the grower to raise more broods per year.

Turkey growers copied the idea of houses from broiler growers, and turkey houses are virtually indistinguishable from broiler houses. James Parsons is the extension poultry specialist in the leading broiler- and turkey-producing area in eastern North Carolina. I asked him how you can tell a turkey house from a broiler house just by looking at it from the highway. He thought a moment, and then he said, "You really can't. You've got to get a look at the birds inside them, but the sign at the farm entrance might be a good clue."

Turkey houses, like broiler houses, are long, low, narrow buildings. Over the years growers have built them larger and larger, and modern turkey houses measure up to 900 feet long and 60 feet wide. Their capacities vary far more than the capacities of broiler houses, because turkeys are so much larger than broilers. The houses often are in clusters of three or four, because each brooder house needs two or three grow-out houses.

Converted school buses bring day-old poults from the hatchery to the brooder house, which has heat lamps suspended about twelve inches above the floor to keep them warm (fig. 10.2). After seven weeks the grower divides the flock in half and moves the birds to grow-out houses. Hens stay in the grow-out house for seven weeks, until they weigh 15 pounds, toms for eleven weeks, until they weigh 30–35 pounds. Hens need 0.6 square foot each in the brooder house and 1 to 2 square feet in the grow-out house; toms need 1 square foot in the brooder house and 2 to 3 in the grow-out house.

Grow-out houses, like brooder houses, have automatic waterers and feeding troughs (fig. 10.3). Turkeys use all the common grains cheerfully and efficiently;

the choice depends on cost and availability. Turkey company feed mills have sophisticated purchasing and nutrition departments to ensure least-cost production of the right feed at the right time to birds of the right age and sex.

Feed generally costs least in the Midwest, more in the South, most in the West, but construction and heating costs are higher in the Midwest because the winters are so severe. The South has cheaper labor, which is especially important for processing plants. The West must offset its higher costs by better management, but it enjoys easy access to a large, growing, and highly health-conscious regional market.

The feeding troughs and waterers in grow-out houses are suspended on wires, and they are winched up and out of the way when the crew comes to load the birds onto the trucks that will haul them to the processing plant. The crew sets up a mechanical loading chute in the door at one end of the house. They start at the far end and slowly drive the birds toward the chute, which has an inclined conveyor that carries them up into coops that are fixed on the truck. The chute

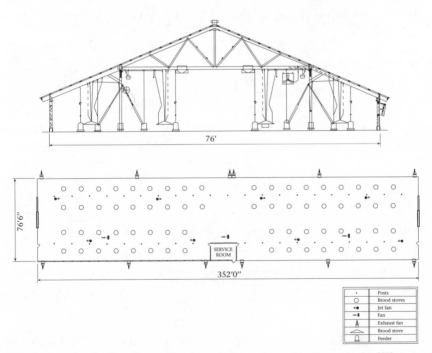

·	Posts
O	Brood stoves
◂●	Jet fan
→❙	Fan
▲	Exhaust fan
△	Brood stove
◻	Feeder

Figure 10.2. A turkey brood barn. (Based on a diagram prepared by George Raab of The Turkey Store Company; used by permission.)

has side walls that flare out into a V shape inside the house to funnel the birds onto the conveyor.

After the flock has been loaded, the grower must scrape up and remove the litter, wash down the entire inside of the house, and let it stand vacant for a month or so to control disease. A grower normally expects to put through three flocks of toms or four flocks of hens in a year. Before the next flock arrives, the grower must spread four inches of clean new litter, wood shavings or wheat straw, on the floor of the house to absorb their droppings.

Growers sell the used litter to crop farmers, who prize it as a rich source of fertilizer, but they must test their soils carefully to be sure they are not wasting money by applying too much. Turkey houses are environmentally sensitive. They contain all of the manure until it is hauled to the fields to be spread, they are well ventilated to control odors, and even the rainwater that runs off their roofs is held in containment basins until it can be discharged responsibly.

Their neighbors rarely are bothered by turkey houses, although a few may complain about the traffic and dust from the daily feed trucks. Turkey growers are more likely to be bothered by their neighbors, because their birds are highly sus-

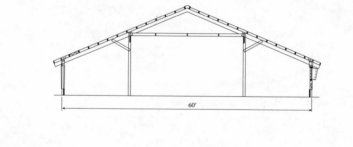

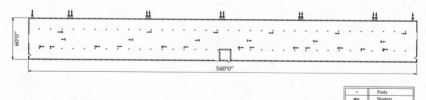

·	Posts
▣←	Heaters
◄●	Jet fan on posts
→▮	Circulating fans

Figure 10.3. A turkey finishing barn. (Based on a diagram prepared by George Raab of The Turkey Store Company; used by permission.)

ceptible to a multitude of diseases. Growers try to site their houses as far from their neighbors as possible to reduce the risk of infection, and they closely control entry to their farms. No one is admitted except on business, and even legitimate visitors and their vehicles must be carefully disinfected before they are allowed to enter.

Growers have held down the cost of turkeys by enlarging the scale of their operations and by using modern technology to make them more efficient. Between 1945 and 1995 the farm price of turkey increased only 20 percent while the farm price of beef quadrupled and overall consumer prices increased nearly 750 percent.[3] In 1945 a pound of live turkey cost more than two pounds of beef, but in 1995, when beef prices were relatively low, you could buy a pound of live turkey for the same price as eleven ounces of live beef.

Low prices have encouraged Americans to eat more turkey. Our per capita consumption in 1980 was ten pounds a year. It rose rapidly in the early 1980s, "when cardiologists did a great job of recommending our products," said Dan Blackshear, president of Carolina Turkeys, "and people became far more health-conscious." Per capita consumption leveled off at nineteen pounds a year in 1989, and it has not changed much since then. Development of new products offers the best opportunity for future growth, and processors have risen to the challenge with enthusiasm and ingenuity.

Turkey processors have come a long, long way from the days when they only killed, defeathered, eviscerated, and chilled whole birds for a seasonal market. The seasonal market for whole birds still is extremely important, but since the 1960s turkey has changed from a commodity product that is only minimally processed to a further-processed product to which value has been added by deboning, cutting, and cooking.

Modern processors use turkeys as the raw material for a bewildering variety of precooked and packaged products that include parts (whole breasts, drumsticks, and wings), boneless cuts flavored with various seasoning mixes, slices, patties, nuggets, sausages, hot dogs, bacon, and ground meat. By-products from turkey-processing plants and spent hens from turkey breeding farms go to rendering plants to be made into food for pets and feed for other animals.

The turkey business has evolved from a production-driven business to a market-driven business. Once growers hoped they could sell what they produced, but now processors produce only what they know they can sell. They prepare delicatessen products in convenient tray packs or pegboard packs for direct sale to consumers in retail stores. They sell food-service products in bulk to restaurants and to institutions such as schools, prisons, and the armed forces, but they have not yet really managed to crack the fast-food market.

The export market for turkey products grew rapidly during the 1990s, and accounted for 5 to 10 percent of total production.[4] The leading export markets are Mexico, Korea, Russia, and Hong Kong, which has the world's highest per capita consumption of turkey frankfurters. The export preference for dark meat nicely complements the domestic preference for white meat.

Most retail turkey products are sold under specific brand names that the processors advertise heavily. Retailers prefer to handle precut and prepackaged products, because they save space and labor and reduce clutter. Consumers prefer processed products that are easy to use, and they are willing to pay more for brands they know and can trust. Processors can promote new products by attaching on-package coupons to their established products, so everyone is happy.

Modern turkey-processing plants must be large and highly specialized to produce the necessary variety of products. Large, well-financed firms have taken over the business, and most small, old, inefficient plants have closed down. Many of the plants that remain in operation have grown like Topsy, with numerous additions, expansions, and upgrades, so it is hard to put a price tag on them, but in 1998 the cost of building a sophisticated modern plant from scratch would have been well over $50 million.

A modern multimillion-dollar turkey-processing plant must run close to capacity fifty-two weeks a year to pay for itself. It must have a continuous, steady flow of live birds of uniform weight and quality, but growers produce the birds in batches, and the processing company must schedule the operations of laying hens, hatcheries, and grow-out farms with exquisite precision to ensure that a steady flow of tens of thousands of turkeys is delivered to the plant door each working day.

The need for tight scheduling necessitates close coordination between processors and growers. Some processors have long-term contracts with independent growers, but some have their own grow-out houses and thus enjoy better control, and many have a mixture of company-owned houses and contract growers.

The processor likes to have the grow-out houses close to the plant, to reduce the cost of hauling birds and feed, and it is easier for the processor to deal with a small number of large growers than with a large number of small individual growers. As a result, turkey production is moving toward a concentration of fewer growers who produce greater numbers of birds in larger houses, and toward greater vertical integration by the processing companies.

Processors in the older turkey-producing areas of the North and West had an early start. They have grown gradually, and they are more likely to have had the time and the capital to have built their own grow-out houses. They are also in areas where farmers have a strong tradition of independence and are suspicious of contracting. Processors in the South are newer. They have grown more rapidly, they have needed grow-out houses faster, and they are in areas where it has been easy to borrow the tradition of contracting from broiler growers.

The top people in turkey-processing companies generally are gracious to inquisitive outsiders, or at the very least they have become aware of the importance of good public relations, but the managers of company-owned farms are some of the spookiest members of the human race; often they are unwilling to say anything to anyone.

Sometimes the workers were willing to talk to me if the manager was not looking, but how often did a turkey farm manager tell me, "I'm not going to say one word to you unless I have permission from my boss"? This attitude is understandable, both because of the severe and often unfair way these and other types of large-scale livestock operations have been criticized and because of their very real concern about disease, but it does increase the difficulty of trying to understand what is happening on the farm.

The map of turkeys sold in the United States in 1997 is also a map of entrepreneurs such as Charles Wampler, Earl Olson, Wallace Jerome, Ottis Carroll, Marvin Johnson, Bruce Cuddy, Max Foster, and Samuel Zacky (fig. 10.1).

Charles Wampler

Charles Wampler was the entrepreneur who started the nation's first major turkey-producing area, in the Shenandoah Valley of northwestern Virginia. He was the agricultural extension agent in Rockingham County in 1922, when he opened a feed and seed store and a turkey hatchery as a sideline, and in 1927 he built a feed mill. One year one of his best customers, a man named Frank Yancey, could not pay his feed bill, so he offered to raise a flock of birds with Wampler and split the profit with him.

This arrangement worked so well that Wampler began to contract with other local farmers to raise turkeys and broilers for him, and he turned the Shenandoah Valley into the leading turkey-producing area east of the Rocky Mountains. In 1984 he merged with Horace Longacre, a poultry producer and processor in southeastern Pennsylvania. Longacre had gotten into processing the way Wampler had gotten into contracting. In 1958 he had sold a load of birds to a scrapple manufacturer who could not pay for them, so the manufacturer gave Longacre his scrapple-making equipment.

In 1988 Wampler-Longacre acquired the Rockingham Poultry Marketing Cooperative. The new name was much too long, so the company changed it to WLR Foods, then to Wampler Foods. Wampler Foods, a completely vertically integrated company, ranked fourth in the nation in turkey production and thirteenth in broiler production in 2000.[5] It contracted with more than 500 growers and employed 4,000 workers in two plants near Harrisonburg, Virginia, and two in southeastern Pennsylvania to process an average of 1.5 million live turkeys and 13 million pounds of broilers a week.

Earl B. Olson

Earl Olson of Willmar, Minnesota, was the entrepreneur who consolidated the turkey business along U.S. 71, the turkey trail that runs northward through west-central Minnesota from Willmar to Wadena. He was the manager of a small country co-op creamery and had developed a flourishing sideline trucking business buying eggs, cream, and poultry from farmers and selling them feed, seeds, and fertilizer, but in 1938 he decided that his future was in turkeys.

He started with only 300 birds in 1941 and slowly built up to 30,000 in 1949, when he bought his first processing plant, in Willmar, and processed 1.5 million pounds of New York–dressed turkeys. The farmers from whom he bought turkeys produced primarily for the Thanksgiving-to-Christmas holiday market, but he wanted to keep his plant in operation for as much of the year as possible, so he organized his own farms for production in the off-season. Then he needed a market for his off-season production, so in 1953 he began eviscerating and further processing, and he named his branded products Jennie-O after his only daughter, Jennifer.

Olson continued to build, buy, and expand processing plants, and in 1963 he began to manufacture his own feed. In 1968 he shifted from free-range to confinement production, which made year-round operation feasible. In 1986 he realized that he did not have the capital or the marketing and distribution system he needed, and he sold his company to the Hormel Foods Corporation, although it retains its own identity and brand name.

In 1998 Jennie-O passed Butterball to become the nation's leading turkey producer.[6] It produced one-third of its birds on twenty-five company farms and contracted for the rest with 45 growers (down from a peak of 300). Individual growers had three to fifty standard 70' × 500' houses, which handled three and a half flocks of 10,000 birds a year. In 2000 the nine Jennie-O plants processed 880 million pounds of turkey, a far cry indeed from the 1.5 million pounds of 1949.

Wallace Jerome

Wallace Jerome built a tom and two hens into the nation's seventh largest turkey company, The Turkey Store. Wally was born in 1909 on a dairy farm near Barron, in northwestern Wisconsin. He was fascinated by turkeys, and in 1922 he bought fourteen turkey eggs from a neighbor and put them under two old broody hens to try to hatch them out. Only one hatched. It was a tom, and it seemed so lonesome that Wally's parents bought him a couple of hens to keep it company.

Wally remembers, "I knew some people in town, bankers' wives and so on, might like a turkey for Thanksgiving, so I made the rounds and took orders." The first year he raised five turkeys, then twenty-one, then seventy. When he had more than he could sell locally, he shipped them by Railway Express to Chicago. In 1930 he bought a pair of prize breeders, got into the turkey-show business, and won a number of national awards. By 1941 he was producing 4,000 to 5,000 birds, and "I was all fired up to become one of the biggest turkey operations in the nation," he said.

In 1941 Wally bought the Barron County Farm and Old People's Home. On his parents' farm he had only 30 to 40 acres, but his new farm had 160 acres. He immediately jumped to 25,000 to 30,000 birds, and doubled the number in the second year. He rotated range by moving the shelters, feeders, and waterers to a clean piece of ground every week or ten days.

In 1943 the army requisitioned all turkeys and imposed a strict new set of sanitary regulations on processors. Wally set up a plant that qualified in the basement of the old dairy barn at the Old People's Home. It had the capacity to dress far more than his own turkeys, so he solicited business from other growers. He employed up to seventy people. They scalded the carcasses, men pulled off the heavier feathers, and women picked the pinfeathers.

His farm did not have city water or good electricity, so after the war Wally bought the old pea cannery in Barron and converted it into a processing plant, which subsequently has been expanded and upgraded many times. He had been selling New York–dressed turkeys, but when he heard about oven-ready turkey he made a trip to Omaha to learn how to make it, and he started selling it in 1951. "I always wanted to be a year or two ahead of things," he said.

In 1953 he realized that people would buy properly prepared turkey all year round, so he shifted his farms from free range to confinement houses. "I always did a lot of traveling to see what other people were doing," he said, "and I suppose I got some ideas from the chicken broiler people in the South, but I had a lot of innovative ideas of my own."

Wally was the first breeder in the Upper Midwest with broad white turkeys, and poults from his hatchery found a ready market. A feed company was expanding aggressively in the area, and it financed growers to buy feed and poults. Wally dressed most of their turkeys. "We processed for anybody we could buy turkeys from," Wally said, "but we didn't need to do much contracting, because the feed company was willing to finance independent growers."

Then the feed company opened its own hatchery and processing plant in Faribault, Minnesota, and it took the growers for whom Wally had been processing, so he had to expand his own grow-out facilities to keep his processing plant running. He did not get into contracting, because the feed company had already tied up most growers, and he could not find new growers who could achieve his standard of performance.

Eventually the feed company went broke, and it sold its hatchery and processing plant to Wally. "The bankers in Wisconsin were all dairy-oriented," he said, "and they couldn't see lending money to anybody foolish enough to raise turkeys. I wasn't able to expand very fast until I moved to Minnesota, where the bankers were more familiar with turkeys."

In 1998 Wally still owned most of his farm production facilities. He would obtain financing for a contracting farmer to put up a set of buildings and pay him a fee to grow out the turkeys, but he has never gotten more than 15 to 20 percent of his birds from contract growers. He had thirty-five company farms and twelve contract farms near Barron and thirty company farms and fourteen contract farms near Faribault. A company farm is an eighty-acre complex with two 72,000-bird brood barns and six 12,000-bird finish barns. The birds are in a brood barn for their first seven weeks and then are transferred to a finish barn. Most contracting farmers have only one or two finish barns.

In the 1970s Wally's company, Jerome Foods, became one of the first turkey companies to produce and brand value-added convenience products at the processing plant, and it advertised and distributed them nationally. In 1984 the company began using The Turkey Store as its brand name, and it completely stopped selling whole birds. In 1998 Jerome Foods officially changed its name to The Turkey Store, and in 2000 the entire company was sold to Jennie-O.

North Carolina

Marvin Johnson, Ottis Carroll, and Bruce Cuddy were among the entrepreneurs who played important roles in increasing North Carolina's turkey production from 1.6 million birds in 1959 to 14 million in 1974 to 31 million in 1982, when the state first led the nation, and to 56 million in 1997.[7]

Marvin Johnson's father, Nash, was a strawberry and tobacco farmer near Rose Hill, in Duplin County. "When my brother and I got out of the service in 1946," said Marvin, "we didn't had nutt'n' to do. We didn't own no land, we didn't own no allotments, so we couldn't grow tobacco, we didn't own nutt'n'! My mom was growing about 150 turkeys a year, and we used to take them down to the tobacco sales barn to sell them, so we decided to get into the turkey business."

They started with a little Sears, Roebuck incubator, about the size of two refrigerators. Their father thought they were crazy and refused to sign a note for the $4,000 they needed to get started, but an old bachelor uncle loaned them the money. They grew turkeys on range, 50,000, 75,000 up to 100,000 a year. Soon they were making more money than their father, but they did not let him into the business until 1956, when they had to have his backing to build the feed mill they needed, and they changed the name of their company from Johnson Brothers to Nash Johnson and Sons.

In the early days all of their feed was in gaily colored bags from which farmers could make shirts and dresses. They had the first bulk feed truck in North Carolina. Once again, said Marvin, "Dad thought we was crazy to buy the truck, but we were the ones humping the bags, and that made a lot of difference." They bought a truck that was made to spread lime, but they took the spreader off the back, replaced it with an auger, and drove the truck into the fields to fill the feeders.

"We got into processing in 1962," said Marvin, "because the company we was selling to went broke, and I had to buy the plant or quit growing turkeys." They have built The House of Raeford, in Raeford, North Carolina, into the nation's tenth largest turkey processing company, with annual production of around 250 million pounds.[8] The House of Raeford is owned by Nash Johnson and Sons, which still operates the feed mill and hatcheries at Rose Hill and contracts with more than 200 Duplin County farmers to grow out turkeys.

In 1939 Ottis Carroll built a feed mill in Warsaw, North Carolina, twelve miles north of Rose Hill. He sold livestock feed to farmers and contracted with them to raise broilers, turkeys, and hogs. In 1967 he realized that eastern North Carolina was overrun with Dennis Ramsey's broiler farms, so with the help of a feed salesman named Bill Prestage he began to concentrate on growing turkeys.

At first his birds were on range, but in 1970 he shifted to total confinement for year-round production. By 1972 his operation had gotten so big that he bought a hatchery, and by 2000 he was contracting with 220 growers to grow out 15 million turkeys a year. Initially he sold the birds to processors, but in 1986 he realized that he could not be competitive unless he had his own processing plant, so he joined Goldsboro Milling Company in forming a new company, Carolina Turkeys, that would process turkeys for the two partners.

The huge Carolina Turkeys plant is out in the middle of nowhere, fifteen miles east of Mount Olive on the Woodland Chapel Road. The partners sited it at the center of their live turkey production, where one of them just happened to own some property. In 2000 the plant employed 1,900 hourly workers in three eight-hour shifts to process 70,000 turkeys a day, 505 million pounds a year, making it the fifth largest turkey company in the United States.

"With this much invested in plant and facilities," said Dan Blackshear, president of Carolina Turkeys, "you've got to run close to capacity fifty-two weeks a year. We process what we can sell, because this is a market-driven business, not a production-driven business. We package about 15 percent for sale as whole birds and the rest go to a cutting or boning operation for further processing. We have one peak at Thanksgiving and Christmas for whole birds and another in summer for cold cuts."

The plant works two eight-hour shifts and then the third shift completely disassembles, cleans, and inspects it for sanitation. "We have more than depleted the supply of people in the neighborhood that want to work here," Dan said. "Slightly more than half of our workers are now Hispanic, and the number moves up a few percent each year." The company has developed three trailer parks nearby with 300 units, and the Hispanic workers consider themselves permanent residents of eastern North Carolina.

The second major turkey-producing area in North Carolina centers on Union County, southeast of Charlotte, and spills over into South Carolina (fig. 10.1). Bruce Cuddy came here in 1970, fresh out of college, to operate a turkey hatchery his father had bought. He was the right person in the right place at the right time, because the price of turkeys was going up, the price of feed was going down, and feed companies were happy to help him with finance and promotions.

Bruce expanded aggressively. He bought and enlarged small feed mills. He bought and modernized small seasonal processing plants that had run turkeys only from May through Thanksgiving, then switched to broilers for the rest of the year. He contracted with farmers to raise turkeys. Union County has many undersized farms with thin infertile soil. The farmers were delighted to augment their meager income by contracting with Cuddy and to enrich their shallow soil with litter from their turkey houses. The number of turkeys produced in Union County skyrocketed from 771,000 in 1969 to 6.6 million in 1978.

In the 1990s Bruce Cuddy's father, A. M. Cuddy, sold Cuddy Farms to Wampler Foods, which subsequently closed down the turkey-processing plant in Union County, and turkey production in the county plummeted from 11.4 million in 1992 to only 6.0 million in 1997.[9]

California

California has a long history of turkey production, and the state still is home to Nicholas and Orlopp, two of the world's leading primary breeders, who sell to the commercial breeders who sell poults to producers. Around 1900 turkey farmers were droving flocks of birds up into the hills, where they gorged on grasshoppers. After the rice harvest they drove the birds onto the rice fields to fatten on leftover grain, and then they drove them to Sacramento for slaughter.

In the 1930s California had many small independent growers who raised turkeys on range, and it was the leading turkey state until 1949, when it produced 7 million birds, 19 percent of the national total, but the industry was plagued by cycles of good and poor price years. Good prices in one year encouraged overproduction in the next, which depressed prices.

In poor years banks would not finance growers, so the growers had to borrow from the feed and processing companies, and many became so deeply indebted that they lost their farms to the company. By the 1960s the industry was dominated by large companies, which produced most of their birds on their own farms but contracted some with independent producers. The companies themselves were consolidated by acquisitions and mergers, and after Louis Rich left the state in 1992, only three were left: Foster, Zacky, and Butterball.

In 1939 Max Foster was the city editor of the *Modesto Bee*. He and Verda borrowed $1,000 to buy an eighty-acre farm that was so rundown their banker was reluctant to lend them the money. They built a small poultry house and Verda raised 3,000 turkey poults, with help from Max evenings and weekends. They did so well that they built a second house, and a feed company asked them to start a hatchery.

They bought a second farm and planted it to clover. They bought forty cows to use the clover and have expanded their herd into one of the largest dairy operations in California, with more than 4,000 cows. They brooded turkeys in the spring and started raising broilers the rest of the year to keep the house busy. By 1950 chickens had crowded out turkeys, and they concentrated on developing a totally integrated broiler operation. That operation has become the leading broiler producer on the West Coast.

In 1982 Foster Farms returned to its roots by buying a major turkey-producing company. Foster Farms broilers already had strong brand recognition on the West Coast, and a line of turkey products built on it nicely. In addition to its dairy and broiler operations, in 2000 Foster Farms was the nation's thirteenth largest turkey producer, with annual production of more than 7 million birds on eleven company farms and thirty-five contract farms.[10]

Samuel Zacky was born in Russia in 1897. His family immigrated to Los Angeles, where he opened a poultry market in 1928. He bought live chickens from local farmers and killed and dressed them on his premises. After World War II his sons, Bob and Al, moved into broiler production. In 1955 they bought a small processing plant, and in 1963 they began developing their own grow-out farms. In 1967 they bought a hatchery, and they became completely integrated when they bought a feed mill in 1971. They expanded into turkey production when they bought two turkey companies in 1984 and 1985, and by 2000 they had become the nation's sixteenth largest turkey producer, with 150 million pounds of live-weight production.[11]

The number of turkeys produced in California plummeted from 29 million in 1992 to only 23 million, less than 8 percent of the national total, in 1997. The turkey industry in the state seems beleaguered. California is a feed-deficit area, even though unit trains of 75 to 110 cars have cut the cost of hauling feed from Nebraska. Prices are highly volatile, financing is difficult, and independent producers are no longer willing to take the necessary risks.

Companies have had to develop their own farms because growers cannot afford to maintain and upgrade their old houses, and no independent grower has put up new turkey buildings since 1990. The old buildings must be destroyed when a farm is sold, and the county approval process often impedes the development of new farms. Even farmer neighbors sometimes object to change. All farmers are obligated to complain about government regulation and bureaucratic incompetence, but California has earned its reputation for having tougher environmental restrictions than other states.

Companies have cut back on production, which has not been particularly profitable in good years, and I sense that they would like to buy in bulk from turkey producers in other areas and to concentrate their resources on further processing and marketing, where the profit is greater.

Turkey people in California seem unusually suspicious of outsiders. Some companies are less than cooperative, to be as polite about it as possible, and many independent contract growers are reluctant, even afraid, to talk to outsiders. Perhaps they have been burned. Paul Orlopp said to me, "A lot of people that come out to talk to us have an ax to grind, animal rights or the environment or salmonella in the product or some other doggone thing they really don't know anything about, and what they write about us shows a complete total lack of understanding of anything we are doing."

Large-scale turkey production has been quintessentially entrepreneurial, and each of the clusters on the turkey map (fig. 10.1) can be associated with one or two individual entrepreneurs. Turkey producers ran their birds on free range until the 1960s, when they began to adopt the broiler model, and by the turn of the twenty-first century they grew their birds in structures that look like broiler houses.

Turkey companies in the South have contracted with farmers to grow out their birds, but in the North and West, where farmers are less willing to contract, the companies have developed their own grow-out facilities.

Whole turkeys are highly seasonal fare, but turkey meat is exceptionally malleable, and turkey processors have been leaders in further processing meat into an astonishing variety of specialty value-added branded products for year-round consumption.

11
Hogs

Over the years, as I have watched the increasing scale of cash-grain farming, of beef cattle feeding, of dairying, of broiler production, egg production, and turkey production, I have kept wondering when hog production in the United States was going to be modernized. As late as 1975 it was still at the horse-and-buggy stage. Each year hundreds of thousands of small independent farms each produced a few hundred animals of mysterious genealogy and quality in nondescript facilities as a casual sideline operation. Hogs were prized for their lard back in the days before soybean and other vegetable oils replaced it. Modern hogs have less fat and more lean meat, even though the standard marketing weight is inching up from 225 to 325 pounds.

In the 1980s hog producers finally began to emulate broiler producers. They have better genetics, better feeds, better buildings, better management, and better processing plants. Today most of our pork is produced by large, new, highly specialized farms that produce hundreds of hogs of nearly identical size, shape, and quality each week. American consumers have driven the change. They want leaner cuts of meat, even if it is tougher and less tasty, because they are concerned about their health, and they want these cuts in convenient ready-to-use packages because they don't want to waste time in the kitchen preparing food.

Meatpacking companies must have a steady supply of uniform, top-quality hogs to produce the cuts their customers demand. Breeders have developed prolific varieties of hogs that grow faster and produce leaner meat with less feed, but these animals require expensive production facilities and top-notch management that only large farms can afford. Furthermore, packers prefer to deal with a few large producers who can regularly deliver large numbers of uniform animals, and many small producers have been squeezed out of the hog business.

Small pig producers complain that the large operations are cannibalizing them. They extrapolate present trends into dire predictions that a mere fifty companies soon will produce all of the hogs the United States can use, and these hogs will be processed in only twelve packing plants.[1] Such concerns have prompted the traditional hog-farming states of the Midwest to pass restrictive laws, so hog production has stagnated in the Corn Belt states and flourished in states such as North Carolina, Missouri, Oklahoma, and Utah, which are more sympathetic to the changing nature and needs of the pork business (fig. 11.1).

The modernization of hog production began in eastern North Carolina, which has rocketed to the fore as the nation's leading pig-producing state (fig. 11.2). The U.S. *Census of Agriculture* says that in 1949 the state had 70,500 hog farmers who sold 750,000 hogs, or an average of only 11 per farm, and they produced hogs mainly for local consumption. In 1997 the state had only 2,666 hog farmers, but they sold 36.43 million hogs, or an average of 13,665 per farm. In that same period the U.S. average per farm rose from 31 to 1,400 and the Iowa state average from 83 to 1,500.

Wendell Murphy

Experience with contract production of broilers and turkeys undoubtedly preconditioned farmers in North Carolina for contract production of hogs, but hog production must be so heavily capitalized that its development has required some truly courageous entrepreneurs who have been willing to take great risks. Wendell H. Murphy of Rose Hill in Duplin County, North Carolina, is the entrepreneurial genius who pioneered the concept of large-scale contract hog production. (Recall that Rose Hill was also the home of Dennis Ramsey, the broiler entrepreneur, and Marvin Johnson of the House of Raeford turkey company, and that Ottis Carroll lived only twelve miles up the road in Warsaw. Must be something in the water.)

When I told Wendell that he was responsible for having gotten me started writing this book, he replied, with characteristic lack of pretension, "I don't know if you're implying credit or blame, but whichever it is, chances are I'm getting entirely too much of both. Consolidation was bound to happen. I don't know that it's necessarily good that it's happening, but when the train's on the track and it's moving, it doesn't stop, and that's where we are headed."

Wendell was born in 1938 and grew up on a small tobacco farm near Rose Hill. He went to North Carolina State, took a degree in agricultural education, and got a job teaching vocational agriculture in the Rose Hill high school. "I knew I didn't want to be a teacher for the rest of my life," he said, "but it was the only job I could get near home, and I wanted to go back home." It took him less than

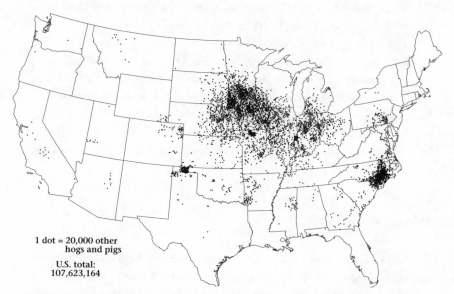

1 dot = 20,000 other
hogs and pigs

U.S. total:
107,623,164

Figure 11.1. Hogs and pigs (other than feeder pigs) sold, 1997. (Source: *1997 Census of Agriculture,* vol. 2, pt. 1 [Washington, D.C.: U.S. Department of Agriculture, National Agricultural Statistics Service, 1999].)

two years to realize that he wanted to get into the feed business. "I love livestock," he said, "and I thought I could build a feed mill and sell feed to the farmers and talk to them every day, which is what I love to do."

He needed to borrow $10,000 to build the mill, and the bank insisted that his father, Holmes Murphy, had to cosign the note. "That was the hardest sale I ever made," Wendell told me. "Of course $10,000 back then was like $100,000 or more now. To me it was a big amount of money, and to Daddy, who was a product of the Depression, it was a huge amount." Holmes finally agreed, on condition that Wendell continue teaching until he had paid off the note. Holmes was at the mill during the day, and Wendell worked there after school until midnight and all day Saturday and Sunday.

"I am so blessed to have had the parents I had," Wendell said. "Daddy's reputation in the community was total honesty, so customers could come to us with full confidence, and he taught me not only to work but to enjoy work. Every morn-

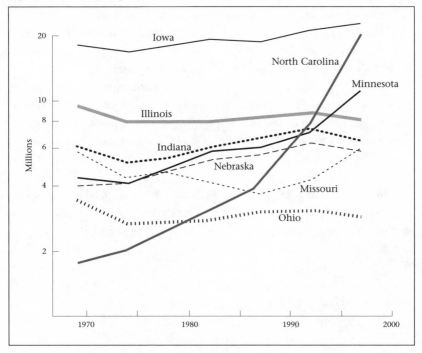

Figure 11.2. Hogs and pigs (except feeder pigs) sold in selected states, 1969–1997. (Data from relevant censuses of agriculture.)

ing when I bounced out of bed I couldn't hardly wait to get going, I was just really enthused. At that time it was all common labor. Everything was done with bags. Daddy wasn't able to throw those heavy bags around, so I did that, and the business management as well.

"He taught me to enjoy my work, and there's no question in my mind that that's what caused us to make it as well as we did. I have tried to communicate that message to our employees. I say to all of them that if you get up in the morning and dread going to work, you are in the wrong profession. You need to find something else. You will do me a favor and you will do yourself a favor if you leave."

Wendell opened his custom-mix feed mill on Labor Day in 1962. Initially he had hoped to sell feed to local dairy farmers, but they were struggling financially. He was not doing enough business to pay his bills and his mill was not operating at capacity, so in 1963 he bought 200 feeder pigs and paid his brother Pete a fee to feed them out on a dirt lot behind the home farm.

He made such a nice profit that he began to contract with other farmers to feed pigs for him. They were delighted to have the income he guaranteed them. All they had to do was put a fence around a piece of property with a few shade trees on it, and they could feed a large number of animals with little capital investment.

After three years they were doing so well that even Holmes agreed that Wendell should quit his teaching job and work full-time at the feed mill. "It didn't take us long," Wendell said, "to see that we were doing a heck of a lot better on the feed we were feeding to our own hogs than on what we were marketing to farmers, and believe it or not, in five or six years we discontinued our feed sales. That was one of the toughest decisions I'd ever had to make, suddenly to start telling these farmer friends whose business we had solicited that we couldn't service them any more."

So Wendell changed from a feed mill operator to a pork producer. At first the business grew slowly, because he was always reluctant to incur debt. "Our method was to use our profits to grow on," he said, "not to go to the bank to borrow money. We never had any government money, either. We did it ourselves. We started out small, and our early growth was not much, even though we were struggling to make it, but we have doubled our net worth and our gross sales every five years, and finally it started to grow pretty fast."

By 1974 Wendell was marketing 40,000 hogs, and he realized that he had to shift from dirt lots to special purpose-built hog houses. Producers had built special hog houses earlier, but many had gone broke because the houses were expensive and poorly designed. They were built to satisfy people, not hogs; they got the people out of the mud of dirt lots, but they did not keep the pigs cool enough in the heat of summer.

Better designs had been developed by 1974, and producers of feeder pigs were building farrowing houses in which their sows gave birth. Wendell was buying feeder pigs that had been reared indoors, and they suffered when he took them outside. By this time he could afford to build houses, and feeding the pigs inside actually saved enough money to pay for the buildings. By 1979 he had to buy sows and start producing his own feeder pigs, because the supply of feeder pigs was dropping. Many small producers were going out of business, and the price had climbed so high that he could produce his own feeders cheaper than he could buy them.

In the 1980s Wendell began to expand into areas that had surplus processing capacity, because processing was tight in North Carolina. He developed breeding farms in Missouri and Oklahoma and contract finishing facilities in Iowa and South Dakota. Jim Stocker, who at various times has been general manager, president, and vice chairman of the board of Murphy Family Farms, was surprised by the tremendous waste and inefficiency in Iowa.

"They were taking 4 pounds of feed to put on a pound of meat," Jim said. "In North Carolina we were down to 2.7, and getting lower. We had appropriate buildings that kept the animals warm in winter, so they didn't have to burn feed just to maintain their body weight, and we have the optimal number of animals per pen. In the Midwest they would have three, four, five hundred animals bedded down with straw in the basement of an old cattle barn. You can't manage them efficiently under those kinds of conditions."

In 1994 Murphy Family Farms opened an enormous feed mill just west of the company's modernistic one-story headquarters building south of Rose Hill. Four sixty-five-car unit trains a week bring corn and soybeans from the Midwest to the gargantuan grain elevator, which holds 1.5 million bushels. The mill loads 125 to 150 feed trucks each day with no fewer than four specialized sow/nursery feeds (gestation, lactation, prestarter, and starter) and four finishing feeds (grower 1, grower 2, developer, and finisher) that are tailored to specific stages of pig growth.

North Carolina Hog Farms

By 1994 Murphy Family Farms had become the nation's top hog producer, with sales of more than $300 million, but it was far from alone in eastern North Carolina. Continental, Cargill, Tyson, Purina, and other national companies were also contracting with local farmers to feed hogs; Carroll's Foods of Warsaw was the second largest pork-producing company; and Prestage Farms of Clinton, ten miles west of Warsaw, ranked fourth. Each company had its own preferred mix of company-owned and contract farms, and they all liked to keep their farms within a comfortable hauling distance, say 50 to 100 miles, of the company feed mill and office (fig. 11.3).

Carroll's was predominantly a turkey company until the early 1970s, when the Smithfield Packing Company of Virginia encouraged it to branch out into hog production. Its hog operations are centered on Warsaw and Laurinburg in North Carolina, and it has a partnership operation with Smithfield in southeastern Virginia. Carroll's has acquired exclusive U.S. rights to National Pig Development (NPD) genetics, which enable it to produce especially lean hogs.

Bill Prestage came to North Carolina in 1960 as the regional sales manager for a feed company. He became heavily involved in helping Carroll's shift from broilers to turkeys and then to expand into hogs; so heavily, in fact, that he bought a half interest in the company from Ottis Carroll in 1967. When Carroll died in

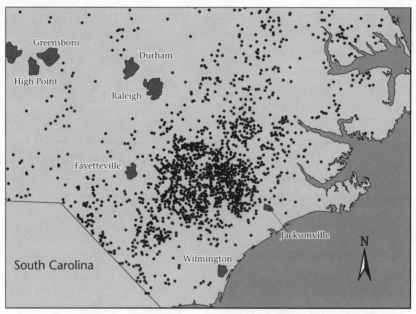

Figure 11.3. Hog farms in eastern North Carolina, 1997. Each dot represents one hog farm. (Data from North Carolina Department of Agriculture.)

1983, Prestage offered the heirs a buy-or-sell option for his half of the company. The heirs bought, and Prestage used his proceeds to start Prestage Farms, which he built from 500 sows in 1983 to 115,000 in 1994. Like Carroll's, Prestage also produces turkeys, and the company is the nation's fifth largest turkey producer.

Modern hog companies organize production into three phases (farrowing, nursery, and finishing) for efficient management, especially disease control, which is critical when so many animals are so close together. The farrowing stage has the breeding house, where the sows are bred, and then they are moved to the gestation house, where each sow has her own individual 2' × 7' stall (fig. 11.4).

When the sow is ready to give birth she is washed with warm soapy water, disinfected, and moved to the farrowing house, where she has her own 5' × 7' "crate" of heavy metal bars. Every five months each sow is expected to produce a litter of ten or eleven piglets, in contrast to only seven or eight on traditional hog farms in the Midwest, and after the fifth or sixth litter she is sold for sausage.

Sows are miserable mothers, so eighteen inches on either side at the bottom of each crate is a "creep" formed of heavy metal bars. The creep allows the piglets to nurse but keeps the sow from rolling over on them and crushing them. In the first two weeks of nursing the sow passes vital antibodies to the piglets, but then she also starts to give them diseases. After two or three weeks, when they weigh ten to twelve pounds and are still cute, the piglets are moved to a nursery to get them started on dry feed and water, and the sow goes back to the breeding barn.

The older pigs in the nursery can give diseases to the younger ones, so after six to eight weeks, when they weigh 45 to 50 pounds, they are moved to a finishing house, where they eat like hogs and reach a market weight of 250 pounds or more in twenty weeks. Both sides of the nursery and finishing houses have long rows of pens that hold twenty-five to thirty pigs each, with a two-foot-wide walkway down the center.

In 2000 a 3,600-sow farrowing house would have cost around $1.5 million, a 2,600-pig nursery around $150,000, and a 1,100-hog finishing house around $100,000. A good producer should have been able to make enough profit to pay for a house in seven years.

Individual producers may specialize in one stage of production or they may have complexes that integrate all three. Farrowing requires more management skill and labor than nursery and finishing, and the company prefers to keep control of breeding on farms it owns. It is more likely to contract nursery and finishing. The company retains ownership of the pigs, provides feed and services, and pays the contracting farmer a flat fee per pig per day, plus an incentive payment,

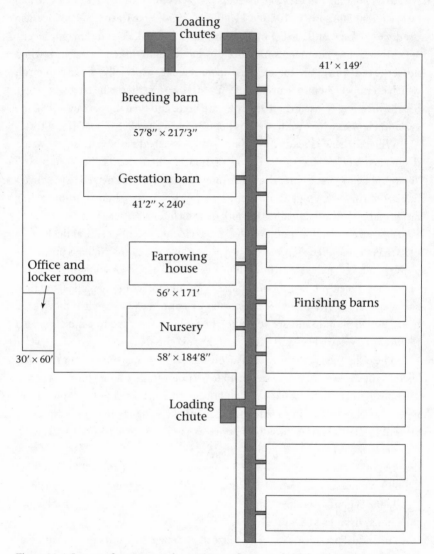

Figure 11.4. Layout of a representative 1,000-sow farrow-to-finish hog operation, with a breeding barn, a gestation barn, a farrowing house, a nursery, and nine finishing barns. (Based on a sketch by Marty L. Manuel of Carroll's Foods; used by permission.)

to feed them to the desired weight. It markets the animals and accepts the risk of price fluctuations.

A modern hog-production complex has ten to fifteen long, one-story cinder-block-and-metal buildings in parallel rows, with large metal feed bins beside each of the buildings, which are 40 to 60 feet wide and 300 to 400 feet long (fig. 11.4). Their sides are studded with circular openings for huge ventilator fans, because hogs generate enormous amounts of body heat, and they are severely stressed by temperatures higher than 80°F.

Hog farmers like to have their complexes screened from the highway by woods to spare them the good offices of animal activists, and the entire complex is enclosed by a waist-high chain-link fence for biosecurity. The only entrance is through a locker room, where everyone who enters, visitors and employees alike, must strip to the skin, shower, wash their hair, and change their clothes completely. You shower when you enter because you have to, and you shower when you leave because you want to.

North Carolina hog farmers have handled the manure from their hog houses the way farmers have always handled manure: they have saved it and spread it on their fields and pastures for fertilizer. Many hog farms have enough pasture to support sizable herds of beef cattle. The floors of hog houses have slatted floors, with one-inch slots every six or seven inches, and the hogs tread the manure through these slots into a shallow pit beneath the building. Every few hours this pit is flushed into an earthen holding basin at the end of the building, where the manure is stored until time to spread it.

The manure holding basins, which are euphemistically known as lagoons, must be larger than football fields, because a mature hog produces four times as much solid waste as a person, so a complex feeding 10,000 hogs will produce as much waste as a city of 40,000 people. Hog manure also smells more like human waste than like cattle manure, because the diet of hogs is more like the diet of people than like the diet of cattle.

Lagoons stink. Their fetid odor has made them an easy and tempting target for critics in an era of intensified environmental sensitivity. It is impossible to describe the dreadful stench of a hog lagoon on a sultry summer day, and you definitely do not want to find out for yourself. Critics have identified no fewer than 168 chemicals that might be released from lagoons, and neighbors have blamed lagoon odors for nausea, headaches, sleep disturbances, shallow breathing, coughing, fatigue, depression, loss of appetite, and increased tension.

Lagoons might seep. They should be lined with impermeable clay or heavy plastic, but some early lagoons were not lined because the builders thought they would seal themselves. Seepage from lagoons could possibly contaminate groundwater with pathogenic microbes in areas of coarse sandy soil, and high levels of nitrates in well water can cause methemoglobinemia, or "blue-baby syndrome," which can be toxic to infants, but it would be hard to tell whether pollutants came from hog lagoons, municipal sewage, or individual family septic systems, which are common in eastern North Carolina.

Lagoons can burst. In fact, only a few older and badly constructed lagoons actually have burst, but even a single break can generate an enormous amount of unfavorable publicity when a great nasty slug of putrefying brown waste washes down the creek to the river and down the river to the bay, and then is sloshed back and forth by the tide at the front steps of the costly summer cottages that line the coast.

In 1996 the *Raleigh News and Observer* won a Pulitzer prize for a series of articles that emphasized the negative aspects of North Carolina hog farms. These articles described all of the environmental disasters the farms might cause, and they quoted farmers who complained that the hog companies had exploited them with contracts, even though the companies had year-long or longer waiting lists of other farmers who were eager to sign up. These articles picked on Wendell Murphy, the largest producer, whom they labeled "Boss Hog," to personify hog producers, and they used him to villainize the entire hog industry.

These articles made much of the fact that Murphy had helped to pass laws worth millions of dollars to his company and his industry during the five terms he served in the state legislature, although they also admitted that these laws passed without a single dissenting vote. I asked Wendell about these laws, and he said, "I represented one of the state's top agricultural areas, and of course I voted in its best interests. The voters kept sending me back, so I must have been doing what they wanted me to do for them."

There can be no question that North Carolina was a congenial area for hog farms, because the state had lenient standards for lagoon construction, for seepage, and for buffer zones around buildings, and even these weak environmental regulations were only minimally enforced. Perhaps the most egregious law, which was passed in 1993, after Wendell had left the legislature, declared that the locations of hog farms were a business trade secret. The state Department of Agriculture could not even divulge their location to the state Division of Environmental Management (DEM), but DEM did not have the personnel to inspect them even if it had known where they were.

The *News and Observer* persisted in its crusade to arouse public opinion against hog farmers in general and Wendell Murphy in particular, and eventually the legislature passed a moratorium on new hog farms, to take effect in 1997. In anticipation of the moratorium, large producers went on the most frenzied expansion spree the U.S. hog industry has ever known, and by the fall of 1998 they were producing more hogs than the packing plants could process.

Ironically, only a year earlier hog farmers had not produced all the hogs that meatpackers needed, and the packers had closed down some of their older and less efficient plants in the Midwest. In June 1997 they were paying 86 cents a pound for hogs and scrambling to get them; in December 1998 the glut of hogs was so bad that they were offering only 9 cents a pound for hogs that had cost 38 cents a pound to produce. Hog producers were losing their shirts, but they had no choice, because they must sell hogs when they reach market weight.

Bill Prestage said that his combination of hogs with turkeys had saved him. "Turkeys were great in 1998," he said. "We couldn't make enough money on them to offset our losses on hogs, but at least they kept us from going broke." Wendell Murphy, who produced only hogs, was not so fortunate. He was marketing 21,000 hogs a day, and for most of December he was losing more than $1 million each day.

The price of hogs eventually rebounded, but when I talked to Wendell in the fall of 2000 he said, "I would be less than truthful if I didn't say these last five years have been hard." The press had calumniated him with charges of environmental abuse that he considered totally unfounded and untrue. Activists had threatened him with lawsuits whose sole purpose was to put him out of business. He had no family members who were interested in taking over, and the abysmally low prices might have been the final straw. He realized that it was not fun any more, and he decided he had had enough.

In January 2000 Wendell Murphy sold Murphy Family Farms to Smithfield Foods for $500 million, including some debt that Smithfield assumed. Smithfield Foods was the meatpacking company to which Wendell had been selling his hogs almost from day one. He had served on Smithfield's board and had great respect for Joseph W. Luter III, Smithfield's CEO. Joe Luter had taken over the company in 1975, when it was virtually bankrupt, and he had built it into the leading hog-slaughtering company in North America. Smithfield markets branded pork products and exports parts of the hog that Americans do not like, such as the rectum, which is considered a delicacy in parts of Asia.

In 1993 Smithfield opened the world's largest pork-slaughtering plant near the hamlet of Tar Heel, twenty miles south of Fayetteville, in southeastern North

Carolina. The Tar Heel plant covers 973,000 square feet and processes 32,000 hogs a day. A plant this large must ensure that it has a steady supply of hogs, and it contracts with producers for more than 80 percent of its supply, but it seems almost inevitable that large meatpackers are going to have to become more involved in the production side of the hog business, as Smithfield did when it acquired Murphy.

The Tar Heel plant employs more than 5,000 people but labor turnover has been more than 100 percent a year, because meatpacking plants are dangerous places to work and they pay low wages. Many of the workers are Hispanic immigrants, and the local community has had trouble accepting them. Most meatpacking companies have histories of bad labor relations and violations of environmental regulations, and Smithfield has been no exception.

Circle Four

In the fall of 1992 Joe Luter, CEO of Smithfield Foods, received a letter from Larry Sower. Larry was the chair of an economic development group in Beaver County, Utah, 170 miles south of Salt Lake City. Beaver County was an economically distressed area on the edge of the high desert. The mines had played out, the Union Pacific Railroad was cutting back on employment, and so many people were leaving that the most flourishing business in Milford was a rental outlet for one-way U-Haul trucks.

The state was pushing agribusiness and Larry had studied broilers, but they didn't look too encouraging. He was sitting in a railroad land shack reading a copy of *Forbes* magazine with an article about Joe Luter and Smithfield Foods just as a train rattled past hauling several carloads of hogs from Nebraska to a packing plant in Los Angeles. "Why not us?" he wondered. "We've got what they need, lots of open space, cheap land, plenty of water," so he sat down and wrote a letter to Smithfield asking if they were interested.

Larry's letter is framed and hanging in the Circle Four conference room in Milford, Utah. At the bottom Luter had scrawled, "Bo, let's go to Utah." In March 1993 Joe Luter and Bo Manley came to Milford and liked what they saw. It was close to the California market, the Pacific Rim export market, and possibly a market in Mexico. There was plenty of land and water and there were few people to complain about hog odors.

Joe Luter went back to North Carolina and organized a new company, Circle Four Farms, to produce hogs in Utah. Circle Four was a consortium of Smithfield Foods, Murphy Family Farms, Carroll's Foods, and Prestage Farms, with management responsibility vested in Murphy. "We probably were lucky," Larry said, "because I think they were already thinking about opening something closer to the West Coast."

The Circle Four feed mill in Milford came on stream in February 1997. The company started with 50 800-sow units, each with its own manure lagoon, and plans to expand to 150 units, which will produce 2.5 million hogs a year. The lagoons have to be larger than those in North Carolina, because the dry climate slows the growth of the bacteria that break down the manure.

Circle Four built, owns, and operates all units, and does not contract with producers. It had originally planned to build its own processing plant in Utah, but found a processor in the Los Angeles area that was eager to buy its hogs. Some local people are delighted that Circle Four has created 750 new jobs in the area and increased tax revenues, but others complain bitterly about the odors from the lagoons.

Lagoon odors, which are undeniably offensive, have made new hog farms easy targets for critics. After Wendell Murphy of eastern North Carolina developed the first modern large-scale hog farms, others imitated his model. They disposed of manure in the traditional way, by storing it for use as fertilizer, but a practice that might have been tolerable at a small scale become objectionable when the number of hogs increased more than fiftyfold in an era of heightened environmental awareness.

Critics also say that hog farm lagoons may seep and pollute groundwater, and badly constructed lagoons have seriously polluted surface water when they have burst. Despite these problems, the large-scale hog farm model developed in eastern North Carolina has been widely adopted in other parts of the United States, but newer generations of hog farms have had to become more sensitive to their waste disposal.

12
New Hog Farms

The cover of the October 13, 1997, issue of *Forbes* magazine had a photograph of Wendell Murphy nuzzling a baby pig and a caption saying that this little piggy had made him $1 billion. This story was not news to Wall Street, which had already discovered that there was big money to be made in pigs, and the business has attracted large amounts of venture capital.

Well-financed companies have developed their own hog farms and built their own packing plants in new areas that have cheap land, low taxes, fewer people to complain, less stringent environmental regulations, and a dire need for economic development of any kind. A cynic might be excused for thinking that the changing geography of the U.S. hog business looks almost as though it were trying to stay one jump ahead of the sheriff, because when it wears out its welcome in one area, it flees to a new area where it is better received, at least initially. Large new hog farms seem to keep popping up in unanticipated places.

In 1989 a battle of billionaires broke out along the South Platte River near

Kersey, twenty miles east of Greeley, Colorado.[1] National Hog Farms, a company owned by the billionaire Bass brothers of Fort Worth, Texas, had begun building a $50 million complex to produce 300,000 hogs a year near ranches owned by Philip Anschutz, owner of the Southern Pacific Transportation Company, and Peter H. Coors, of the brewing family.

Anschutz and Coors sued to stop construction of the farm, financed two small citizens' groups that opposed it, and hired public relations experts to advise these groups. They questioned the hog farm's ability to dispose of its wastes safely, but the farm had a state-of-the-art treatment system that removed the solids and aerated the liquid effluent to reduce its smell before it was sprayed on pastures. The hog farm won.

In 1999 a Nebraska-based company named Sun Prairie, a subsidiary of Bell Farms of Wahpeton, North Dakota, acquired 1,200 acres of land on the Rosebud Sioux Indian Reservation in south-central South Dakota and began to construct a huge hog farm at a cost of $105 million.[2] South Dakota has a law prohibiting corporate farms, but Sun Prairie circumvented it by building on the reservation, which is outside state jurisdiction.

The farm has thirteen sites, each with twenty-four 1,100-hog buildings that will finish two and one-half lots, or a total of 858,000 hogs, a year. It will provide 200 new jobs in one of the poorest areas in the United States. The chief of the Bureau of Indian Affairs tried to block it on environmental grounds, but a federal judge rebuked him scathingly for "arbitrary and capricious" behavior, because the company had already secured approval for its plans from the U.S. Environmental Protection Agency.

Premium Standard Farms

In 1989 Dennis Harms and Tad Gordon formed Premium Standard Farms (PSF) and started to develop one of the nation's largest hog farms in Mercer, Putnam, and Sullivan counties in north-central Missouri. They were a good team. Harms had worked in the feed business and knew how to raise hogs on a large scale. Gordon had been a securities trader on Wall Street and knew how to raise money on a large scale.

Initially Harms and Gordon had hoped to develop a 1,000-sow farrowing farm west of Ames, Iowa. They planned to contract with local farmers to finish their hogs, but local opposition was so strong that they were not able to obtain the permits they needed, so they dropped the Iowa project and moved across the state line into northern Missouri, where they were welcomed. Their northern-most hog farm is so close to Iowa that you can smell it there.

North-central Missouri was in the final throes of abandonment. The countryside is hilly and the heavy clay soils are hard to cultivate. The *Census of Agriculture* says that the total number of farms in the three counties dropped from 6,704 in 1935, the peak year, to 5,280 in 1950, then skidded to only 1,845 in 1992, and most of those that remained were last-generation ma-and-pa affairs. The old folks might be able to eke out an existence on them, because the land was bought and paid for, but these farms could not provide a level of living that young people would find acceptable.

According to the census, the total population of the three counties was 51,676 in 1900, but it had dropped to 33,794 in 1940 and then to only 15,128 in 1990. There was nothing for young people to do in the area, and most residents were commuting seventy miles or more to jobs in Kansas City or Des Moines. The people were so poor and tax revenues were so pathetic that Mercer County officials seriously wondered whether they could afford to keep the courthouse open.

Missouri had a family farm law prohibiting corporate farms, but the state welcomed PSF by exempting Mercer, Putnam, and Sullivan counties. The company received no other special treatment, no government financing, no subsidies, no waived fees, no streamlined approvals. The only public money it has required was spent on roads during the hectic construction phase in the early 1990s. Harms, Gordon, and other senior executives made their homes in the area, and the company made a special effort to be a good neighbor and a good citizen.

Harms and Gordon realized that there were too few local farmers with whom they could contract to finish their hogs, and they would have to finance all of their finishing barns. "We took $25,000 we really didn't have," Harms remembers, "made a video to tell our story, and hit the road. We met with more than thirty different financial institutions, and many of them showed tremendous interest." They had no trouble raising the $800 million they needed to start their operation.

They bought 40,000 acres of land in the three counties and built a handsome headquarters building and training center in Princeton, seat of Mercer County (fig. 12.1). Princeton also has a feed mill that employs twenty people to make 700 tons of feed a day, and a second feed mill in Lucerne employs seventy people and produces 2,200 tons of feed a day. In 1997 the company had four highly specialized breeding farms that produced sows and boars for breeding, 75 sow farms, and 500 grow-finish units.

It started with 10,000 sows, jumped to 60,000 in 1991, and had more than 100,000 by 1995. In 1991 it was putting up a building a day or better. Each sow farm had 1,100 sows, employed five people, and had separate buildings for breeding, gestation, farrowing, nursery, and the office (fig. 12.2). Each grow-finish unit had eight 1,100-hog buildings that kept two people busy. Grow-finish units were grouped in sites, some of which had as many as twenty complexes of eight 1,100-hog grow-finish buildings plus a central office and dining hall.

Local groundwater resources were inadequate, so PSF dammed streams to create reservoirs of clean water (fig. 12.3). Each set of buildings had a rectangular manure lagoon into which waste from the buildings was flushed every two hours with water recycled from the lagoon. Eventually the manure was spread on land planted to grasses, which reduce erosion and stabilize the topsoil. The grass was cut for hay and sold to cattle producers.

Harms and Gordon realized that they needed a processing plant. Harms knew hogs and Gordon knew finances, but neither knew how to make hogs into meat, so they bought a small family-owned pork-processing plant in Indiana to

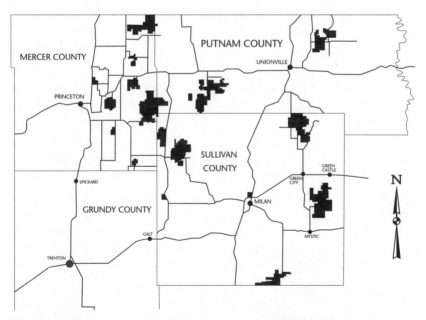

Figure 12.1. Areas where Premium Standard Farms has developed hog farms in Mercer, Putnam, and Sullivan counties, north-central Missouri. (Used by permission of *Southeastern Geographer.*)

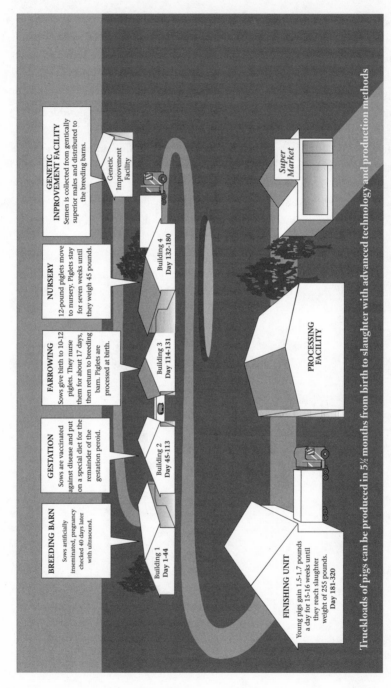

BREEDING BARN
Sows artificially inseminated, pregnancy checked 40 days later with ultrasound.

GESTATION
Sows are vaccinated against disease and put on a special diet for the remainder of the gestation peroid.

FARROWING
Sows give birth to 10-12 piglets. They nurse them for about 17 days, then return to breeding barn. Piglets are processed at birth.

NURSERY
12-pound piglets move to nursery. Piglets stay for seven weeks until they weigh 45 pounds.

GENETIC IMPROVEMENT FACILITY
Semen is collected from genetically superior males and distributed to the breeding barns.

Building 1
Day 1-44

Building 2
Day 45-113

Building 3
Day 114-131

Building 4
Day 132-180

Genetic Improvement Facility

Super Market

PROCESSING FACILITY

FINISHING UNIT
Young pigs gain 1.5-1.7 pounds a day for 15-16 weeks until they reach slaughter weight of 255 pounds.
Day 181-320

Figure 12.2. A modern pork production system, from genetics to supermarket. (Used by permission of Premium Standard Foods.)

learn processing and to acquire its management team and skills. In 1992 PSF built a $55 million processing plant in Milan in only eleven months. Its facade was so fancy that some local people thought it was going to be a shopping mall.

The 300,000-square-foot PSF processing plant employed 700 workers to process 8,000 hogs a day. The company preferred to use local workers as much as possible, and paid good wages to attract and keep them, because training new workers costs so much money. It also had recruited some Hispanic workers, but never more than 20–25 percent of its labor force. It encouraged them to come with their families and to become permanent residents of the area.

The PSF payroll of around $40 million a year has been the salvation of north-central Missouri. Local young people have been able to return to the area,

Figure 12.3. Vertical aerial photograph of Premium Standard Farms (PSF) hog farms in north-central Missouri. Each unit is a set of parallel buildings with a dark rectangular manure lagoon next to it. PSF has dammed streams to create lakes for storing water for use in the hog houses. (U.S. Department of Agriculture, National Aerial Photography Program exposure 8526-196, March 15, 1996.)

or to remain in it, but not everyone is happy with the new hog farms. Some people have complained about odors, even though most buildings are set back two miles or more from the property line. Church leaders and politicians have complained that large farms are killing "the family farm," even though family farms were long gone before PSF ever set foot in the area. Critics of PSF invited the country singer Willie Nelson to perform at a protest meeting, which they scheduled in Des Moines rather than in Princeton or Milan to ensure maximum attendance and publicity.

In 1996 the ownership of PSF changed hands. Harms and Gordon had been unwilling to settle for less than the best, even though they were operating with borrowed venture capital. Then in 1995 hog prices plummeted, corn prices sky-rocketed, and extreme summer heat killed massive numbers of hogs throughout the Midwest. Harms and Gordon lost so much money that they were forced to file for bankruptcy, restructure the company, and turn over ownership to their financial backers, but they boasted that no supplier or vendor who had done business with them had lost so much as a single penny because of their restructuring.

Colette Schultz Kaster, director of technical services at PSF, said, "Restructuring had been rumored for so long that it was pretty much a nonevent when it finally happened. We read about it in the papers, same as you did, but it didn't change anything we did." In 1997 PSF was sold to Continental Grain Company, but day-to-day operations have continued pretty much as before.

PSF had maintained a sales office in Kansas City to make it easier to bring in customers and to attract salespeople who were unwilling to live in the remote rural area near the farms. Most of the new senior officials of the company live in Kansas City, "but most of us who work in production like living in rural areas," said Colette. "People need to understand that we all came from family farms. I did, my husband did, everybody I know came from a family farm. It's not just PSF, but every pig company is staffed with people that came from family farms. We came here because we want to work in agriculture, and right or wrong, this is the future of agriculture."

One of the more ambitious ventures of PSF before it was restructured was an aggressive expansion program in Texas. In 1994 PSF bought from National Hog Farms a 19,000-sow farrow-to-finish operation at Perico, twenty-five miles northwest of Dalhart, in the far northwestern corner of the Panhandle. Perico itself is no more than a sign beside the Burlington Northern Railroad, and does not even warrant the dignity of being called a whistle stop.

In 1991 National owned a 15,600-acre grain farm with sixty-five center-pivot irrigation systems and a 10,000-head beef cattle feed yard at Perico, but had decided to sell it, even though it was a good grain farm, because the company wanted to get out of grain production. Harold Meyers, National's hog farm manager in Nebraska, argued that the high, dry climate made Perico a dandy place to develop a hog farm. It is 4,500 feet above sea level, averages only three days a year when the temperature hits 100°F, and cools off rapidly at night.

"We do have a problem with hot weather when we ship hogs on the highway," he said. "The blacktop pavement gets the bottom of the truck trailer so hot you can't even bear to touch it, and the hogs get blisters if they lie on it. In real hot weather we don't load any hogs in the morning when they would have to travel through the day. We load them in the evening and get them there first thing in the morning when it is still cool."

National sent Harold to Perico to develop a $50 million hog farm. It still had not been completed in 1994 when PSF bought it, and he decided to stay with the farm rather than with the company. He sited hog buildings on the unirrigated land at the corners of the circles (fig. 12.4). They are in groups of four, with a far-

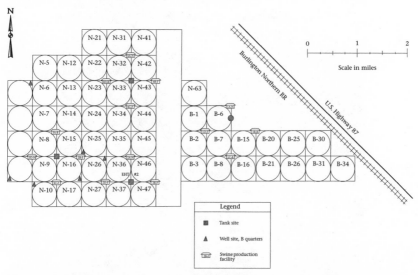

Figure 12.4. Premium Standard Farms hog production facilities at the Perico site, northwest of Dalhart, Texas, with hog-production facilities at the apices of cropland circles and circular tanks for collecting liquid manure at the center of each set of four production facilities. This area is also shown on Figure 12.5. (Based on a map provided by Harold Meyers of Premium Standard Farms; used by permission.)

rowing unit, a nursery unit, and two finishing units in each group (fig. 12.5). The manure from all units goes through a system that separates the solids and pumps the liquid into a twenty-foot-high open metal tank at the center of the group.

The liquid is aerated by hundreds of small propellers in the bottom of the tank, and then sprayed to fertilize and irrigate the fields, which are all leased to farmers for a cash rent of $125 an acre. When I visited Perico in 1997, Harold invited me to climb the stairs to the top of one of the tanks. I was not particularly enthusiastic about the thought of gazing soulfully into a huge bubbling vat of liquid hog manure, but I would have been rude if I had declined his invitation.

When we reached the top of the tank I was surprised to discover that it was almost odorless, even though the wind was blowing straight across it into our faces. Yes, it did have a faint fragrance, and yes, it was unmistakably hog manure,

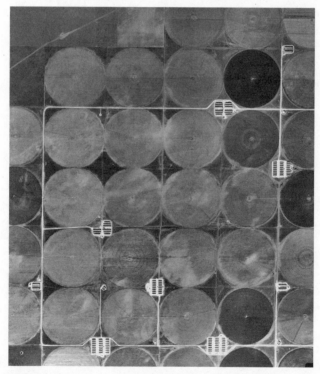

Figure 12.5. Vertical aerial photograph of the north-central part of the Perico site (shown also in Figure 12.4). (U.S. Department of Agriculture, National Aerial Photography Program exposure 9079-126, March 2, 1996.)

but the odor was unobjectionably faint. It occurred to me that other hog producers should consider adopting this system of manure management.

Harold was also proud that he maintains pen integrity. The same pen of twenty-five pigs stays together when it is moved from barn to barn, and the same pens stay on either side. "When you mix them they fight for three or four days," he said, "and they stop eating until they reestablish their social order. Even if you put a different pen next to them, they're biting through the bars and trying to fight, and they get off feed. In ten years everybody will be doing it this way."

When the hogs reach slaughter weight, Harold trucks them to the PSF processing plant in Milan, Missouri. "It's a long way to haul them," said Collette Kaster, "650 miles, a fourteen-to-sixteen-hour trip, but some people haul hogs even farther. A processor in California hauls them all the way from the Midwest." When the Milan plant has taken all it can handle, Harold sells the rest to the new processing plant that the Seaboard Corporation has built in Guymon, in the center of the Oklahoma Panhandle.

Seaboard on the Panhandle

Seaboard is a diversified international corporation that specializes in food production and processing, commodity trading and milling, and ocean transportation, with annual sales of around $1.8 billion. Seaboard stock is traded on the American Stock Exchange and was rated one of the three best stock picks of the year in 1998 by a national stock digest. Seventy-five percent of the stock is owned by the Seaboard Flour Corporation, which is owned by the secretive children of Otto Bresky.

Seaboard was founded in 1918 when Otto Bresky bought a flour mill in Atchison, Kansas. He kept buying other flour mills, and the company focused on flour and feed until 1982, when it sold all its domestic flour mills to Cargill. It still has flour mills in Africa and Latin America. In 1983 it became involved in ocean shipping services and now is the leading carrier of containerized cargo from the Port of Miami, serving eighteen countries in South America and the Caribbean. In the same year Seaboard started producing broiler chickens in the United States and has become the nation's ninth largest broiler company, with 725 contract broiler growers.

Seaboard is constantly searching for good new investment opportunities. "We were making money in our shipping business and in our broiler business," said Mark Campbell, vice president of development, "and we were looking for a good place to invest it. It could just as easily have been a flour mill in Nigeria. We went into it with a lot of thought, research, and analysis."

"We found that the hog industry was highly fragmented," he continued, "with a large number of small producers. We decided there was a tremendous strategic opportunity in hogs by uniting a lot of fragmented pieces, genetics, feed, production, transportation, distribution, sales. We knew agricultural production, processing, and marketing, and we invested in something we knew. Hog production is very capital intensive, but we are an entrepreneurial organization that has the wherewithal to do it, and we thought we could make money on hogs."

Seaboard started in the Midwest, where hog production was concentrated and feed grain was produced. In 1990 it bought an unused pork-processing plant in Albert Lea, Minnesota, but quickly realized that it had made a mistake, because it could not secure a steady and reliable supply of hogs of consistent quality from many small producers, and it faced stiff competition for hogs from established processors. It gradually cut back on production and sold the unprofitable Albert Lea plant in 1994.

"We got out the U.S. map and looked at the key ingredients of grain, climate, land, and people," Mark remembers, and they liked what they saw on the Oklahoma Panhandle. "Grain is the biggest cost in raising a hog," he said, "and we found no packers in an area where a lot of grain is produced. The dry climate reduces the risk of diseases, and copious sunshine with steady strong winds speeds up evaporation from lagoons.

"The land is flat, with no surface streams we might pollute, and the groundwater is 200 feet below the surface, protected by a lot of geology. In North Carolina they have to mound up their lagoons, because the groundwater is so close to the surface, but we could excavate them in the heavy clay soil and not have to lie awake nights worrying that they might burst. It doesn't rain much there anyhow."

The sparsely populated Panhandle had fewer people to complain about lagoons, and they were already preconditioned to livestock odors, because southwestern Kansas has one of the world's greatest concentrations of beef cattle feed yards. Both Oklahoma (1991) and Kansas (1994) have laws that favor corporate farms. They are well placed with respect to the growing metropolitan markets of Texas and California and the new markets in Mexico and around the Pacific Rim that NAFTA and GATT have opened up. Technological innovations allow hogs to be slaughtered in Oklahoma, vacuum-packed, shipped refrigerated by rail to the West Coast and by ship to Japan, and after fifty days still sold as fresh rather than frozen pork.

"Our careful analysis attracted us to building a hog-processing plant in Guymon, Oklahoma," Mark said, and Guymon wanted Seaboard even more than Seaboard wanted Guymon. The town is in the very heart of the notorious Dust Bowl of the 1930s. The area had recovered after World War II, when deep wells and powerful pumps enabled local farmers to tap the water of the Ogallala aquifer for large-scale irrigation of bumper crops of corn, wheat, and sorghum, and deep beneath the Ogallala was one of the world's largest natural gas fields, which provided cheap energy to power the pumps.

By 1991 Guymon had started to hurt once again. The Swift packing plant, which had employed 250 workers, had closed its doors in 1987, cattle and wheat farmers were struggling with low prices, and the petroleum business was in a slump. More than half the stores on Main Street in Guymon were closed and shuttered. The town needed new business and would do whatever was necessary to get it.

Seaboard revived Guymon. The company invested more than $110 million in a new 450,000-square-foot plant on the site of the old Swift plant. The plant employs 1,000 workers to process 1,000 hogs an hour, so two shifts working 40 hours a week without overtime can process 4 million hogs a year. It opened in December 1995 and went to a second shift in 1997.

Finding enough workers in the sparsely populated Panhandle was a challenge, even though Mark assured me that "we pay $16–17,000 a year to workers right off the street, which is well above the minimum wage." A meatpacking plant is a dangerous place to work. The floors are slippery with blood and water, and the knives and saws that cut up hogs and cattle do not play favorites. They can cut through human flesh just as easily, and slice off a finger, a hand, a whole arm, even though the workers wear protective gauntlets of chain-mail steel.

Few local people were willing to take low-wage jobs in such a dangerous industry, so Seaboard had to recruit workers from well beyond reasonable commuting distances. Many were Hispanic and Southeast Asian immigrants. They needed housing, so Seaboard invited a developer named Rob Martin to set up a 195-unit mobile home park. The company automatically deducts their rent payments from their paychecks and sends them directly to the park office. Some of the residents are pretty tough customers. When I was taking a picture in the park, one woman with a car full of kids berated me in the kind of language I have heard only rarely since I left the Navy.

Seaboard had thought of contracting with local farmers to produce the 4 million hogs it needed, but soon found out that it was in cattle country, where hogs are not popular. It realized that it was going to have to produce at least half the hogs it needed on its own farms and buy the rest from other producers in a 250-mile radius who could meet its standards. It began building farms in 1992 but developed them most rapidly in 1995 and 1996. In 2001 it had 106,000 sows and 200 hog farms producing 10,000 hogs a year each.

The individual farms are far enough apart to reduce the risk of disease but close enough together for efficient delivery of feed and efficient management (fig. 12.6). Seaboard was able to buy land at reasonable prices, Mark said, "but each farm had to go through the entire craziness of the permitting process, with landowner notification, hearings, and all sorts of bureaucratic regulations. There was nothing we didn't plan to do anyhow, but it was a cumbersome, time-consuming, and costly headache."

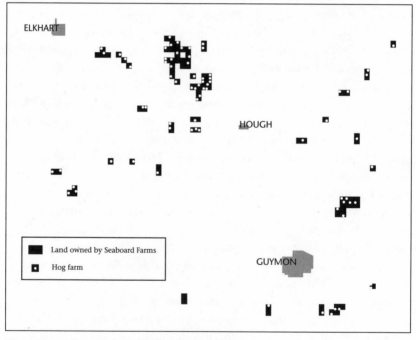

Figure 12.6. Hog-production facilities developed by Seaboard Farms northwest of Guymon, Oklahoma, in the heart of the Oklahoma Panhandle. (Based on a map provided by Mark Campbell of Seaboard Farms; used by permission.)

The new hog farms are highly visible on the flat plains, where you can see the next grain elevator ten miles before you get to it. All Seaboard farms have parallel rows of identical cookie-cutter houses, 40' × 192', but the number of houses varies from farm to farm (fig. 12.7). The end of each set of houses has a manure lagoon 22 feet deep and as large as a football field. Lagoon effluent is sprayed on irrigated cropland. Seaboard decided not to become involved in grain production, so it has sold the cropland to farmers for $750 to $1,100 an acre, and they have free fertilizer from the hog houses.

Paul Hitch, a fourth-generation cattle rancher who also runs one of the oldest beef feed yards in Oklahoma, shocked other cattlemen in 1993 when he agreed

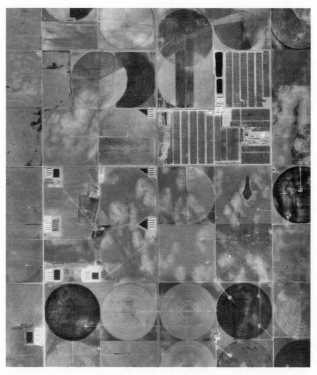

Figure 12.7. Vertical aerial photograph of hog-production facilities developed by Seaboard Farms on the Oklahoma Panhandle. Each set of four to six parallel hog houses is identifiable by a dark triangular or rectangular manure lagoon. Location near an existing beef cattle feed yard did not protect these farms from criticism about the odor of their lagoons. (U.S. Department of Agriculture, National Aerial Photography Program exposure 8464-165, February 10, 1995.)

to start producing hogs for Seaboard. Initially he had been skeptical. "Why would I want to help a company that's going to compete for my feed grain and my employees?" he wondered. "The more I looked at it, though, the more it looked like hog production might be viable for us, and they were going to come anyhow, no matter what we did.

"We had been looking at the down side. When we looked at the up side, we realized that we had everything we needed—land, water, equipment, management, credit line, computers, a veterinarian, a nutritionist—everything, in fact, but pig expertise, and you can always buy expertise. When we crunched the numbers, they showed that pig production could be quite profitable for us.

"We also realized that Seaboard needed the Good Housekeeping seal of approval, so to speak. If Hitch does this, maybe everybody else would say it's OK because Hitch is doing it. Maybe Seaboard is willing to pay for our approval." Seaboard did agree to contract with Hitch to build two fourteen-building hog farms, but then he decided to develop his own farrow-to-finish hog operation that would produce 300,000 hogs a year on six farrowing sites, eight nurseries, and thirty-six finishing farms.

Other hog-producing companies have flocked into the Panhandle area. They include well-known American companies such as Cargill, DeKalb, Land O'Lakes, and Murphy, as well as Kroneseder from Germany, Vall from Spain, Pig Improvement Company from England, and Nippon Meat Packers, Inc., the largest meatpacking company in Japan and fourth largest in the world. Nippon has developed an operation near Perryton, Texas, that is specifically designed to produce 500,000 pigs a year for export to Japan.

Hog farms have brought the Panhandle area out of its economic tailspin. Main Street in Guymon is bustling again, and the new fast-food joints along the highways have all the business they can handle. Sales taxes and building permits are up, births are up, school enrollment is up, crime is up. The mayor of Guymon may have been a bit optimistic when he told the state legislature that Seaboard has created 5,000 new jobs on the Panhandle, but a front-page story in the *Daily Oklahoman* on May 18, 1997, said that "corporate hog farms possibly have been the greatest economic boon for Oklahoma agriculture since statehood."

Of course not everyone has been happy with the new hog farms, and the opposition has been vocal, persistent, and highly emotional. Some critics have been concerned about lagoon odors and possible pollution of groundwater. Some have been troubled by the large influx of immigrant workers who have been willing to work for low wages, because they have required greatly increased school, police, health, and other social services, but they have not paid enough taxes to support these services.

Some critics have flayed Seaboard for gorging itself at the public trough. On November 30, 1998, *Time* magazine published an article attacking Seaboard because, "like other profitable businesses, it collects subsidies—or more accurately, corporate welfare—from local, state, and federal governments." This article accused Seaboard of having secured a tax incentive package worth $21 million from Guymon and the state of Oklahoma, without adding that the company had invested $800 million in processing plant and hog farms on the Panhandle between 1992 and 1997.

Seaboard might rejoin that the company would have been remiss if it had failed to accept the financial incentives that were available to it, and it seems unfair to blame the company because economic development warfare has broken out among states, cities, and counties that are competing to attract new industries.

Seaboard has played into the hands of its critics, however, because it has made little apparent effort to be a good neighbor, and has ridden roughshod over those who oppose it. The company offices are 400 miles away in Kansas City, and its top executives are perceived as arrogant, heavy-handed, and out of touch with local people. Some of them are afflicted with a corporate mind-set, and they can reduce everything to numbers. They are hard-eyed believers in the despotism of the dollar, and they worship the bottom line, but they are singularly insensitive to other human values.

Furthermore, Seaboard has not hesitated to play hardball with its critics. The company has invested such huge amounts of money that it cannot afford to let anyone get in its way, and it does not hesitate to use its economic and political muscle to crush any opposition. It hires the best lobbyists and lawyers to protect its interests, and the legal process is not always nice and fair. Small wonder that critics of the new hog farms feel so totally frustrated and helpless.

Minnesota

Hog production has stagnated since 1970 in the traditional hog-producing states of the Midwest, where many farmers are suspicious of contracts, but it has increased steadily in Minnesota, which rose to become the nation's third largest hog-producing state in 1997 (fig. 11.2). Individual hog farmers in Minnesota who treasured their independence have shown that they can still compete with large corporate producers by forming alliances to use the best genetics and the most advanced management practices. Dr. Allen D. Leman, a charismatic member of the faculty of the College of Veterinary Medicine at the University of Minnesota, played a major role in nurturing the modernization of hog production in the state.

Dr. Leman realized that veterinarians were well placed to advise farmers about the latest innovations in livestock production and to help them develop sophisticated business plans and marketing arrangements. He encouraged veterinary clinics to take the lead in helping producers form alliances to upgrade pig production, especially by introducing top-quality genetics, because "back in those days farmers were raising pigs that were no good," remembers Dr. Gordon Spronk of the Pipestone Veterinary Clinic. The message of the clinics resonated especially well with forward-looking young farmers, who were keenly sensitive to the necessity of upgrading from traditional diversification to large-scale specialization.

Martin County in central southern Minnesota has become the state's leading pig county, and it ranks eighth in the United States (fig. 12.8). In 1997 it produced 934,000 pigs, or more than two pigs for every acre in the county (fig. 12.9). Dr. Kent Kislingbury of the veterinary clinic in Fairmont, the county seat, said, "A lot of things came together for us. We have smart young farmers. We have markets as good as any place in the country, six processing plants within 150 miles, and there's nothing like getting competitive bids.

"We have bankers who understand livestock," he added, "and they were willing to lend money to get this thing started. We have good implement dealers, and local manufacturing firms that have been eager to take great new ideas from farmers and make even better equipment. Without computers producers could not have kept track of their livestock, and their records would not have been good enough for their bankers to stick with them.

"When I came here in 1964," he continued, "Martin County had 15,000 to 18,000 milk cows on small dairy farms, but now it's down to only 1,200. We have a better environment for pigs than for cows, because we have mostly cropland and not a lot of pasture. We have a good source of feed, some of the best crops and lowest prices in the country, and feed is 60 percent of the cost of production. These old dairy barns are good barns, and we have been able to convert them into farrowing barns as well as anybody in the entire country, because we have done it time and again. Some of them have been converted to something different inside three times.

"Hog manure is darned good fertilizer for corn and soybeans," he added. "It cuts your chemical bill by $30 to $40 an acre, and our producers have learned how to handle it properly. They don't flush it into lagoons but store it in deep pits, because you lose an awful lot when you put manure in a lagoon, especially the nitrogen. Martin County has only six lagoons for hog manure but thirteen municipal sewage treatment lagoons. Our new hog houses have pits deep enough to store all the manure the pigs can produce in fourteen months."

In 1987 the Fairmont Veterinary Clinic pioneered the concept of a producer-owned sow production system using the very best genetics available. The clinic helps independent producers form limited partnerships to buy sow farms, which

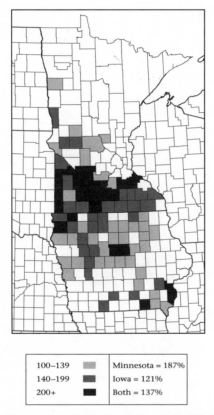

100–139		Minnesota = 187%
140–199		Iowa = 121%
200+		Both = 137%

Figure 12.8. Number of hogs and pigs (other than feeder pigs) sold in Minnesota and Iowa, 1997, as a percentage of the number sold in 1987. Hog production increased rapidly in southern Minnesota between 1987 and 1997, whereas production in Iowa stagnated or declined. (Data from Minnesota and Iowa state volumes of the *1987 Census of Agriculture* [Washington, D.C.: U.S. Department of Commerce, Bureau of the Census, 1989] and *1997 Census of Agriculture* [Washington, D.C.: U.S. Department of Agriculture, National Agricultural Statistics Service, 1999.)

the clinic manages for them. Each year each producer-partner takes delivery of a certain number of gilts for breeding from the sow farm, and upon delivery they become the property of the producer.

The clinic has organized a complete management service that is available to anyone who wishes to use it. It manages 40,000 hogs for producers, and is attractive to older producers who are ready to ease back a bit. Four of the eight veterinarians in the clinic also produce pigs as a sideline activity, and they hire the management service just as other producers do.

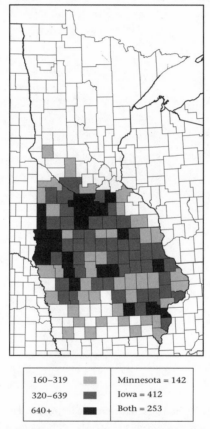

160–319	▨	Minnesota = 142
320–639	▨	Iowa = 412
640+	▨	Both = 253

Figure 12.9. Number of hogs and pigs (other than feeder pigs) sold per square mile in Minnesota and Iowa, 1997. The greatest concentration of hog production in 1997 was in central southern Minnesota, northwestern Iowa, and scattered counties elsewhere in Iowa. (Data from Minnesota and Iowa state volumes of *1997 Census of Agriculture* [Washington, D.C.: U.S. Department of Agriculture, National Agricultural Statistics Service, 1999].)

The clinic also manages two producer-owned 300-boar farms that sell semen to producers. "We were buying good boars," said Dr. Kislingbury, "but now we have the top 5 percent. Top genetics cost 10 to 15 cents more per pig, but the pigs sell for $1.50 to $2.00 more. That's the difference between just buying a good boar and buying the very best boar. The pigs are leaner and cheaper to produce, too, because putting on a pound of fat takes far more feed than putting on a pound of lean, and our feed conversion ratios have been dropping steadily."

The first modern, large-scale pig producers in Martin County were crop farmers who wanted to increase the size of their farm business, but many newer producers are more specialized on hogs, and around 1990 some producers started contracting with their neighbors to feed hogs for them. "I think guys from Carolina came up here and started it," said Dr. Kislingbury, "but we could also have borrowed the idea from turkey producers in Minnesota, who were doing a lot of contracting. A lot of the Carolina hog people actually started off with turkeys."

Whatever its origin, contracting to feed hogs has lost its stigma in Martin County, and in 2001 most producers were eagerly looking for contractors to feed pigs for them. A contractor needed only a little chunk of land on which to build houses, and eight 600-head houses could provide a reasonable living. The producer paid the contractor $36 per pig place per year for a 600-head house that costs around $100,000. The contractor should be able to pay for the house in ten years, and has the benefit of its manure while paying for it.

Can Martin County and southern Minnesota continue to produce enough pigs to keep five or six packing plants in business? Can small old packing plants compete with large new plants elsewhere? "A little guy with only a thousand sows doesn't cut much weight with a processor when a big guy can come in with half a million pigs," said Dr. Kislingbury, "and the prospect that processors will consolidate is really scary. Our producers can't stay in business if they don't have any place to market their hogs."

In 1990 the veterinary clinic at Pipestone, in the far southwestern corner of Minnesota, adopted and modified the Fairmont model. The Pipestone clinic has developed twenty producer-owned sow farms with 25,000 sows to serve 150 pig producers in Minnesota, South Dakota, and Iowa. The clinic realized that many farmers wanted weaned baby pigs rather than gilts, however, because breeding requires far more management than finishing, and breeding barns cost around $1,000 per sow, so the Pipestone clinic developed the concept of the "ten-pound weaner pig," which is the cornerstone of the Pipestone system.

"The farmer takes ownership of the ten-pound weaned pig when we deliver it to his farm," said Dr. Gordon Spronk of the Pipestone clinic, "and he can do whatever he wants to do with it, but we are happy to help him with advice and recommendations. Individual farmers using top-quality genetics can do better than the big corporate pig producers because they have pride of ownership in their pigs, and the corporate manager can never have that."

Bob Christensen

The veterinary clinics in Minnesota have fostered the formation of producer alliances, but some producers have contracted successfully with individual farmers. Bob Christensen is an entrepreneurial genius who grew up on a cattle and row-crop farm near Sleepy Eye. In 1974, when he was 13 years old, a neighbor gave him two bred gilts. When the pigs were born he sold the barrows and bred the gilts, and by 1980, when he graduated from high school, he had built up a herd of 200 sows. By 2001 he had developed Christensen Family Farms—which Bob, his brother, and his parents still own—into the nation's eighth largest pork producer, with 80,000 sows, 520 employees, and annual sales of $200 million.

Bob built a sow barn on the home farm in 1977, and he added another each year for the next ten years. During the farm crisis of the 1980s many pig buildings on neighboring farms were empty, because bankers wouldn't advance farmers money to buy pigs. Bob would take fifty-pound feeder pigs to neighbors who had empty buildings and pay them 6 to 9 cents per pig per day. There was one period when he added a new contract producer each month for twenty-seven months straight.

I asked Bob if other farmers were happy about contracting with him, and he said, "At first they accepted reluctantly, but now more than 90 percent are making a conscious decision to build new pig facilities. There's so much synergy with small row-crop farmers who have only 400 to 700 acres they need to fertilize. The manure is a value to them rather than a disposal problem. They get $4,000 worth of fertilizer value from each barn, and with machinery getting bigger, they have excess labor."

Then I wondered if he was "saving the small family farm," and he replied, "The vast majority who have contracted with us have been trying to expand, not desperately trying to save the farm. They could have made it without us, and we have been more of an addition on top that has made them more comfortable.

Adding hog finishing often has expanded the farm business enough to enable a son to stay on the farm with his father."

Bob told me that in the early 1980s he could raise a pound of pork for 34 or 35 cents, when the average was 47 or 48, by using very high quality genetics, top-notch management techniques, and good cost management, primarily the feed side. "We knew we could put a pound of pork out there for 10 to 12 cents less than everyone else," he said, "and for twelve to fourteen years we borrowed every penny we could get to expand. We had a clear picture of our performance, so we could make decisions based on hard facts. We standardized the fundamentals we had proved would work, and we looked for every opportunity to systematize, automate, and keep our costs just as low as feasibly possible.

"Our goal is the outcome," he continued. "There may be things that influence it that are beyond our control. That's why it's so critical to have an information system and management talent that can ascertain what they are. When the outcome isn't acceptable, what made it that way? Was it within our control? We have to be able to arrive at the right answer the first time, because sometimes you don't even get a second time. With our contractors it's more of an education process that supervision. We tell them what's worked for us, and if they can do it in a different way and get the same or better outcome, go for it!"

Bob is a keen student of trends in the pork business, and he told me that he has been served fairly well by not going in the same direction as everyone else. "In the eighties and up until '92 we were the only ones expanding in southern Minnesota," he said. "In 1990 we built a 12,000-head sow complex and began contract sow production, but we slowed down in the mid-nineties when everyone else was expanding. We decided we had better build our own assets instead of contracting, so we decided to own our feed mills, our sow farms, and our nurseries, and to contract only the finishing. In 1997 we even started to shift from contracting to company-owned finishing.

"By 1996," he said, "uneconomical rates were being paid for hogs, and everyone was building barns. There were banks where if you had a production contract or a packer contract and they took your pulse and thought you were going to live for ten years, you could get a million-dollar loan, and if you could somehow justify it with the auditors, it would be even better to do $10 million.

"There were people that thought it would be easy money, and too many people got into the business in the mid-nineties for the wrong reasons. You don't take 2,000 pigs and walk through them for fifteen minutes before you go to work and ten minutes at night when you get home from work. They need consistent attention. You don't need to spend your whole day in there, but they need a quality hour in the morning and a quality hour in the evening. And they don't quit on holidays and weekends.

"From '95 to '98 the majority of the industry lost focus on the importance of cost containment and made a lot of investments that are not going to be sustainable. In '96 and '97 we didn't borrow a cent, when the business invested $3.5 to $4.0 billion, because we knew it was going to take an extended period of losses and weed out a lot of the high-cost producers. For the next few years the business is going to have to live painfully with some bad investment decisions that were made in the mid-nineties. It's not the decisions we make when things are bad that hurt us, it's the decisions we make when times are good.

"Part of our problem was our own making," Bob admitted, "because of compromises we made. Say we needed 120,000 head spaces. The first 80,000 we contracted were high-quality management, but the last 40,000 we were compromising, and we decided to build our own rather than compromise. So in 1999 we became very aggressive again when everyone else was standing still."

Bob told me that in 2001 he had 36 sow barns, 140 contractors, and 700 finishing barns, about two-thirds contracted. "I am perfectly happy with a contractor who has 2,000 pigs," he said, "because he is going to give them more attention and care than if he has 4,000 or 6,000. Our goal is set by our management talent and how close we are to capturing our maximum potential. There's no point to adding 10 percent to our production base if we're missing 10 to 15 percent of our potential, but it's time to add to our business when we are in the mid-nineties of capturing our potential."

Dave Preisler, executive director of the Minnesota Pork Producers Council, said, "Christensen is a very well managed company. It has done a very good job of hiring good people, and has put a premium on that. The organization has really impressed me from the standpoint of the people they've got there. They've got some very, very sharp people. Their average age of employee is pretty young, but they are sharp."

ValAdCo

Not all pig farms in Minnesota, unfortunately, have been managed as well as Christensen Family Farms. "Pigs have gotten a bad name in Minnesota," said Dr.

Kislingbury, "and some of it was earned, but not very much." ValAdCo, a co-op formed to produce hogs in Renville County, ninety miles west of Minneapolis, probably has received more publicity than all other pig farms in the state combined, and virtually all of it has been negative.

Animosities had smoldered in rural Renville County long before ValAdCo had ever been invented, and they burst into open flame when it was formed. Some local farmers had been arrogant and ruthless in acquiring land, and they had done other things that had not endeared them to their neighbors. In 1992 they urged their local grain co-op to get into pigs, but the other members voted them down, so they formed ValAdCo to produce pigs on their own.

Their neighbors accused them of trying to steal the pig market, and from its very start ValAdCo has been saddled with controversy and acrimony. This controversy caught the eye of the news media, and ValAdCo was as arrogant to the press as it was to everyone else, so it virtually guaranteed itself maximum negative publicity.

ValAdCo took four years to get its permits and to get its system in place, and it did not start pig production until 1996. By 2001 it had 11,000 sows on seven sites, sold 200,000 hogs a year, and grossed $20 to $25 million. All of its facilities were permitted and constructed in strict compliance with the letter of the law when they were built. Initially they flushed manure into open lagoons, a 10-acre primary and a 7.5-acre secondary at each site. Five of the seven sites released excessive levels of toxic gases, and hydrogen sulfide levels regularly exceeded the state standard; one reading was 600 times the permitted level.

Neighbors had little recourse against the odors until Julie Jansen, who lived near one of the sites, took matters into her own hands. She had to close down her home day-care operation because the kids were getting sick, and her own six children began suffering ills that she blamed on the hogs. "My whole house smelled like a backed-up sewer," she told a reporter. "You get a sore throat, and your eyes water. You can smell it on the kids' breath, and when they cough it smells like the lagoon odor."

Julie Jansen discovered that she had a genius for milking the media for maximum publicity. In March 1999 I was at a legislative committee hearing to which she brought five covered buckets of liquid hog manure. She planned to uncap them to reinforce her testimony against a feedlot air emission standards bill. The committee chairman sternly admonished her not to open them, and she complained, "You won't even let me open 23 quarts of manure, but I have to live next to 23 million gallons of it." Her efforts paid off when the legislature passed a bill requiring the Minnesota Pollution Control Agency to monitor hydrogen sulfide gas from large livestock operations. The gubernatorial candidate Mark Dayton demonstrated his commitment to agriculture by picking her as his running mate for lieutenant governor, but they failed to win the primary.

In 1999 ValAdCo was reeling from the hog price crisis of December 1998, which had exacerbated problems caused by poor management and a seriously flawed strategic plan. The members of the co-op were successful crop farmers, but they did not know how to manage large-scale pig production. The mostly new board of directors that took over in May 1999 realized that they needed a good professional manager who knew what he was doing. They hired Eddie Crum, who had been a production manager for Seaboard Farms hog farms in southwestern Kansas.

"Before I took this job," Eddie said, "I exercised due diligence to assure that they hadn't done anything wrong, either through mistake or willfulness, and I found that it's basically just another pig company, no better or worse than any other pig business in the United States, but it hadn't done anything in particular that was effective in managing the odor. And southern Minnesota and northern Iowa is the best place on the face of the entire planet to grow pigs. This is the heart of corn and soybean country, we have wonderful weather, and we have readily accessible markets, so we just went back to the basics of good hog production."

Eddie brought an evangelical zeal to his job. "It was important to give the staff a sense of pride in what we do," he said, "and we have made some tremendous and truly remarkable successes in developing new ways to control odor. Today we're the finest environmental stewards in the pork business."

In 2001 Eddie had placed a solid impermeable cover over each lagoon basin, and he anchored and sealed it around the edges. A set of pipes run underneath the cover, which can rise or fall to contain the manure gases until fans can pump them out. The manure gases are treated with ozone to turn them into simple harmless compounds. The basins have little odor. The principal source of odor on the farms now is dust from the buildings, which is controlled by an elaborate system of large straw filters that trap the dust from the exhaust fans.

Despite these efforts, the ValAdCo farms remain a prime target for the Minnesota Pollution Control Agency (MPCA), the Minnesota Health Department, and the state attorney general's office. These farms violated state air-quality standards for hydrogen sulfide 113 times in 1999 and 158 times in 2000. A spokesman for the MPCA primly explained that agency's failure to take action by saying, "Odor is not pollution, and we have no authority to regulate odor," but Patricia Bloomgren of the Minnesota Health Department said, "We are taking this very seriously," and the Renville County commissioners asked the attorney general's office to become involved because it has legal authority to control public nuisances.

Eddie Crum defends ValAdCo by saying, "The Minnesota hydrogen sulfide standard is a silly standard based on questionable science. OSHA says you can have 10,000 parts per billion in the workplace and be safe, but Minnesota has a 50 parts per billion rural standard. We were 99 percent compliant, but for that 1 percent we were singled out in the papers and called a terrible polluter. I don't believe we have polluted anything. We were singled out when we didn't have the resources to fight back against a rule that I don't believe is either right or fair. What has been done to us is just flat wrong."

Nevertheless, in December 2002 ValAdCo agreed to pay a $125,000 penalty to settle a suit brought by the Minnesota attorney general and the state Pollution Control Agency alleging that it had violated state standards for hydrogen sulfide emissions more than 150 times in 2000 and more than 100 times in 2002. ValAdCo wanted to settle the suit because it was eager to sell its hog operations to Christensen Family Farms, which was party to the negotiations. As part of the settlement Christensen agreed to drain the largest manure lagoon, bulldoze its walls, and replace it with two concrete storage pits with impermeable covers. Christensen also agreed to replace earthen lagoons at the five other ValAdCo farms with concrete storage pits, at an estimated total cost of around $2 million.[3]

Like Eddie Crum, many other operators of new large-scale hog farms feel that they have been treated unfairly. Some undoubtedly have, because rural animosities antedate hog farms, but some have asked for trouble, because they have not made an effort to be good neighbors. They have been insensitive to complaints and they have not hesitated to use their economic and political power to ride roughshod over those who have gotten in their way.

Most of the new large-scale hog-producing companies have developed all of their own facilities and have not contracted, but producers in Minnesota have demonstrated that contract hog feeding can complement cash-grain farming on small Corn Belt farms. Specialized sow farms do all of the breeding, which requires the highest level of management, and they deliver feeder pigs to the contracting farmers. Small cash-grain farmers have been willing to build finishing houses and contract to finish hogs both because of the value of hog manure as fertilizer and because the additional income enables farmers to keep a child on the farm.

13
Critics

Many people are genuinely concerned about the way American agriculture is changing, and they are especially critical of large new livestock farms, for a variety of reasons. Some people simply seem to detest anything that is new; they would like to repeal the twentieth century, and are not too sure about the nineteenth. Some people are concerned about pollution of air and water. Some are worried about human health. Some fear that large farms are cannibalizing small farms and destroying rural communities. Some distrust large organizations. Some are suspicious of new technology. Some are concerned about maltreatment of farm animals, and some are repulsed by the very idea that anyone would eat meat or use animal products.

Different groups have taken different approaches in attempting to address these issues. The Water Keeper Alliance, led by Robert F. Kennedy Jr., is a group of concerned citizens who have taken matters into their own hands because they believe enforcement of environmental laws has broken down. In December 2000 they used law firms experienced in litigation against tobacco companies to file lawsuits against large hog producers in seven states, alleging they have violated the federal Clean Water Act and other laws. They would like to put the large hog farms out of business.[1]

A number of states have passed laws that ban or strictly control large livestock farms, despite concern about losing competitive advantage if they act unilaterally. In Minnesota in 1998, for example, critics alarmed proponents by pressing the legislature to enact a moratorium, because the proliferation of large feedlots, particularly hog farms, had overwhelmed the ability of state and local pollution-control agencies to inspect, monitor, and regulate them.

Feedlots were the hot-button issue of the 1998 legislative session. In dozens of rural communities across the state farmers were fighting farmers, neighbors were fighting neighbors, and worst of all, rural Republicans were fighting each other. The Republican governor finessed the issue by securing funding for a three-year, $3 million generic environmental impact study of the livestock industry in Minnesota. (Disclosure: I was one of the twenty-five members of the citizens' advisory committee for this GEIS.)

Pollution

Manure lagoons on hog farms have been a major flashpoint for critics of large-scale animal agriculture, because their odor makes them an easy and inviting target. It is offensive to everyone, and it can make some people physically ill. Hog manure smells far worse than the manure of any other kind of farm animal. Other large-scale livestock operations have not been criticized nearly as vehemently as hog farms, perhaps because they do not smell as bad, perhaps because they were developed before the era of heightened environmental and social activism. One wonders how other forms of livestock would have fared if hog production had been the first to be modernized, rather than the last.

The first-generation large-scale hog farms clearly were not concerned about odor, because they flushed their manure into open-air lagoons, but hog farmers quickly realized that they had to do everything possible to control and reduce it. Odor is hard to measure scientifically, but good techniques are now available for estimating the frequency of annoying odors at different distances from particular feedlots, and they provide a basis for recommending desirable setback distances. The better hog farmers have made good progress in controlling odor, even though it adds considerably to their costs of production. Before long the odor of hog farms will be no more contentious than the odor of any other kind of livestock operation.

Some newer hog farms have replaced lagoons with concrete pits beneath their barns. These pits are deep enough to hold fourteen months of manure. The farmer hires a specialized contractor to pump the manure out of the pit and inject it into the soil before the time to plant crops each spring. Concrete pits help to control odor, and they also reduce concern about the possibility that seepage from earthen lagoons could contaminate groundwater. Nobody really knows for sure whether seepage from earthen lagoons is a problem, but one might expect it to be most severe in areas of porous sandy soil or in karst areas underlain by soluble limestone.

Earthen lagoons can wreak havoc if they overflow or break and spill large quantities of manure into surface streams. Manure contains high levels of nitrate or phosphate, which encourage algal blooms. The algae consume the water-dissolved oxygen on which fish depend, and the result can be massive fish kills.[2] Nutrient-enriched water can also encourage the multiplication of toxic microorganisms such as *Pfiesteria piscicida,* which has been blamed for killing large numbers of fish in Chesapeake Bay (broiler farms) and in eastern North Carolina (hog farms).[3] High levels of nitrogen in drinking water may cause methemglobinemia, or blue-baby syndrome, but the World Health Organization (WHO) found only 2,000 cases of methemglobinemia worldwide between 1950 and 1970.

Lagoon bursts and spills have enjoyed the most publicity, but inefficient municipal treatment plants and domestic septic systems, unchecked runoff from open feedlots, and row-crop agriculture are more important sources of stream pollution. Feedlot operators must have nutrient management plans that show they own or have permanent access to enough land to spread all the manure their animals produce, but more than 99 percent of stream pollution by agriculture is from manure application on farmland at excessive rates, say on ground that is snow-covered or frozen, or on rain-soaked ground that is already saturated with moisture. Some people suspect that the cost of hauling manure encourages operators of large feedlots to spread more manure close to the lot and less farther away, but the greatest agricultural source of stream pollution is small- and medium-sized farmers who cannot afford to upgrade their facilities.[4]

Subtherapeutic Antibiotics

One of the most compelling criticisms of modern livestock operations is their use of small amounts of antibiotics as feed additives to increase growth and feed efficiency, and to help control disease. Apparently the antibiotics suppress subclinical levels of infection, and the animals can use all of their feed energy to grow, because they do not have to devote any to fighting infection. A highly undesirable effect is that bacteria eventually seem to develop resistance to these antibiotics, and the antibiotics can no longer control them effectively.

To make matters worse, many of the antibiotics that are used subtherapeutically in animals are also used to treat people, and there is a serious danger that some antibiotics will not be effective just when people need them most. For example, the standard treatment of campylobacter, which causes severe gastrointestinal illness in people, is fluoroquinolones, but the use of fluoroquinolones in broiler feed seems to be fostering a resistant strain of campylobacter bacteria.[5]

Some people have proposed banning the use of antibiotics in livestock feed, but such a ban would reduce production prohibitively, and it would hurt small marginal farms the most, because subtherapeutic antibiotics are most effective on poorly managed farms with substandard sanitary conditions. One can argue, however, that we should stringently limit and control the use of all newly developed antibiotics that will be used to treat people. Some people suspect that even physicians and hospitals might have been guilty of overprescribing antibiotics.

Large Farms

Technology has trashed the Jeffersonian ideal of the small family farm, whether we like it or not. Many people do not. Farmers who have failed to expand their operations have been forced to find off-farm jobs to supplement their meager farm income, and many have left the land completely. The United States needs to confront and answer an ideological question that has no right answer: Should small farms be encouraged even though they probably cannot provide an acceptable level of living for the farm family?

Some critics seem to dislike large farms simply because they are large. They take it for granted that family farms must be small and large farms must be corporate farms, an attitude of "any farm larger than mine is a corporate farm." They fail to realize that more than 97 percent of all farms in the United States are still family owned and operated, although many have incorporated to facilitate inter-generational transfer of assets. Their scale of operation has increased so greatly that they have had to hire many farm workers, instead of the single hired man who was a fixture on the traditional family farm.

Many small farmers, especially the older ones, bemoan the loss of a way of life. They lament the decline of neighborliness, shared equipment, exchange of labor, and socializing in general. Many have an infuriated feeling of powerlessness before the juggernaut of change, but some have organized grass-roots groups to fight specific projects. Sometimes members of state and national environmental and sustainable agriculture groups have joined them, but the outsiders rarely seem to have much in common with local people except a shared distaste for the idea that bigger is better.

Outside activists who advocate restrictions on livestock production may actually create problems for small farmers, because small producers cannot afford the expense of complying with new regulations and are unwilling to endure the often byzantine ordeal of securing permits. Exempting small farmers from new regulations can doom them to remain small, because having to comply with the regulations is an additional expense if ever they wish to expand.

Some small farmers who have spoken out publicly against large new farms complain that they have been ostracized and even harassed by neighbors who want development. On the other hand, large producers, who have expanded to keep their children on the farm, claim that their critics are motivated by envy of their success. Some large producers also have problems with city people who have moved to the country but are insensitive to the imperatives of modern farm operations.

The number of farms has declined as their size has increased, and the decline started long before anyone ever thought of large-scale livestock production. The number of farms in the United States dropped from 6.8 million in 1935, the peak year, to only 1.9 million in 1997. The farm population has declined in tandem with the decline in number of farms, and many rural areas no longer have enough people to support their churches, schools, hospitals, and other institutions. Many people think that the decline in the farm population has hurt small towns, but these people fail to understand that Henry Ford killed Main Street, which has been dying a slow and lingering death ever since he started selling his Model T.

Automobiles enabled farm people to travel farther to buy the goods they once had bought in the small town, and the retailing function has been steadily working up the urban hierarchy to larger places and out to the edges of most places. At the same time, the manufacturing function has been trickling down the urban hierarchy, and the small towns that originated as agricultural service centers have now become tiny cogs in the national manufacturing network. You have to look hard to find the new small-town "factories," because most are in recycled older buildings, such as old schoolhouses that were built solidly enough to keep the kids from trashing them.

Some, but far from all, of the new factories have been built to process agricultural commodities that are produced on the large new livestock farms, and some of the criticism of large farms seems tinged with xenophobia, because many of the new processing plants employ large numbers of dark-skinned workers whose first language is not English. At first the plants employ young single men, who get into and make more trouble than married men, and tension seems to simmer down a bit when more married men are employed. Some critics also complain that the new plants have foreign owners, and their profits leave not only the community but the country.

Large Organizations

Most of us distrust large organizations, even or perhaps particularly those we know best because they employ us, whether land-grant universities, government agencies, or corporations. This distrust, always latent, was intensified by the Vietnam War and has been festering ever since. That war ruptured the fabric of American society, turned us into a nation of cynics, and legitimized disrespect for duly constituted authority. Our political and military leaders lied to us about the war. The tobacco companies lied to us about the dangers of smoking. The FBI and the CIA seem willing to lie to us about anything, and the list goes on and on. Who can anyone trust any more?

Our distrust of large organizations is aggravated by their bureaucracies, which seem specifically designed to frustrate us. Many individual bureaucrats are admirable human beings, but on the job the organization seems to endow them with an infuriating spinelessness that is exceeded only by their bumbling incompetence. It is easier for them to say no than to try to help us. They can always blame company or agency policy when they don't want to do anything, and if they say no or do nothing, they can always blame someone else if anything goes wrong.

Large organizations have trapped us in a dehumanized world. They have deprived us of our individual identity and reduced us to mere strings of numbers:

Social Security, credit card, PIN, password, e-mail address. "If you are calling from a touch-tone phone, press 1." If you are foolhardy enough to press 1, you are challenged by an interminable string of numerical options. If perchance you finally are fortunate enough to break through to another real live human being, "I am sorry I can't help you."

Small wonder that we seethe with free-floating anger at the system, that "road rage" has become part of our commonplace vocabulary. Society as a whole has become more confrontational and less deferential, "me first" behavior has become the norm, and civility, tolerance, graciousness, and good manners seem to have fallen by the wayside. We vent part of our anger at the large organizations we distrust.

Some critics of large-scale animal agriculture do not trust large land-grant universities, which they accuse of having extremely narrow vision. The critics claim that university programs and research are heavily biased toward large-scale producers, and that they are in thrall to the corporations and producer associations that fund their research. Critics say that the land-grant universities will do nothing that might jeopardize their funding, and they are hostile to alternative modes of production and the whole concept of sustainable agriculture.

Government agencies are always an easy target for critics, because their activities must be so transparent to the public. Critics claim that the rapid growth of large-scale animal agriculture has overwhelmed many of the state and federal agencies that should be policing it. They have inadequate staff to inspect and monitor feedlots, and often do nothing until they receive complaints from neighbors, who may be reluctant to complain for fear of retribution.

Producers are equally critical of regulatory agencies. They have to deal with too many, whose authorities may overlap or even conflict, and the process of requesting permits for new or enlarged feedlots takes so long that it engenders distrust in the competence of the agency. Everyone, producers and complainants alike, complains that the agencies are unresponsive, failing to return phone calls or answer letters, and many people complain that the agencies ignore them and are not interested in their concerns.

Everyone distrusts corporations. Some of this distrust stems from anticapitalist ideology, and some of it is a reaction against the impersonal, coldblooded, cutthroat, competitive corporate culture. All companies try to take the risk out of capitalism by crushing their competitors and creating a monopoly for themselves, but some corporate climbers seem to enjoy the power of crushing others just for the fun of it. "Destroy the other" might be an appropriate military strategy, but it corrodes personal relationships in a civilized society.

In their early days the entrepreneurs of large-scale animal agriculture had friendly personal relations with their individual producers, but a corporate culture takes over the business as it grows larger, and it alienates their producers. The corporation doesn't care. Many people are alienated by the arrogance of corporate executives who work in ostentatious headquarters buildings and pay obscene salaries to themselves but minimum wage to their workers. People are also alienated by the take-it-or-leave-it corporate attitude that limits our choices to the products that the corporation can sell to the greatest number of people.

Small livestock producers complain that corporate processors have reduced their access to markets with fair prices. The processor prefers to deal with a few large producers who can deliver a steady supply of standard animals, and it contracts with such producers for a guaranteed price. The marketing function of price discovery is compromised when more and more animals are sold under private contract, and no one knows what the true market price should be. In the year 2000, for example, less than 20 percent of all hogs were sold on the open market, and producers without contracts could not be sure that they were receiving a fair price for their animals.

Animal Welfare

Some critics say that large-scale animal agriculture can be detrimental to the welfare of farm animals, as they define it. Most people would say that farm animals should not be neglected, abused, or otherwise maltreated. Most producers would agree emphatically, because their livelihood depends on their animals, and they cannot afford to employ cruel, untrained, or impatient workers who might harm them. Producers realize that some normal and necessary procedures, such as vaccination, beak-trimming, dehorning, tail-docking, castration, and branding, may be painful, but people do not like to be vaccinated either, and producers believe their animals are happy and healthy because they are productive.

Advocates of animal welfare do not agree. They argue that performance alone is not an adequate indicator of welfare, because high levels of production may actually create poor welfare conditions, and production systems designed without regard for the basic behavioral and psychological needs of animals may distress them mentally. They argue that farm animals should be free from thirst, hunger, malnutrition, disease, injury, pain, fear, discomfort, and boredom, and they should be able to behave normally and naturally. How does one know when a pig is bored? How does one identify normal and natural behavior?

Advocates of animal welfare believe they can determine the psychological state and mental well-being of farm animals by studying their neuroendocrine changes and by carefully observing their behavior in seminatural parks that are as close as possible to natural conditions. The advocates believe that animals are happiest and can behave most naturally in an environment most nearly similar to that of their wild ancestors, although human animals seem to be happier living in houses than they would be living in caves.

The theory of animal welfare is that farm animals suffer mentally when they are not allowed to do things their wild ancestors did. In the wild, for example, sows build nests in which to farrow, and chickens flop around in the dust to get rid of parasites and excess lipids in their feathers; the theory says they become frustrated when they are confined and cannot engage in these activities. This theory also has a tinge of anthropomorphic transference, because people cringe at the thought of living in a crate like a sow or in a small wire cage with four other individuals, and they assume that the animals must feel the same way.

Modern egg-producing farms with hundreds of thousands of laying hens in batteries of cages have been an especially tempting target for criticism by animal welfare advocates. The hens cannot dust-bathe and they do not have enough room to flap their wings. The poorly chosen name of "forced" molting implies that the producer is doing something unnatural to the hens, and animal welfare activists have stampeded McDonald's into announcing that it will buy no more eggs from producers who force-molt their hens.

When their laying days are done, the spent hens also may suffer, because they have little value, and the producer is interested only in getting them out of the house as fast as possible so he can replace them. The handlers may hurt them when they are pulling so many out of the cages as rapidly as they can. The hens may also suffer from heat or cold en route to the processing plant, because so few plants handle them that they may have to be hauled great distances in inclement weather.

A large literature on animal welfare has blossomed in Europe since the 1960s, and some countries, Sweden and Switzerland among them, have imposed the animal welfare model on all farmers.[6] Hog farmers, for example, may not keep sows in individual stalls or in crates, but must keep them in groups, with permanent access to straw, and in buildings where part of the floor must be solid, with separate areas for eating, lying, and dunging. This model has had little impact in the United States, where farmers are free to adopt any model they like and are quick to adopt the one they consider the best.

Many American farmers accuse animal welfare advocates of insensitivity to the imperatives of successful livestock production. Louis Long, a rancher and hog farmer on the Oklahoma Panhandle, spoke for many farmers when he said, "They are basically a bunch of people that want you to pet all your animals. They have never had to chase a cow, to try to get her back in the fence, when you really feel like taking a shotgun to her. They have never had to load a hog that didn't want to be loaded. They think you can just pat it and talk to it and it will do what you want it to do."

Animal Rights

Animal rights, like animal welfare, is an ideology. An ideology is a set of beliefs and objectives that are taken on faith. Debating them is pointless, because they cannot be proved or disproved. Either you believe them or you don't, and ideologues believe them passionately. Most ideologues are strong-minded, self-righteous, and rarely given to critical analysis of their beliefs. They may try to persuade others by philosophical argument or by confrontation. Animal rights advocates have used both strategies.

Peter Singer is probably the best-known philosopher of animal rights.[7] He believes that causing pain to any animal, whether human or nonhuman, is immoral. He says that the human species of animal oppresses, exploits, and causes pain for the nonhuman species, just as white males treated women and black people for centuries, and he uses the term "speciesism" as a parallel to "sexism" and "racism." He has found special favor with feminists.

Singer argues that the basic moral principle of equality should be extended beyond sex and race to include all species of animals, human and nonhuman alike. This principle does not assume that humans and nonhumans actually are equal, nor does it even require equal treatment. It merely requires that they be considered equally. Equal consideration can lead to different treatments and different rights for different beings.

Singer believes that the vital characteristic that gives nonhuman animals the right to equal consideration is their ability to feel pain, and he dismisses as trivial their inability to use language to tell us how they feel. Infliction of the pain animals feel is just as immoral as infliction of the pain people can describe. Singer adds that the relative suffering of different species cannot be compared, but that is not important, because the basic moral principle is that no suffering should be inflicted on any animal.

He has surprising difficulty trying to decide whether and when it is right to kill animals and people painlessly, because he can identify no agreement about the moral principles that should guide our thinking about euthanasia and abortion. He concludes that all animals have a similar right to life, but he is more interested in the moral principle of minimizing suffering and in promoting complete abstinence from meat-eating.

Singer has assembled an anthology of horror stories about the use of animals in laboratory experiments and about the treatment of animals on large farms in his attempt to make everyone so uncomfortable when they eat meat that they will all become vegetarians. He draws his line somewhere above oysters, which show no apparent signs of pain, and thus may be eaten by vegetarians, and below shrimp, which vegetarians should not eat. His apparent goal, however, is to convert us all into vegans, who refuse to eat all animal products (including eggs, milk, butter, cheese, and gelatin) and refuse to use leather, wool, and fur.

Singer's descriptions of some farm practices are such caricatures that they would be laughable if people who know no better did not take them seriously (fig. 13.1). Like many animal rights activists, he seems to feel obligated to overstate his case to get his message across. Most of us, if we stop to think about them at all, probably are kindly disposed toward farm animals, and we feel that they should not be mistreated, but concern for their rights and welfare rarely is high on our agenda, and some activists think they have to scare the wits out of us to get our attention.

They feel that the normal channels of protest and political action are not adequate to effect the changes they think are necessary, and they must create negative publicity to arouse public opinion and pressure supermarkets, fast-food chains, politicians, and government agencies. They manipulate the news media, because they know that the American news media and the American people have an apparently insatiable appetite for news of disaster, plus a short memory. Periodically our fears are inflamed by sensational accounts of the latest food scare, with a follow-up story several months later at the bottom of page 12 saying that it was only another false alarm.[8]

The extreme animal rights activists have actually undermined their cause by antisocial behavior. Some members of People for the Ethical Treatment of Animals (PETA), believing they are justified in breaking laws they consider unjust, have vandalized research laboratories, destroyed fields of experimental crops, and committed other acts of eco-terrorism to generate publicity and provoke discussion, while claiming high moral authority for their illegal activities.

The campaign for animal rights has cloaked anti-American and anticapitalist sentiments. On March 14, 2000, the *New York Times* reported on a conference at The Hague on genetically modified food. "The discussion among 300 participants in the hall was serious science—intelligent, earnest, and a bit dull. Outside, things were livelier," and of course the television cameras lingered on the protestors outside, who numbered fewer than twenty but secured maximum publicity.

"Two protestors dressed as headless chickens strutted. A gorilla wailed over

Figure 13.1. The cover of the December 5–11, 1997, issue of *Isthmus,* the alternative weekly newspaper of Madison, Wisconsin. (Used by permission of Brian Reeves, Slop Mountain College.)

his pox-speckled bananas, and a mutant apple in a radiation suit passed out leaflets. The demonstrators played a tape of bubbling cauldrons and vile belches, and the perfect fillip was the stench that hung in the air—which was not even their idea, just dumb luck that a sewer crew was working nearby."

Inside the hall Benedikt Haerlin of the Greenpeace movement said that many scientists are liars who are at the beck and call of global agribusiness corporations, and Pierre Lellouche, a French politician, said, "The general sense here is that Americans eat garbage food, that they're fat, and they don't know how to eat properly. The strawberries and asparagus in America look beautiful, but they have no flavor." An official from Africa quietly reminded the group that "organic farming is practiced by 800 million poor people in the world because they can't afford pesticides and fertilizer—and it's not working."

In Europe, where standards of sanitation, hygiene, and food safety regulation are more casual than in the United States, the debate about genetically modified food is as much about passion and perception and politics as it is about science. By sheer bad timing, the first shipments of genetically modified soybeans arrived in Europe just when people were terrified of mad cow disease, and many jumped to the totally erroneous conclusion that the two were somehow related. Europe has also suffered recurrent outbreaks of foot and mouth disease, which have been rare in the United States.

Bruce Friedrich, the vegan campaign coordinator for PETA, traveled to the United Kingdom during the outbreak of foot and mouth disease in May 2001 and said it would be a positive thing if someone would infect animals with the disease at the World Dairy Exposition scheduled for Madison, Wisconsin, in October. "Introducing the disease into the United States is not something PETA would do intentionally," he said, "but it's something we would welcome." One must wonder how inflicting a painful disease on animals would enhance their rights and welfare.

Few are as extreme as Friedrich, but many people are seriously concerned about the transformation of American agriculture. Their concern may lead to conflict and confrontation with farmers, who feel that some critics do not understand normal farm practices. Many farmers also believe that technological innovation is forcing the transformation to larger farms, and they are afraid of missing the boat if they fail to adopt the new technology, although they realize that any technological innovation must be policed with great care to ensure that it does not have unintended and undesirable consequences.

14
The Rim

The third segment of the new tripartite macrogeography of American agriculture is the outer rim of the nation, where crops became increasingly important in the second half of the twentieth century (fig. 1.2). In the Northeast farmers have been moving toward greater emphasis on the production of highly specialized crops for direct sale to the residents of nearby cities. In the Southeast cotton has enjoyed an impressive comeback. In California and the West large-scale vegetable farmers are accounting for an ever-increasing share of our total agricultural production. In all of these areas the scale of crop production on modern farms is vastly greater than it was on their predecessors of half a century ago.

The Nursery and Greenhouse Belt

Megalopolis is the densely built-up area that extends from Washington 400 miles northeast to Boston. This great conurbation has spawned the nation's principal nursery and greenhouse belt (fig. 14.1). The *Census of Agriculture* says that more than 44 percent of all farm income in this belt in 1997 was derived from the sale of nursery and greenhouse crops, mushrooms, sod, and other crops that the producers sold directly to their customers (fig. 14.2). This belt produced 11 percent of the total national value of these products, although it produced only a shade more than 1 percent of all our farm sales.

All of our major cities have nurseries and greenhouses on their rural-urban fringes, where the built-up area of the city feathers into the adjacent countryside, and of course our largest "city" has our most highly developed nursery and greenhouse belt. The rural-urban fringe is an irregular, discontinuous zone of dissonance where the least intensive urban uses of land are steadily displacing the most intensive rural uses. Sparkling new subdivisions sprout next to fields of

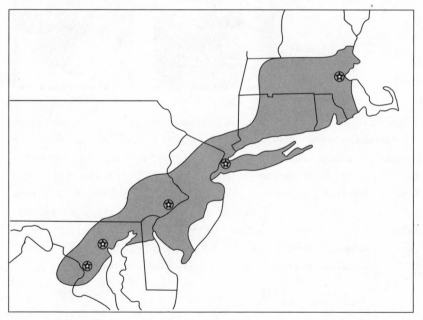

Figure 14.1. The nation's nursery and greenhouse belt has developed in the rural-urban fringe of Megalopolis. (Based on data in *1997 Census of Agriculture,* vol. 2, pt. 1 [Washington, D.C.: U.S. Department of Agriculture, National Agricultural Statistics Service, 1999].)

sweet corn and vegetables. Former dairy barns have been converted into riding stables and boarding kennels. Glasshouses perch in parlous proximity to driving ranges, golf courses, and country day schools. Gleaming new single-story warehouses, factories, and office buildings sit next to unkempt vacant lots with "For Sale" signs amidst their weeds and brush.

This mélange of land uses is not as confused as it may first appear, however, because certain rural land uses cling to the built-up edge of the city. Most cities are encircled by discontinuous concentric rings of nurseries and greenhouses at the urban edge and of vegetable farms a bit farther out. These rings retain their geographic relation to the city as its built-up area expands, like the bow wave of a ship speeding through the water.[1]

Nursery and greenhouse farmers can afford to pay higher prices for land than other farmers because they produce our most valuable crops. To get a sense of the relative value of different crops, I divided the total national value of sales of each crop by the total national acreage of that crop to estimate its average gross value per acre (table 14.1). These crude estimates are gross values, not net values, and the actual return per acre varies with the cost of production, but they do indicate that

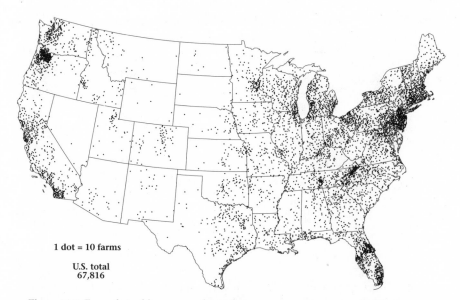

1 dot = 10 farms

U.S. total
67,816

Figure 14.2. Farms that sold nursery and greenhouse crops, mushrooms, sod, and cut Christmas trees, 1997. (Source: *1997 Census of Agriculture,* vol. 2, pt. 1 [Washington, D.C.: U.S. Department of Agriculture, National Agricultural Statistics Service, 1999].)

one acre of nursery and greenhouse crops produces as much value as 2.5 acres of tobacco, 3.7 acres of vegetables, 33 acres of field corn, or 38 acres of soybeans.

When the owner of a nursery or greenhouse sells the land to an urban developer, as is inevitable, the owner uses the windfall profit from the sale to move the business to a new and larger site a bit farther out, but still as close to the city as possible, because the success of the business depends on being near its customers. This transfer of urban capital to rural owners drives up the price of farmland, and the nursery and greenhouse areas on the rural-urban fringes of our cities have some of our highest-priced agricultural land. Some people confuse price with quality, but the high price of this land is merely a product of its geographic location at the urban edge; it is quite unrelated to the inherent quality of its soil.

The new site of the nursery or greenhouse often is a former vegetable farm, because vegetable farms form the next ring outside the nursery and greenhouse belt. In years gone by the vegetable farmer also used the windfall profits to buy a new farm a bit farther out, but today vegetable farmers are a dying breed in Megalopolis, because even the largest are too small to compete with large-scale pro-

Table 14.1
Average gross value produced by one acre of
selected crops, United States, 1997

Nursery and greenhouse	$8,864
Tobacco	3,489
Fruits and berries	2,454
Vegetables	2,374
Cotton	451
Corn	271
Soybeans	236
Sorghum	135
Wheat	122
Hay	77
Oats	45

Source of data: *1997 Census of Agriculture,* vol. 1, pt. 51 (Washington, D.C.: U.S. Department of Agriculture, National Agricultural Statistics Service, 1999), 193, 202, 436, 437, 442, 445, 459, 462, 488, 507.

ducers in other parts of the country who can deliver larger lots of standard quality over a much longer growing season.

The supermarket chains would rather deal with a few large producers than with many small ones, and the remaining vegetable growers of Megalopolis have had to scratch to find markets for their crops. Some have set up their own roadside stands, some sell at the weekly farmers' markets in the city, and some have developed personal relationships with produce managers and restaurant owners who are willing to pay premium prices for high-quality local products.

Cotton

The resurgence of cotton as a major crop in the old cotton belt of the plainsland South is a truly remarkable story.[2] In 1929, the peak year, 1.7 million farmers in the South grew 42.6 million acres of cotton and produced 12.1 million bales (fig. 14.3). By 1982 the erstwhile Cotton Belt had shrunk to a mere shadow of its former self, and only 27,660 farmers grew 7.1 million acres of cotton and produced 7.1 million bales. In 1997 24,860 farmers grew cotton on 11.8 million acres and produced 12.7 million bales, more than 1.7 million farmers had produced in 1929.

In 1929 cotton was king of the South. Everyone grew the crop, with a mule or two and endless hours of backbreaking stoop labor under the broiling sun. Few families could handle more than fifteen to twenty acres, and even the youngest children had to pitch in and help. By 1982 cotton had been reduced to the status of just another specialty crop. In the eastern South it had become little more than a curiosity outside a few small vestigial islands of production, and many children in this area had never even seen a boll of cotton.[3]

By 1982 cotton had virtually disappeared except in the Delta area of Mississippi-Louisiana-Arkansas and on the High Plains of west Texas. By 1997 production had increased in these two areas, and the crop had made an astonishing comeback on the inner coastal plain of Georgia and the Carolinas, where farmers grew 500 to 600 acres of the crop with the latest farm machinery and state-of-the-art center-pivot sprinkler irrigation systems.

Some people assume that better prices triggered the resurgence of cotton in the South. An aggressive promotional campaign by the cotton industry certainly helped to increase demand, and world production slumped in the 1970s. An adequate price obviously was necessary and a good price was an additional incentive,

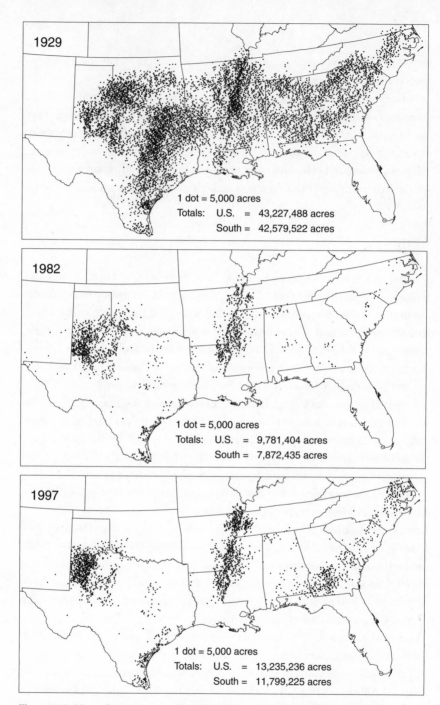

1929

1 dot = 5,000 acres
Totals: U.S. = 43,227,488 acres
South = 42,579,522 acres

1982

1 dot = 5,000 acres
Totals: U.S. = 9,781,404 acres
South = 7,872,435 acres

1997

1 dot = 5,000 acres
Totals: U.S. = 13,235,236 acres
South = 11,799,225 acres

Figure 14.3. Maps of cotton acreage in 1929, 1982, and 1997 show the demise and
metempsychosis of King Cotton. (Used by permission of *Southeastern Geographer*.)

but the price alone would not have been good enough if the boll weevil eradication program had not reduced the cost of production so dramatically. In fact, the price of cotton was favorable from 1975 on, but its acreage did not start to surge until boll weevils had been eradicated in northeastern North Carolina in 1987.

The cooperative federal-state-farmer program to eradicate boll weevils was started in northeastern North Carolina in no small measure because of the initiative and leadership of Marshall Grant, an early chairman of the Southeastern Boll Weevil Eradication Foundation, whose family has farmed near Gaston, north of Roanoke Rapids, since the 1780s. This area is peanut country, and cotton was never a major crop. It was able to hang on because farmers needed a crop to break their continuous cultivation of peanuts, and no other crop worked as well as cotton.

For years entomologists have known how to eradicate boll weevils, and they have demonstrated their ability in selected test areas, but the voracious insects have immediately swarmed back into the test areas from all sides as soon as the program has ended. Marshall Grant is the one who said, "Let's start at the corner, in northeastern North Carolina. There's nothing to the east of us but the ocean, there's nothing to the west of us but the mountains, and there's nothing north of us but Virginia. Let's eradicate the boll weevils in northeastern North Carolina and then work southwestward."

His suggestion was a brilliant success. Three years of precisely timed spraying completely eliminated boll weevils from the area, and careful monitoring has detected no signs of subsequent reinfestation. The monitoring program has green metal traps mounted on sticks at the edges of cotton fields. These traps are baited with pheromones, the sex odors of boll weevils, which attract them irresistibly, but only one or two a year have been trapped. They have sneaked into the area on used cotton machinery that was not properly cleaned before it was brought here from other areas.

The eradication program was gradually extended to the southwest, and it is anticipated that the boll weevil will have been eradicated from the entire South by the year 2004. Marshall said that the elimination of boll weevils has cut his cost of growing cotton by at least $50 an acre, because he has to spray only twice a year for budworms rather than ten to twelve times a year for boll weevils, and his yields have increased by 25 to 72 pounds per acre.

Other farmers told me that the eradication of boll weevils has cut their costs as much as $200 an acre, and they plant genetically modified seeds that reduce the threat of budworms and help them to control grass and weeds. The cessation of spraying for boll weevils has also encouraged the growth of beneficial insects that help control other pests.

Cotton has always been a good crop for the subtropical South, where the total annual precipitation is adequate but much of the rain comes in summer thundershowers, which are notoriously erratic and spotty, and individual fields can suffer periods of drought that last from a few weeks to the entire summer. Unlike other field crops, the cotton plant is a perennial that sheds its squares (immature fruit) when it is stressed by drought, and it produces new squares if and when the rains resume.

Cotton farmers have learned that they can increase their yields by irrigating the crop during the inevitable dry spells, and center-pivot sprinkler irrigation systems have become a common sight in cotton fields even in areas that have abundant annual rainfall. The use of such systems testifies that cotton farmers have been eager to adopt the latest and best agricultural technology, and they have had to enlarge their scale of operation accordingly.

For example, farmers have to grow at least 250 acres of cotton to justify the expense of a mechanical cotton picker, but machines now enable them to handle 500 to 700 acres of cotton with only a hired hand or two, greatly reducing their dependence on an often unreliable labor supply.

Farmers who decide to start growing cotton have had to "plant out of program to build a base." The "base" is the acreage for which the farmer is guaranteed a price by the government price-support program. It is the average acreage of cotton the farmer has grown in the three preceding years, so the first three years are unusually risky for a farmer who decides to start growing cotton without a base.

The spectacular increase in cotton production in the South has severely taxed existing gin capacity. Groups of farmers have built cooperative gins, which cost $500,000 or so, but the shortage of gin capacity has forced farmers in many areas to shift from wagons to modules. Traditionally cotton farmers have unloaded their pickers into cotton wagons with wire-mesh sides and hauled the wagons to the nearest gin, but the gins simply cannot handle the huge new volume, and the loaded wagons have had to wait in long lines at the gin when the farmer desperately needed them back in the field.

Cotton farmers have turned to hydraulic module builders to ease the gin problem. A module builder is a large metal trough that is filled with cotton. It can compact 6,500 to 12,000 pounds of cotton into a long, rectangular, boxlike module that looks like a stranded semitrailer without wheels. The farmer covers each module with plastic and leaves it in the field until a truck can haul them all to a gin that is ready for them. These large white plastic-capped modules sitting in the fields are a vivid manifestation of the resurgence of cotton in the South.

Vegetables

Vegetable production in the United States has migrated from the backyard garden to the urban edge to ever more distant producing areas, pushed outward by the expanding city, pulled by the necessity of enlarging scale of production, and facilitated by improvements in transportation. Before World War II many people ate only the fresh vegetables they had grown themselves, and most commercial vegetables were grown only in the warm season, close to the cities where they were consumed.

According to the *Census of Agriculture,* 10 percent of all the market-garden products sold in the entire United States in 1860 were produced within the current limits of New York City. The growth of the city pushed production eastward on Long Island, then south into New Jersey, Delaware, and Maryland. The sandy soils near the coast warm earlier in the spring, and hitting the market even a week ahead of competitors was a tremendous advantage.

In 1900 nearly one-third of all the market vegetables grown in the entire United States were produced in the belt between Long Island Sound and the mouth of Chesapeake Bay (fig. 14.4), and as late as 1950 significant quantities of vegetables were grown for sale only near large cities, in pockets scattered through the East and South, and in the irrigated oases of the West (fig. 14.5), but by 1997 the East Coast belt produced less than 5 percent of our vegetables, and production had moved to new areas (fig. 14.6).

By 1950 improved transportation had divorced vegetable growers from the necessity of proximity to urban consumers, and Florida had become a major area of commercial vegetable production, especially winter vegetables. The leading winter vegetable area in Florida was the Everglades Agricultural Area, south of Lake Okeechobee, which at most has only one or two brief freezes each year, and many years none at all.

The 750,000-acre Everglades Agricultural Area, which is slightly smaller than the state of Rhode Island, was a vast marsh of gently waving sawgrass, six to ten feet tall, before it was diked and ditched and drained. The remains of the sawgrass plants gradually accumulated when they died and fell into the water, because the normal microorganisms of decay require oxygen, and they cannot work on

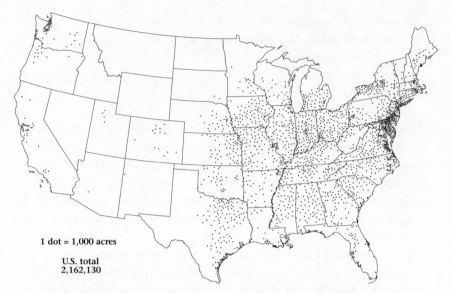

Figure 14.4. Acres planted in vegetables, 1899. Most vegetables were grown during the warm season near the places where they were consumed. (Source: *1950 Census of Agriculture,* vol. 5, pt. 6 [Washington, D.C.: U.S. Department of Commerce, Bureau of the Census, 1952], 93.)

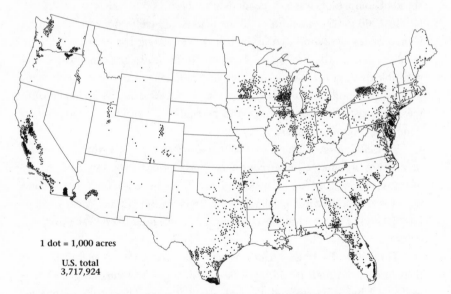

Figure 14.5. Acres of vegetables harvested for sale, 1949. By 1949 the migration of vegetable production was well under way. (Source: *1950 Census of Agriculture,* vol. 5, pt. 6 [Washington, D.C.: U.S. Department of Commerce, Bureau of the Census, 1952], 29, 93.)

vegetative matter that is under water. The residues of partly decomposed sawgrass form one of the world's largest deposits of organic soils, peat and muck. This deep, rich, black, spongy soil is almost ideal for growing vegetables and sugarcane.

In 1949 Ray Roth came to the Everglades from Cleveland, where his father had a truck farm. Ray leased ten acres and grew endive. He gradually expanded by leasing more land, and he bought land when it was available and he could afford it. By 1983 he owned 3,060 acres. He grew sugarcane on part of his land and rotated three years of cane with three years of vegetables to control diseases, but he was a vegetable grower. "I do grow some cane for disease control," he told me, "but there's more profit in vegetables. This is a major producing area, and we control the amounts produced, so a disaster here is reflected in good prices. If California controls the supply, we can have a bad year and also get a poor price."

In summer, when it was too hot to grow vegetables, Ray had flooded his bare fields to keep bacteria from attacking the dry muck, but in 1980 he realized that he could grow a commercial crop of rice in the flooded fields. His son, Rick, took over the operation in 1986. Rick downscaled vegetables, increased sugarcane,

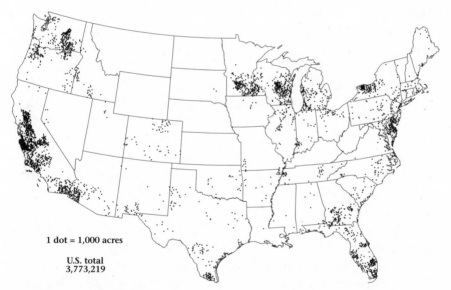

1 dot = 1,000 acres

U.S. total
3,773,219

Figure 14.6. Acres of vegetables harvested for sale, 1997. By 1997 most vegetable production had migrated to California, but Minnesota, Wisconsin, and New York produced a goodly share of the nation's green peas, snap beans, and sweet corn. (Source: *1997 Census of Agriculture,* vol. 2, pt. 1 [Washington, D.C.: U.S. Department of Agriculture, National Agricultural Statistics Service, 1999].)

and started growing sod for new lawns and new golf courses in Palm Beach and in other rapidly growing urban areas only thirty miles away on the east coast. He harvests three crops of sod every two years.

"Our two most profitable crops are sugarcane and sod," Rick said, when I visited him in 1997, "because they have price stability year in and year out. Vegetables have wild swings in prices because of their perishability, but sod has stable prices and no shelf life problem. With sugarcane and sod you can do projections and budgets and all that sort of thing and come pretty close to knowing how much money you are going to make this year, but vegetables will drive a bookkeeper crazy."

Rick said he almost got out of vegetables completely because his margins were getting thinner and thinner. "We were down to 20 percent of our original volume," he said, "but we have come back up. I have people employed with me for twenty or thirty years, highly skilled, very specialized in what they do, but with almost no marketable skills in another vocation. That's one of the reasons we stay in the vegetable business.

"It's tough," he said. "Our cooperative packinghouse went out of business. I use an independent broker who used to sell for the packinghouse, but our customer base has shrunk. It's hard to compete with the big vegetable corporations that have their own packinghouses and distribution systems, their own networks of salespeople and connections. The margins are going to keep getting thinner, and the cost of production is going to continue to go up."

In 1997 Rick had 1,000 acres of leafy vegetables, "all kinds of lettuce, salad vegetables, all produced in similar fashion," 1,500 acres of radishes, 700 acres of sod, 2,300 acres of sugarcane, and 800 acres of rice. He had bought an additional 850 acres, but 400 acres of his land had been condemned by the water management district, which was going to turn it into an artificial wetland to filter runoff water. "We have much tighter water control in this area," Rick said, "which makes it even riskier to grow vegetables."

The control of water is only one of many highly emotional environmental and political controversies in the Everglades. The rapidly growing cities on the east coast demand a reliable supply. Farmers in the agricultural area have replumbed the seasonal pattern of flow, and the change has seriously harmed animal and plant life to the south, in one of the world's most endangered ecosystems, including the Everglades National Park, at the southern tip of the state. The park could be flooded and turned into a saltwater marsh if global warming raises sea levels.

In November 2000 Congress approved a twenty-year, $7.8 billion plan to "restore" the Everglades, but parts of the agricultural area may be abandoned before the plan can be completed, because the soil is steadily subliming.[4] Aerobic bacteria begin to attack the muck as soon as it is exposed to air, and in some areas four or five feet have already vanished, with only three or four feet remaining above the limestone bedrock.

Sugarcane is the principal crop in the agricultural area, and two huge corporations produce 80 percent of it, more than 300,000 acres. They do not hesitate to play hardball politics, and they contributed a total of $2.3 million to both political parties in the last three presidential elections.[5]

The vegetable business in the Everglades is sort of lost in the shuffle, and it is fading away. Some farmers blame government regulations and restrictions, but the basic problem is that they are too small to compete with large-scale growers in the West. The vegetable farm that seemed large in 1980 was undersized and noncompetitive by 2000, and American vegetable production is migrating once again to a new area.

The Salinas Valley

The Salinas Valley of California, about seventy-five miles south of San Francisco, is the world's leading vegetable-producing area. According to the *Census of Agriculture,* in 1997 growers in the valley harvested more than 250,000 acres of vegetables, one of every fourteen acres harvested in the entire country. Sere brown ridges of the Coast Ranges rise steeply on either side of the valley, which is six to ten miles wide and fifty miles long. The flat valley floor is intensely cultivated, but vast stretches look deserted, because farmsteads and other settlements are on the less valuable land on the lower slopes of the hills.

In the early days most Salinas vegetable growers had small, intensively cultivated farms of twenty to fifty acres, and they sold their crops as best they could. Eventually groups of growers formed co-ops and hired professional managers to pack and ship their crops, while entrepreneurs formed packing/shipping companies and bought crops from individual growers. Crops were hauled from the field to the packinghouse, packed in wooden boxes, covered with top ice, and shipped by rail to terminal markets, where grocers came to buy them. After 1950 cardboard boxes began to replace wooden boxes, and they were vacuum-cooled rather than iced.

Since 1998 nearly everything has been packed in the field rather than in the shed. John D'Arrigo, president of the D'Arrigo Brothers Company, said, "With the advent of new mobile equipment, new transportation methods, all-terrain and all-weather vehicles, you really set up mobile packing sheds out in the field. You only bring in the product that has already been packed, so you're not hauling culls around. You leave all the refuse and the cutting out there, and you plow all that back into the ground, so it's good for the ground."

A bewildering variety of arrangements has evolved as growers and shippers have become larger and more specialized in growing, harvesting, packing, shipping, and selling specific crops. The arrangements vary from crop to crop, from grower to grower, from shipper to shipper. The list of crops seems interminable: it includes everything you can find in the produce area of your supermarket, plus quite a few you have never even heard of. A few independent growers may grow a single crop for a single shipper, but most grow several different crops for several different shippers.

Some shippers own no cropland, but others want to own as much as possible. Most Salinas shippers also have plants in the San Joaquin Valley and in irrigated areas in the desert near Yuma, where the growing seasons are different. They have different financial arrangements with different growers, and they ship to all the major supermarket chains and independent warehouses in the United States and Canada. I asked Gary Tanimura of Tanimura and Antle how close to the Everglades they could compete, and he said, "Publix, the grocery chain in Florida, is one of our good customers."

Salinas shippers also have developed a substantial export business in the Orient, where they compete with Australia, and they are starting a European business from Yuma. They ship mostly by cargo container, but they have air-freighted when Japan ran short after a series of typhoons or when Europe was suffering severe cold weather, and they air-freight some high-value products fairly consistently.

Shipment of fresh vegetables in the United States is almost 100 percent by truck. John D'Arrigo said, "A fast truck and two drivers can be in New York the fourth morning, while a rail car with a perishable commodity is still sitting on a siding somewhere in Nebraska. Half the time they lose the darned thing, and even if they do manage to get it to New York, I am looking at the tenth morning or the twelfth morning. Today's customer isn't like yesterday's. You had better deliver fresh products, properly cooled, properly iced, in good condition, or you're out of business."

Growers and shippers alike are concerned about the consolidation of supermarket chains, which reduces the number of customers to whom they can sell, and raises the specter of a monopoly that might dictate prices. The large chains are already forcing shippers to consolidate, because they want to load as much as possible at a single place, and are reluctant to deal with small shippers. "Every time a truck stops it costs you fifty bucks," they say, "so we want to make as few stops as possible."

Smaller shippers also are threatened by the shift to value-added, ready-to-eat, microwaveable, fresh-cut vegetables in convenient plastic bags, which began in the early 1990s. Only four or five of the twenty-five to thirty shippers in Salinas have been able to shift from boxed commodity to value-added, because the capital costs are great, but one-quarter of the vegetable business in 1998 was value-added. Many people seem willing to pay a little extra for the convenience, and some of the smaller shippers who do not market ready-to-eat may have to close.

Three operations suggest the variety in the Salinas Valley in 1998. Bill Ramsey, president of the Mann Packing Company, said, "I am strictly a broccoli shipper. I schedule 11,898 acres of broccoli a year. I have thirty-five growers here, in the San Joaquin Valley, and near Yuma. They plant 230 acres of broccoli a week, and I pack and market it. They harvest their crop under my direction, in terms of how I have to market it. Sometimes you have to disk perfectly good, beautiful fields of broccoli, just plow it right back into the ground, because you know you can't sell it for what it would cost to put it in the box."

The Tanimura and Antle Company both grows and ships. When Gary's father and uncle were released from the internment camp after World War II, they worked as laborers until they had saved enough money to buy a twenty-acre ranch and start growing head lettuce. They saved their pennies and invested in land. Every two or three years they bought another ranch, which turned out to be a good idea. They bought land in the 1960s for $3,000 an acre, which seemed like a lot at the time, but some of the last sales of land in the area have been close to $35,000 an acre.

In 1982, when they had around 1,000 acres, a friend named Bob Antle, with whom they had been shipping, invited them to join him in forming a company that has become one of the largest independent growers and shippers in the United States, with gross sales of around $400 million. They double-crop 9,000 acres near Salinas, have an 8,000-acre satellite farm company in the San Joaquin Valley near Coalinga, and split costs and returns with eighteen growers near Salinas, seventeen near Yuma, and five near Oxnard.

"We hit some pretty good markets and kept growing in the 1980s," Gary said, "but we almost missed the boat getting into the prepackaged salad business, and we got into it when the window was just about closing. We are now roughly number three in that area. A large company like ours had the financial resources to get into it. A lot of guys would like to get into it now, but it's probably already too late, because the brand names are pretty well established. Right now ready-to-eat and box are in a tug-of-war."

John D'Arrigo said that the D'Arrigo Brothers Company is a shipper, with gross annual sales of $150 to $160 million in 2002, but its strength is owning 70 percent of its own ground. Andrew D'Arrigo migrated from Italy to the United States in 1907, and Stephen joined him in 1911. In 1923 they formed a company in Boston to sell fresh grapes to first-generation Europeans who wanted to make their own wine, and Stephen moved to California to buy grapes.

Stephen saw Italians in San Jose growing broccoli, and he thought Andrew might be able to sell it on the East Coast, so in 1924 he started shipping him boxes of iced broccoli by rail. They did so well that in 1925 Stephen bought 28 acres of land in San Jose, and in 1927 he planted 100 acres of broccoli near Salinas. He plowed all of his profits into acquiring more ground, buying it in good years and borrowing against it when times were lean.

Stephen continued to grow broccoli, and he expanded into other crops and other areas. He bought 500 acres near Salinas in 1951, shortly before his prema-ture death, and his son, Andy, took over the company at the age of 27. Andy kept adding, and by 1960 he was growing a cornucopia of crops (including peas, toma-toes, cactus pears, celery, table grapes, sweet anise, broccoli rabe, asparagus, soft fruits, and lettuce) in seven areas spread over 700 miles in California and Arizona.

In 1991 Andy turned the business over to his son, John. "Seems like all the fun's gone out of it now," Andy said. "I didn't have all the regulation, all the con-straints, all the laws and the pesticides and all that sort of thing. The customers have turned into big corporate customers. You used to make a million-dollar deal with some buyer back east with a simple handshake, but now it's all lawyers and contracts and paperwork. It was hard work back then, but it was easier."

John said, "I have consolidated and expanded. I've sold all the tree fruits and the grapes, because we're a grower and shipper of fresh vegetables. I had to be very sensitive, because my dad has strong emotional ties to different pieces of ground, but eventually he reluctantly bought off on it. Back then you could afford to do stuff like that, but we have consolidated on bigger plots of land in the same area for economies of scale."

John expanded from 24,000 crop acres in 1998 to 30,000 in 2002. His goal was 2.5 crops per acre per year (fig. 14.7). In 1997 he was at 2.3. "We have learned that the Salinas Valley is full of microclimates," he said, "and we need to have ranches on both sides of the valley, all the way down, so we get diversification of temperature and risk. The wine industry from Napa is coming into the foothills in the southern end of the valley, and they have jacked up prices."[6]

"Getting ground is tricky," John said, "because this is a very risky business. We had a bad contraction a few years ago. Seven families just like us went out of business, and we barely made it through. We had to sell a few ranches, and then we tried to make some money to pick up some of that available ground. That's when you have to do it. Another guy's disaster can be your boom if you've got the nuts in the closet. If you want to pick up more ground, you've got to do it when your neighbor, your friend, the guy you grew up with, is having really tough times and has to sell off a piece of his operation.

"For us getting ground is also relationship-related," he added. "We have some long-term leases with longtime Salinas Valley families that aren't farming anymore. We even have one landlady that is a descendant of the Spanish land grants. They know we farm responsibly and keep their ground clean, and they want us to have it when they pass on. You can't go out actively and try to get it, because that would be sending the wrong message, but eventually we hope to get it."

John likes to farm big blocks of ground. "We prefer to have thousand-acre ranches all in one spot," he said, "with these big D-75 Challenger tractors working it on a big scale. I made a deal with Caterpillar, bought four D-75s all at once, saved tremendous money. I also cut down from six carton suppliers to two. I want

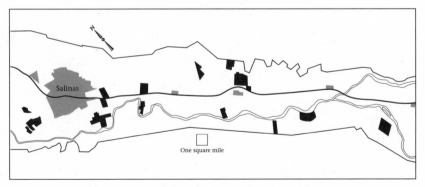

Figure 14.7. In 1998 the D'Arrigo Brothers farms extended more than 35 miles along the Salinas Valley of California. (Based on data provided by John D'Arrigo; used by permission.)

to deal with the guys that own the trees. I was afraid to go with only one, in case he has a forest fire. I tell them long in advance what I'll need and when, so they can schedule their plants for maximum efficiency and save money for both of us."

John told me that he has about 135 management people and 1,200 to 1,500 field workers. "The key to our growth and our success is our people," he said. "We're a family corporation, 100 percent owned by the family, and we have tried to focus on having all of our employees part of the family. We try to take care of our people, keep them motivated, keep them happy, take care of them. We have people that have been here their entire lives. In the last ten, fifteen years we've brought in a new crop of young people with new ideas. I have seen the value of keeping a constant influx of new people coming in, and it has really been one of the keys to our success."

John D'Arrigo harvested 55,000 acres of vegetables in 1997. The *1997 Census of Agriculture* says that the total area of vegetables harvested in the entire state of New Jersey in that year was only 64,000 acres. This remarkable contrast reflects the shift to large-scale, highly specialized crop production in the nation's rimland. Different areas specialize in different crops—nursery and greenhouse in Megalopolis, cotton in the South, vegetables in California—but all have greatly increased their scale of production. The migration of vegetable production in the United States is an especially nice example of the push of urban encroachment and the pull of greater opportunity created by improved transportation and the changing scale of the market.

Conclusion

At the dawn of the twenty-first century entrepreneurs were transforming American agriculture from a cottage industry into an efficient, modern, streamlined, and ever more tightly integrated system of large-scale food-supply chains linking producers with processors and retailers. The consolidation of smaller units into larger units, whether producers, processors, or retailers, has achieved impressive economies of scale that generate better food at lower prices for consumers. The share of the consumer dollar spent to buy food dropped from 21 cents in 1950 to only 11 cents in 2000.

American consumers have driven this transformation. We assume that the shelves of our grocery stores will be well stocked with food we can afford. We take for granted an awesomely elaborate and efficient food distribution system that moves thousands of food products from millions of farms to the shelves of 127,000 grocery stores. This system draws food from all over the globe, as a stroll through the fresh fruit and produce aisles of any supermarket will easily demonstrate.

Americans want food that we think is nutritious, healthy, and good for us, and we expect it to be free of dangerous chemicals and pathogens. We want food that is convenient and ready to eat, or at least ready to pop into the microwave, because we are reluctant to spend time preparing it, and we like to eat out. We spend 40 cents of our food dollar in restaurants and other convenient eating places, and supermarkets have added prepared food and take-out counters to compete with them. We expect the quality of our food to be consistent, and we are willing to pay premium prices for reliable brands we have learned we can trust.

Some people are concerned about the conditions under which their food is produced, and they seek assurance that farmers have been as kind as possible to their land, to their livestock, and to their labor. They are concerned about pollution of water and air by farm operations. They are concerned about the welfare and humane treatment of farm animals. They are concerned about the use of chemicals and biotechnology to enhance the growth of crops and animals. They are concerned about the working and living conditions of farm workers and about the wages they are paid. Like everyone else, they express their concerns at the checkout counter.

Food-Supply Chains

All of us, whether we realize it or not, send signals loud and clear to supermarkets when we buy bar-coded food. The bar codes tell the supermarket computer what we buy, when, and how much. The supermarket uses this information for inventory control, and its ideal is to save warehouse costs by placing items on its shelves "just in time," just before we enter the store to buy them.

The consolidation of small retail grocery stores into large supermarket chains has concentrated the buying power of the chains, and they have used their economic muscle to dictate to the food processors who supply them. Instead of meekly taking whatever the processor has to offer, they tell the processor what they will buy, because they know their customers want it, and they have pushed the cost of warehousing back onto the processor.

The bar-code scanner at the checkout counter in the supermarket tells the store's computer that the supply of an item is running low. The store computer sends a signal to the computer in the processor's warehouse, which prints out a resupply order to the driver of the delivery truck, who is the first real live human being who even knows about the transaction, which means a significant saving in labor costs.

Food processors have had to satisfy the demands of supermarkets for healthful, convenient, consistent products, and they have transmitted these demands of consumers back down the food-supply chain to the farmers who produce the commodities they process. Processors have closed down their small, old, high-cost plants and consolidated their activities in fewer, larger, more efficient new factories. The closure of small old processing plants deprives farmers of some of their options for selling their commodities. In 1975, for example, the state of Minnesota had 86 butter and cheese plants where dairy farmers could sell their milk, but the number had dropped to 44 in 1985 and only 20 in 1998, and not a single new plant had been built since 1968.

Food processors have located their new plants in the rural areas that produce the commodities they process, where land and labor are cheaper. They have cut their high labor costs by breaking down their processes into simple tasks that low-skill workers can perform, but they have had to recruit large numbers of low-skill workers, many of them immigrants, to do unpleasant work. The influx of large numbers of immigrant workers has created serious social problems in the rural areas where the new plants are sited.

The new processing plants must operate at full capacity to achieve their maximum efficiency, and they must have a steady and reliable supply of the commodities they process. A meatpacking plant, for example, cannot afford to adjust its machinery for each new truckload of animals. It would rather contract with a few large producers who can deliver a regular supply of uniform animals instead of having to dicker with large numbers of small independent farmers who deliver an irregular supply of heterogeneous animals when they feel like it.

Farmers must enlarge their scale of operations to produce what processors and retailers need, and those who fail to link into a food-supply chain will have difficulty staying in business. They no longer enjoy the luxury of producing whatever they like, taking it to market, and assuming someone will buy it. They must choose between controlling all of a small and probably faltering business and becoming part of a larger business organization.

Modern farmers, who are not willing to accept a lower level of living or a poorer lifestyle than city people, realize that the profit in farming today lies not in producing commodities, as in years gone by, but in adding value to commodities by processing them into products. They are well aware that the farmer's share of the consumer's food dollar dropped from 33 cents in 1970 to only 20 cents in 2000, and the rest goes to pay for processing, packaging, transportation, and marketing.

Successful modern farmers must tap into these sources of value-added profits by developing formal contracts with processors and retailers, even though these contracts will cost them some of their cherished independence. Some small producers have tried to retain some of their independence by forming cooperative alliances that will give them greater power in bargaining with processors, but most farmers have had to enlarge the scale of their operations in order to stay in business.

Enlarging farm operations should generate economies of scale and reduce costs of production. The lowest-cost producer never has to worry about the price of the commodity, but increasing scale also increases risks. Large-scale production requires large amounts of capital and labor, and the ability to acquire and manage them as skillfully as crops and livestock. The large-scale producer must do almost everything right almost all the time, and has precious little margin for error.

Some small producers have been able to retain their independence by identifying and serving specialized niche markets for products such as organic foods and exotic vegetables. Niche production requires highly specialized knowledge of marketing, however, and if it succeeds, it risks attracting too many producers, who may destroy the market for everyone by producing an oversupply.

Entrepreneurs and Communities

The people who have transformed American agriculture have been entrepreneurs. They have believed in themselves and they have been willing to take great risks, albeit risks they have calculated with minute precision. They have been charismatic leaders who have been able to identify, hire, and inspire dedicated lieutenants. They have demonstrated the ability to grow a one-man band into a rational and orderly business organization of closely collaborating specialists.

Many entrepreneurs have problems of succession. Their children have grown up in an atmosphere of ever-increasing affluence as their parents have prospered. The children are quite willing to spend the money their parents have made, but they have never had to learn to work as hard as their parents had to work. Good entrepreneurs must be clever or wise enough to know when to hire a professional manager to run the business, or when to sell it.

Selling the business in which they have invested their entire lives can be traumatic for the entrepreneurs, and it can be equally traumatic for the business. The original entrepreneurial business is a highly personal affair, and the entrepreneurs see their producers and clients in church on Sunday as well as on their farms during the week. When the original owner sells a business, the good old boy atmosphere of mutual trust and friendship may be replaced by a cold-eyed, cutthroat corporate culture that worships only the bottom line and cares nothing about people. Aggressive young masters of business administration move in and take over, and their style can quickly turn the business into a less pleasant place to work and do business.

Many entrepreneurs have problems of success as well as succession. Their less successful neighbors often envy them, and long-standing feuds have intensified. The increasing size and decreasing number of farms have decimated the population of rural areas. Some large farms are owned by absentees. Many absentee owners are accused of taking their profits out of the community because they do not patronize traditional local businesses, but they may spawn successful new businesses with their needs for specialized consultant support and advisory services for everything from crops through agrichemicals to nutrition, animal health, custom machine work, accounting, and global positioning systems.

Large farms and rural depopulation often are blamed for changes that actually were triggered by Henry Ford and his Model T. Affordable automobiles enabled rural people to travel far and wide in search of the goods and services they needed, and the Main Streets in small central places that serve rural areas have been losing businesses for nearly a century, but so slowly that many people fail to understand that they have long since lost their original reason for existence. The idea of rural areas consisting of tight six-mile communities is a hangover from the horse-and-buggy era.

Some people complain that entrepreneurs and their large farms are oversubsidized. On May 14, 2001, the *New York Times* (p. A10) reported that the top 10 percent of American farmers received 61 percent of all federal farm subsidy payments, but added that "8 percent of the country's farms produce 72 percent of the country's harvest." The largest farms, then, actually receive less than their share of farm subsidy money, even though their risks are greater. Too many small inefficient farmers would rather blame others and seek scapegoats than accept responsibility for their own inadequacies. These are the kinds of farmers who complain bitterly about their taxes when they enjoy a good year and then hope for a government bailout when they suffer a poor year.

Too many politicians seem unable to put such complainants in proper perspective. Perhaps it is socially desirable to spend public dollars to subsidize undersized farms that are inefficient and uneconomic, but it seems unjust for farm programs to discriminate against successful farmers by capping the amounts of subsidy dollars they may receive.

The New Tripartite Macrogeography

The transformation of American agriculture has rewritten the agricultural geography of the United States. The nation now has a cash-grain core in the agricultural heartland in the Midwest, specialized livestock-producing areas around its peripheries, and specialized crop-producing areas in the rimland (fig. 1.2).

Farmers in the agricultural heartland have shifted from mixed crop-and-livestock farming to large-scale production of corn and soybeans, feed grains they can sell directly for cash instead of feeding them to animals. Some farmers in the heartland capitalize on the ready availability of these high-energy crops by specializing in livestock production, but livestock feeding has lost its erstwhile preeminence in the region and has shifted to its peripheries.

Unit trains and interstate highways carry enormous quantities of high-energy feed grains from the heartland to the peripheries, where entrepreneurs have developed modern large-scale livestock operations that specialize in producing a single commodity. The spotty distribution of these new livestock operations reflects the decisions of entrepreneurs, because they have not been developed in other areas that seem just as suitable as the areas in which they have been developed.

Large-scale production of cattle and of poultry and pigs developed along two parallel tracks, with much interchange of ideas and technology between tracks. Large-scale feed yards for beef cattle, which are concentrated on the southern High Plains in Kansas, Oklahoma, and Texas, use open dry lots. Beef producers were early in starting large-scale production, but subsequently the beef industry has lagged, because it has not been able to standardize and deliver a consistent reliable product. Beef feed yards are at the mercy of many small independent cow-calf producers, who keep cattle for pleasure and prestige as much as for profit and like exotic genetics that produce a wildly heterogeneous variety of feeder animals.

The first large-scale dairies near Los Angeles adopted a modified version of the open dry lots used by beef feed yards. The dairy producers who have been displaced by urban encroachment have transplanted their operations to the Central Valley, Texas, Idaho, and other parts of the United States, where they are more likely to house their cows in long, one-story, curtain-sided structures similar to those used for poultry and pigs. In the traditional dairy-farming areas of the East, producers have lagged a bit in adopting modern large-scale technology.

Broiler producers in northeast Georgia and on the Eastern Shore were the first to develop a true modern system of large-scale food production, with food-supply chains that stretch from genetics to grocery store and deliver convenient healthy food of consistent high quality at attractive prices. Broiler production has become widespread throughout the South, and chicken has gained market share at the expense of beef to become our leading meat.

Turkey and egg producers have emulated the broiler model, and they house their animals in purpose-built structures that look like broiler houses. The maps of the distribution of turkeys and of laying hens are the best examples of maps that show entrepreneurial patterns. Laying hens especially are ubiquitous throughout the East.

Pig production was the last major form of livestock production to be modernized in the United States. Wendell Murphy started the process in eastern North Carolina, which has become the nation's second leading pig-producing state. Entrepreneurs have developed new centers of production in Missouri, Oklahoma, Utah, and other widely scattered areas, and in the Corn Belt pig production has shifted toward northern Iowa and southern Minnesota.

Pig production has been modernized in an era of heightened environmental sensitivity, and pigs are the most malodorous form of livestock, because their waste smells so much like human waste. The stench of the new pig farms gave environmental activists an easy weapon with which to attack them, and pig producers seem to have jumped from state to state in pursuit of the most permissive environmental regulations. We need national environmental standards to reduce unhealthy competition between states to recruit undesirable facilities.

On the nation's rimland the production of specialized crops has become more important. Vegetables have given way to nurseries and greenhouses on the fringes of Megalopolis, and vegetable production has migrated to New Jersey, to the Eastern Shore, to Florida, and finally to California, whose large-scale producers compete to place fresh vegetables in every supermarket in the United States. In the Southeast cotton has made a dramatic comeback, and Florida now has extensive citrus groves in areas that were considered unsuitable for citrus before the Great Freeze of 1985.

Sweeping changes, such as those that are transforming American agriculture, offer great opportunities, but they also have serious adverse consequences. They beget losers as well as winners, and some producers will suffer while others prosper. Some people fear change and try to halt it by political means, but they will be no more effective than the legislator who proposed a law to change the value of pi to an even 3.0 because he could never remember 3.14159265.

Change is inevitable, and it is foolhardy to try to halt it. Somebody somewhere is going to use new technology as soon as it becomes available, and no individual, no state, no nation is going to be able to force the genie back into the bottle once it has emerged. No country can long support domestic prices above the world price of a commodity, as the United States learned to its sorrow when it tried to protect the price of cotton, but some politicians still seem to think that we can maintain and protect an artificially high domestic price for other crops.

Change is global. The best equipment for egg houses is made in Germany. The best swine genetics were developed in England and are licensed to producers in the United States. Manufacturers in Europe have developed competitive technology for producing, processing, and packaging other agricultural commodities. As Gary Allen said to me, "In Minnesota agriculture our competition is no longer the guy down the road. In dairy it's California or Idaho or New York. In hogs it's Iowa or North Carolina or Chile, and in beef and soybeans it's Brazil."

The future of American agriculture is in the hands of those who realize that they must embrace change instead of trying to halt it, the entrepreneurs who have learned that they need to add a zero or two to the way they think about farming. The farm that seems large in 2002 will seem small in 2022.

Notes

Preface

1. *Minneapolis Star Tribune,* May 30, 2002, E3.

1. Background

1. Most farmers laugh at this figure and say it is far too low, but it is the best break-point in census data on sales of farm products. "Only farms with sales of $200,000 or more earned returns adequate to provide substantial equity growth," according to Dale Nordquist and Kent Olson, "Agriculture Finance Trends: Real Data From Real Farms," *Minnesota Agricultural Economist,* no. 690 (Fall 1997), 5–7; but "many lenders now believe that a financially viable commercial farm must have $500,000 or more in annual sales," according to Marvin Duncan and Richard D. Taylor, "Opportunities for Rural Community Banks in Farm Lending," *Economic Review* (Federal Reserve Bank of Kansas City) 78, no. 4 (Fourth Quarter 1993): 44.

2. *1997 Census of Agriculture,* vol. 1, pt. 51 (Washington, D.C.: U.S. Department of Agriculture, National Agricultural Statistics Service, 1999), chap. 2, table 11, "Tenure and Characteristics of Operator and Type of Organization: 1997 and 1992," 300.

3. John Fraser Hart, "Half a Century of Cropland Change," *Geographical Review* 91, no. 3 (July 2001): 525–543.

4. John Fraser Hart, "Nonfarm Farms," *Geographical Review* 82, no. 2 (April 1992): 166–179.

5 John Fraser Hart, "Part-Ownership and Farm Enlargement in the Midwest," *Annals of the Association of American Geographers* 81, no. 1 (March 1991): 66–79.

6. Gary L. Benjamin, "Industrialization in Hog Production: Implications for Midwestern Agriculture," *Economic Perspectives* (Federal Reserve Bank of Chicago) 21, no. 1 (January/February 1997): 2–13.

2. Change in the Corn Belt

1. For more on the evolution of the Corn Belt, see John Fraser Hart, "Change in the Corn Belt," *Geographical Review* 76, no. 1 (January 1986): 51–72.

2. Sharon Schmickle, "Plowing Ahead with Biotech Crops," *Minneapolis Star Tribune,* April 30, 2001, A7.

3. John Fraser Hart, "Part-Ownership and Farm Enlargement in the Midwest," *Annals of the Association of American Geographers* 81, no. 1 (March 1991): 66–79.

4. *1997 Census of Agriculture,* vol. 1, pt. 51 (Washington, D.C.: U.S. Department of Agriculture, National Agricultural Statistics Service, 1999), chap. 1, p. 24.

5. I should also express my deep admiration of and appreciation for the farm wife. She has always managed the household, raised the family, milked the cow, fed the chickens, tended the garden, kept the books, and had a hot meal waiting whenever the farmer came in from the field. More recently she has taken the place of the hired man as mechanization has reduced the need for brute strength and increased the importance of intelligence and skill. She is so quietly efficient that it is easy to underestimate her contribution, but the farm could not function without her.

6. Appropriate censuses of agriculture.

7. I described their farm operations in the early 1980s in *The Land That Feeds Us* (New York: Norton, 1991), pp. 149–161. Here I have updated those descriptions, with the permission of the Commonwealth Fund Book Program and the W. W. Norton Company, to show how Corn Belt farming has changed.

3. Beef

1. U.S. Department of Agriculture, *Agricultural Statistics,* appropriate years.

2. Charles M. Wilson, "The Cattle Feeding Industry in the High Plains," *Business Review* (Federal Reserve Bank of Dallas), July 1969, 4.

3. Russell L. Lamb and Michelle Beshear, "From the Plains to the Plate: Can the Beef Industry Regain Market Share?" *Economic Review* (Federal Reserve Bank of Kansas City) 83, no. 4 (Fourth Quarter 1998): 58.

4. See Ann Lee Harris, *Load the Wagon: The Story of Jack A. Harris* (Albuquerque: Charles Stocks, 1987), for a biography of Jack Harris.

5. Gladwin Hill, "Planter Taking $965,595 Gamble," *New York Times,* January 19, 1958, 1.

6. Lamb and Beshear, "From the Plains to the Plate," 58n.

4. Dairying from Farm to Dry Lot

1. I described the evolution of the traditional dairy belt in *The Land That Feeds Us* (New York: Norton, 1991), 172–185. In the first part of this chapter I have paraphrased

and updated that background material, with the permission of the Commonwealth Fund Book Program and the W. W. Norton Company.

2. Calculated from the appropriate censuses of agriculture.

3. L. B. Fletcher and C. O. McCorkle Jr., *Growth and Adjustment of the Los Angeles Milkshed: A Study in the Economics of Location,* Bulletin 787 of California Agricultural Experiment Station, 1962.

4. Samuel A. Hart, "Manure Management," *California Agriculture,* December 1965, 5–7.

5. Joel Splansky, "A Geography of Dairying in the Los Angeles Basin: Past and Present," unpublished paper, April 22, 1997.

5. Dairying in Other Areas

1. Calculated from the appropriate censuses of agriculture.

2. L. B. Fletcher and C. O. McCorkle Jr., *Growth and Adjustment of the Los Angeles Milkshed: A Study in the Economics of Location,* Bulletin 787 of California Agricultural Experiment Station, 1962.

3. Conversation with Bill Baxter, August 1998.

6. Can Midwest Dairying Thrive?

1. *1997 Census of Agriculture,* vol. 2, pt. 1 (Washington, D.C.: U.S. Department of Agriculture, Agricultural Statistics Service, 1999).

7. Broilers

1. *1954 Census of Agriculture* (Washington, D.C.: U.S. Department of Commerce, Bureau of the Census, 1956), vol. 1, pt. 1, p. xx, and vol. 2, chap. 6, p. 528

2. *1997 Census of Agriculture,* vol. 1, pt. 51 (Washington, D.C.: U.S. Department of Agriculture, Agricultural Statistics Service, 1999).

3. Gordon Sawyer, *The Agribusiness Poultry Industry: A History of Its Development* (New York: Exposition Press, 1971), is the classic history of the heady early days of the broiler business. George Watts and Connor Kennett, "The Broiler Industry," *Poultry Tribune Centennial Edition* (September 1995), 6–18, is also an extremely informative historical account.

4. D. Gale Johnson, "World Food and Agriculture," in *The Resourceful Earth: A Response to Global 2000,* ed. Julian L. Simon and Herman Kahn, 67–112 (Oxford: Basil Blackwell, 1985), graph on 84.

5. Watts and Kennett, "Broiler Industry," 14.

6. Ibid., 18.

8. Broiler Areas and Broiler People

1. Marvin Schwartz, *Tyson from Farm to Market: The Remarkable Story of Tyson Foods* (Fayetteville: University of Arkansas Press, 1991), tells the Tyson story well.

2. <http://www.tyson.com/corporate/info/today.asp>.

9. Eggs

1. Donald Bell, "Forces That Have Helped Shape the U.S. Egg Industry: The Last 100 Years," *Poultry Tribune Centennial Edition,* September 1995, 30–43, is a useful historical account.

2. Ibid., 33.

3. Ibid., 42.

4. Ibid.

5. Ken Looper, "Egg Marketing in the United States," in *Watt Poultry Yearbook,* USA ed. (Mount Morris, Ill.: Watt, 1997), 65–71.

6. Bell, "Forces That Have Helped Shape the U.S. Egg Industry," 40.

7. "Nation's Top Egg Producers," *Watt Poultry Yearbook* (1997), 62.

8. Ibid., 62–63.

10. Turkeys

1. Bernard Heffernan, "Leading Companies Plan 'Modest' Increase in '97," in *Watt Poultry Yearbook,* USA ed. (Mount Morris, Ill.: Watt, 1997), 49.

2. Robert E. Moreng, "Development of the Turkey Industry in the United States," *Poultry Tribune Centennial Edition,* September 1995, 19–27, has useful background material.

3. "A Turkey in Every Pot?" *Fedgazette* (Federal Reserve Bank of Minneapolis), April 1998, 5.

4. Jim Sumner, "Turkey Exports: Fastest Growing Turkey Market," *Watt Poultry Yearbook* (1997), 44–47.

5. "Top Turkey Companies in the USA," *Watt Poultry USA,* January 2000, 20.

6. Bernard E. Heffernan, "Jennie-0 Solidifies Top Ranking," *Watt Poultry USA,* January 2000, 19.

7. Appropriate censuses of agriculture.

8. "Top Ten Turkey Companies in the USA," *Watt Poultry USA,* January 2000, 20.

9. *1997 Census of Agriculture,* vol. 2, pt. 1 (Washington, D.C.: U.S. Department of Agriculture, Agricultural Statistics Service, 1999).

10. "Top Ten Turkey Companies," 22.

11. Ibid.

11. Hogs

1. Gary L. Benjamin, "Industrialization in Hog Production: Implications for Midwest Agriculture," *Economic Perspectives* (Federal Reserve Bank of Chicago) 21, no. 1 (January/February 1997): 11.

12. New Hog Farms

1. Keith Schneider, "Billionaires in Duel over a Hog Farm," *New York Times,* November 28, 1989, A14.

2. William Claiborne, "Despite Opposition, Plans Proceed for Hog Farm on Tribal Land," *Minneapolis Star Tribune,* April 7, 1999, A7.

3. Tom Meersman, "Operator of Large Hog Lot Agrees to Fine," *Minneapolis Star Tribune,* December 21, 2002, B1–B2.

13. Critics

1. "Environmentalists Sue Hog Operations in Seven States," *Minneapolis Star Tribune,* December 7, 2000, A24.

2. Michael A. Mallin, "Impacts of Industrial Animal Production on Rivers and Estuaries," *American Scientist* 88, no. 1 (January/February 2000): 26–37.

3. Mary Hager and Larry Reibstein, "The 'Cell from Hell,' " *Newsweek,* August 27, 1997, 63.

4. D. J. Mulla, A. S. Birr, G. Randall, J. Moncrief, M. Schmitt, A. Sekely, and E. Kerre, "Technical Work Paper: Impacts of Animal Agriculture on Water Quality," prepared for the Minnesota Environmental Quality Board and Citizens' Advisory Committee, St. Paul, April 3, 2001, esp. vi and 104.

5. Marlene K. Halverson, "Farm Animal Health and Well-Being," Supplementary Literature Summary and Technical Working Paper for the Minnesota Generic Environmental Impact Statement on Animal Agriculture, April 23, 2001, 61–66.

6. Ibid., 210–249.

7. Peter Singer, *Animal Liberation,* 2d ed. (New York: Random House, 1990).

8. For Alar, see Stephen Glass, "Congress Listens, Too, to Its Star Witnesses," *Minneapolis Star Tribune,* January 8, 1998, A14; and Jane E. Brody, "Health Scares That Weren't So Scary," *New York Times,* August 18, 1998, F7. For Bt corn, see "EPA Says Biotech Corn Seems Safe for Monarch Butterflies," *Minneapolis Star Tribune,* July 25, 2001, A12.

14. The Rim

1. John Fraser Hart, "The Perimetropolitan Bow Wave," *Geographical Review* 81, no. 1 (January 1991): 35–51.

2. John Fraser Hart, "The Metempsychosis of King Cotton," *Southeastern Geographer* 40, no. 1 (May 2000): 93–105.

3. John Fraser Hart, "The Demise of King Cotton," *Annals of the Association of American Geographers* 67, no. 3 (September 1977): 307–322.

4. Lizette Alvarez, "House Approves Plan to Restore Everglades," *New York Times,* November 4, 2000, A11.

5. James C. McKinley Jr., "Sugar Companies Play a Pivotal Role in Effort to Restore Everglades," *New York Times,* April 16, 1999, A20.

6. William Grimes, "Monterey: The Next Napa (or Is It Burgundy?)," *New York Times,* November 30, 1998, F8.

Bibliography

Agricultural Atlas of the United States. Vol. 2, pt. 1, of *1997 Census of Agriculture* (AC97-S-1). Washington, D.C.: U.S. Department of Agriculture, National Agricultural Statistics Service, 1999.

Agriculture 1950: A Graphic Summary. Vol. 5, pt. 6, of *1950 Census of Agriculture.* Washington, D.C.: U.S. Department of Commerce, Bureau of the Census, 1952.

Andreas, Carol. *Meatpackers and Beef Barons: Company Town in a Global Economy.* Boulder: University Press of Colorado, 1994.

Ball, Charles E. *Building the Beef Industry: A Century of Commitment.* Denver: National Cattlemen's Foundation, 1998.

Barkema, Alan, and Michael L. Cook. "The Changing U.S. Pork Industry: A Dilemma for Public Policy." *Economic Review* (Federal Reserve Bank of Kansas City), Second Quarter 1993, 49–65.

Barkema, Alan, Mark Drabenstott, and Nancy Novack. "The New U.S. Meat Industry." *Economic Review* (Federal Reserve Bank of Kansas City), Second Quarter 2001, 33–56.

Barlette, Donald L., and James B. Steele. "The Empire of the Pigs: A Little-Known Company is a Master at Milking Governments for Welfare." *Time,* November 30, 1998, 52–64.

Barnes, C. P., and F. J. Marschner. *Natural Land-Use Areas of the United States.* 1:4,000,000. Washington, D.C.: U.S. Department of Agriculture, 1933.

Becker, Elizabeth. "Far from Dead, Subsidies Fuel Big Farms." *New York Times,* May 14, 2001, A1, A10.

Benjamin, Gary L. "Industrialization in Hog Production: Implications for Midwestern Agriculture." *Economic Perspectives* (Federal Reserve Bank of Chicago) 21, no. 1 (January/February 1997): 2–13.

Biddle, George, ed. *Western Poultry History.* Sacramento: Pacific Egg & Poultry Association, 1989.

Caire, Justinian. *Cattle Feeding and Its Place in Twelfth District Agriculture.* Supplement to *Monthly Review* (Federal Reserve Bank of San Francisco), January 1953.

Caves, Richard E. "From Our Bookshelf." *Regional Review* (Federal Reserve Bank of Boston) 11, no. 2 (Second Quarter, 2001): 5–7.

Drabenstott, Mark. "Consolidation in U.S. Agriculture: The New Rural Landscape and Public Policy." *Economic Review* (Federal Reserve Bank of Kansas City), First Quarter 1999, 63–72.

Drabenstott, Mark, Mark Henry, and Kristin Mitchell. "Where Have All the Packing Plants Gone? The New Meat Geography in Rural America." *Economic Review* (Federal Reserve Bank of Kansas City), Third Quarter 1999, 65–82.

Drache, Hiram. *Beyond the Furrow: Some Keys to Successful Farming in the Twentieth Century.* Danville, Ill.: Interstate Printers and Publishers, 1976.

Effertz, Nita. "Trust Me—Not!" *Beef Today,* June/July 1998, 20–22.

Federici, Brian A. "Broadscale Use of Pest-Killing Plants to Be True Test." *California Agriculture* 52, no. 6 (November/December 1998): 14–20.

Fielding, Gordon J. "Dairying in Cities Designed to Keep People Out." *Professional Geographer* 14, no. 1 (January 1962): 12–17.

Fletcher, L. B., and C. O. McCorkle Jr. *Growth and Adjustment of the Los Angeles Milkshed: A Study in the Economics of Location.* Bulletin 787. California Agricultural Experiment Station, 1962.

Generalized Types of Farming in the United States. Agriculture Information Bulletin no. 3. Washington, D.C.: U.S. Department of Agriculture, 1950.

Greenman, Catherine. "Down on the Farm, Up on Technology." *New York Times,* July 13, 2000, G1, G8.

Gregor, Howard F. "Industrialized Drylot Dairying: An Overview." *Economic Geography* 39, no. 4 (October 1963, 299–318.

Hammond, Edwin H. *Classes of Land-Surface Form in the Forty-eight States, U.S.A.* 1:5,000,000. Map supplement no. 4. *Annals of the Association of American Geographers* 54, no. 1 (March 1964).

Harris, Ann Lee. *Load the Wagon: The Story of Jack A. Harris.* Albuquerque: Charles Stocks, 1987.

Hart, John Fraser. "The Demise of King Cotton." *Annals of the Association of American Geographers* 67, no. 3 (September 1977): 307–322.

———. "Change in the Corn Belt." *Geographical Review* 76, no. 1 (January 1986): 51–72.

———. *The Land That Feeds Us.* New York: Norton, 1991.

———. "The Perimetropolitan Bow Wave." *Geographical Review* 81, no. 1 (January 1991): 35–51.

———. "Part-Ownership and Farm Enlargement in the Midwest." *Annals of the Association of American Geographers* 81, no. 1 (March 1991): 66–79.

———. "Nonfarm Farms." *Geographical Review* 82, no. 2 (April 1992): 166–179.

———. *The American Farm.* New York: Barnes & Noble, 1998.

———. *The Rural Landscape.* Baltimore: Johns Hopkins University Press, 1998.

———. "The Metempsychosis of King Cotton." *Southeastern Geographer* 40, no. 1 (May 2000): 93–105.

———. "Half a Century of Cropland Change." *Geographical Review* 91, no. 3 (July 2001): 525–543.

Hart, John Fraser, and Ennis L. Chestang. "Turmoil in Tobaccoland." *Geographical Review* 86, no. 4 (October 1996): 550–572.

Hart, John Fraser, and Chris Mayda. "The Industrialization of Livestock Production in the United States." *Southeastern Geographer* 33, no. 1 (May 1998): 58–78.

Hill, Gladwin. "Planter Taking $965,595 Gamble." *New York Times,* January 19, 1958, A1.

Hinton, Mick. "Lawmakers Not Ready to Blow Pig Farms Down." *Sunday Oklahoman,* May 18, 1997, 1-A.

Johnson, D. Gale. "World Food and Agriculture." In *The Resourceful Earth: A Response to Global 2000,* ed. Julian Simon and Herman Kahn, 67–112. Oxford: Basil Blackwell, 1985.

Kennedy, Robert F., Jr. "I Don't Like Green Eggs and Ham!" *Newsweek,* April 26, 1999, 12.

Lamb, Russell L., and Michelle Beshear. "From the Plains to the Plate: Can the Beef Industry Regain Market Share?" *Economic Review* (Federal Reserve Bank of Kansas City), Fourth Quarter 1998, 49–66.

Lasley, Floyd A., William L. Henson, and Harold B. Jones Jr. *The U.S. Turkey Industry.* Agricultural Economic Report no. 525. Washington, D.C.: U.S. Department of Agriculture, Economic Research Service, 1985.

Law-Yone, Wendy. *Company Information: A Model Investigation.* Washington, D.C.: Washington Researchers, 1980.

LeDuff, Charlie. "At a Slaughterhouse, Some Things Never Die." *New York Times,* June 16, 2000, A1.

Mallin, Michael A. "Impacts of Industrial Animal Production on Rivers and Estuaries." *American Scientist* 88, no. 1 (January/February 2000): 26–37.

Marschner, F. J. *Major Land Uses in the United States.* 1:5,000,000. Washington, D.C.: U.S. Department of Agriculture, 1950.

———. *Land Use and Its Patterns in the United States.* Agriculture Handbook no. 153. Washington, D.C.: U.S. Department of Agriculture, 1959.

Marsden, Stanley J. *Turkey Production.* Agriculture Handbook no. 393. Washington, D.C.: U.S. Department of Agriculture, Agricultural Research Service, 1971.

Mason, Jim, and Peter Singer. *Animal Factories.* New York: Harmony Books, 1990.

Mayer, Lawrence A. "Monfort Is a 'One-Company Industry.'" *Fortune,* January 1973, 90.

McAdams, Christian. "Frank Perdue Is *Chicken!*" *Esquire,* April 1973, 113.

McNeil, Donald G., Jr. "Protests on New Genes and Seeds Grow More Passionate in Europe." *New York Times,* March 12, 2000, A1, A12.

1950 Census of Agriculture. Washington, D.C.: U.S. Department of Commerce, Bureau of the Census, 1952.

1997 Census of Agriculture. Washington, D.C.: U.S. Department of Agriculture, National Agricultural Statistics Service, 1999.

Nordquist, Dale, and Kent Olson. "Agriculture Finance Trends: Real Data from Real Farms." *Minnesota Agricultural Economist* 690 (Fall 1997): 1, 5–7.

North, Mack O. *Commercial Chicken Production Manual.* 3d ed. Westport, Conn.: AVI, 1984.

Plant, Richard E., G. Stuart Pettygrove, and William R. Reinert. "Precision Agriculture Can Increase Profits and Limit Environmental Impacts." *California Agriculture* 54, no. 4 (July/August 2000): 66–71.

Pollan, Michael. "Naturally." *New York Times Magazine,* May 13, 2001, 30.

Poultry Tribune Centennial Edition. Mount Morris, Ill.: Watt, September 1995.

Raisz, Erwin. *Landforms of the United States.* 1:5,000,000. Cambridge, Mass.: E. Raisz, [1957].

Roth, Daniel. "The Ray Kroc of Pigsties." *Forbes,* October 13, 1997, 115–120.

Saito, Isao, Noritaka Yagasaki, Takaaki Nihei, Makoto Hirai, and Taro Futamura. "Changes of Crop Combination Regions and Land Use in the Kansas High Plains." *Science Reports of the Institute of Geoscience, University of Tsukuba,* sec. A, vol. 21 (January 2000): 107–129.

Sawyer, Gordon. *The Agribusiness Poultry Industry: A History of Its Development.* New York: Exposition Press, 1971.

Schlosser, Eric. "Meat and Potatoes." *Rolling Stone,* November 26, 1998, 68.

Schwartz, Marvin. *Tyson from Farm to Market: The Remarkable Story of Tyson Foods.* Fayetteville: University of Arkansas Press, 1991.

Singer, Peter. *Animal Liberation: A New Ethics for Our Treatment of Animals.* New York: Random House, 1975.

Skinner, John L., ed. *American Poultry History, 1974–1993.* Vol. 2. Mount Morris, Ill.: Watt, 1996.

Smith, Everett G., Jr. "America's Richest Farms and Ranches." *Annals of the Association of American Geographers* 70, no. 4 (December 1980): 528–541.

Smith, Jonathan Vaughan. "Premium Standard Farms and the Transformation of Livestock Geography in Northern Missouri." *Southeastern Geographer* 39, no. 2 (November 1999): 161–171.

Soule, George, Martha V. Taber, and Mary M. Kirkwood. *Vertical Integration in the Broiler Industry on the Delmarva Peninsula and Its Effect on Small Business.* Chestertown, Md.: Washington College, 1960.

Splansky, Joel. "A Geography of Dairying in the Los Angeles Basin: Past and Present." Unpublished paper, April 22, 1997.

Swackhamer, Gene L., and Blaine W. Bickel. "Cattle Feeding in the Tenth District: Development and Expansion." *Monthly Review* (Federal Reserve Bank of Kansas City), April 1970, 13–22.

Tyrchniewicz, Ed, Nick Carter, and John Whitaker. *Finding Common Ground: Sustainable Livestock Development in Manitoba.* Winnipeg: Government of Manitoba, 2000.

Vogeler, Ingolf. *Wisconsin: A Geography.* Boulder: Westview Press, 1978.

Wade, Nicholas. "So, How About Those Viruses?" *New York Times,* July 18, 2000, F4.

Warrick, Toby, and Pat Stith. "Boss Hog: North Carolina's Pork Revolution." *Raleigh News and Observer,* February 19–26, 1996.

Wilson, Charles M. "The Cattle Feeding Industry in the High Plains." *Business Review* (Federal Reserve Bank of Dallas), July 1969, 3–9.

Wood-Gush, D. G. M. *Elements of Ethology.* London: Chapman & Hall, 1983.

Index

Italicized page numbers refer to illustrations (tables, maps, or photographs)

activism, social: animal rights and, 155–56, 168, 195, 235–38; animal welfare and, 233–35; in California, 185; Clean Water Act and, 226–27; environmental regulation and, 197; future and the food-supply chain, 258; and genetically modified organisms (GMOs), 17–18; pollution and, 227–29; resistance to change and, 226–27

advertising: beef industry, 60–61; brand name, 141–44, 178; turkey industry, 176, 181

agrarian fundamentalism, 4–7, 230

agricultural chemicals: crop production and, 18; future and the food-supply chain, 258; insect control and, 245–46; organic farming and, 238; variable-rate application of, 19–20

agricultural production: animal welfare and, 233–35; future and the food-supply chain, 259–60; gross return per acre of, *242;* resistance to change in, 226–27; shifts in, 3–4, 262–64; urban encroachment and, 240–43; value-added products and, 11–12; of vegetable crops, 247–56. *See also* disease control; insect control, biotechnology and

Alabama, broiler production, 126–32

Allen, Gary, 107–10

Allen, Linda, *96,* 107–9

alliances, farmer, 216–20. *See also* cooperatives

animal agriculture. *See* livestock production

animal rights. *See under* activism, social

animal welfare. *See under* activism, social

antibiotics, 229

Arizona, dairy industry, 75

Arkansas: broiler production, 116, 125–26, 132; cotton, 243–44; turkey production, 171

asset turnover, 109–10. *See also* profits

Aukeman, Lewis, 74–78

Bacillus thuringiensis (Bt), 17

Baer, Amon, *146,* 156–60

bar-code scanner, 258–60

Baxter, Bill, *40,* 52–55

beef cattle: as business or hobby, 40–42; case studies of, 42–61; concentration of, by state, *49;* Corn Belt farming and, 15–16, 41–42; cow/calf operations, 41, 60–61, 262; per capita consumption of, *121;* transformations in, 262. *See also* livestock production biotechnology, 17–18, 258. *See also* genetically modified organisms (GMOs)

Blackshear, Dan, 175, 182

breeding: corn and plant, 17–18; dairy industry and plant, 65; hog, 187, 192, 216; poultry, 120, 152, 172

broiler production, 127; Alabama, 126–32; Arkansas, 125–26; California, 184; case studies of, 126–45; defined, 112; Delaware, 125; development and growth of, 114–16, 118, *126;* efficiency in, *123;* Georgia, 125–26; Gold Kist, Inc., 124, 130; per capita consumption of, *121;* Perdue Farms, Inc., 141–42; Ralston Purina, 128–32; Texas, 125; transformation of, 124, 263; turkeys and, 172; Tyson Foods, Inc., 143–45; vertical integration of, 12–13, 116–18, 124. *See also* chickens

Brookover, Earl, 48–55

by-products: chicken, 119, 135; egg production, 150, 163–66; turkey, 175; waste as, 100–101, 103–5, 158–59

California: beef industry, 55–60; broiler production, 184; Chino Valley, 68–79; corporate farming, 10; dairy case studies, 71–78, 83–84, 184; dairy industry, 65, 82–83, 96–97, 262–63; dry-lot dairy industry, 67–71, 82–84; egg production, 152; environmental restrictions, 185; Los Angeles milkshed, *68;* Salinas Valley, 251–56; turkey production, 170, 183–85; vegetable crops, 251–56, 263

Campbell, Mark, 210–12

Carroll, Ottis, 181–82

case studies: beef cattle industry, 42–61; broiler production, 126–41; California dairy industry, 71–78, 82–84; Corn Belt transformations, 28–39; dairy industry, 84–95, 98–111; egg production, 156–68; hog production, 187–99, 201–25; turkey production, 177–85. *See also* transformation

cash-crop farming: Corn Belt, 16, 24, *25;* gross return per acre of, *242;* specialty products and, 240–43; transformation from, 102, 161–63, 207–9; transformation to, *26, 262–64. See also* mixed farming

cattle: custom feeding, 51–54; feeder, 41–42, *49. See also* beef cattle; livestock production

center-pivot irrigation, 50–51

centralized control, 2

change. *See* case studies; transformation

chemicals. *See* agricultural chemicals

chickens: early farm production of, 112–14; export markets and, 121; health inspection of, 123; per capita consumption of, *121;* transformations in, 262. *See also* broiler production; egg production; livestock production

Chino Valley dairy, 68–79

Christensen, Bob, 220–22

Circle Four, 198–99

citrus crops, 91, 263

Clean Water Act, 226–27

Colorado, beef industry, 42–48

commodities: beef cattle as, 47; farm size and agricultural, *9;* marketing of, 39; profits from, 58; transformation and, 259–60, 264; vertical integration and, 12–13

community responsibility, 110

ConAgra Foods, Inc., 47, 55, 124

consolidation: in American agriculture, 1–2, 257–60, 263–64; of broiler production, 124; economy of scale, 254–56; of egg production, 150–51; farm size and agricultural, 8–10; of hog production, 188; supermarkets, 252–53; of turkey production, 171, 183; of vegetable crops, 247–56. *See also* transformation

consumers: biotechnology and, 17–18; broiler production and, 120–21; dairy industry and, 66; education, 60–61; egg production and, 148–50; food quality and, 46–47, 59–60; marketing to, 38–39; pork industry and, 187; transformation and role of, 257–58; turkey production and, 175–76; value-added products for, 239

Continental Grain Company, 131, 206

contract production: broilers and, 115–19, 135, 144–45; eggs and, 148, 162, 167–68; family farms and, 35; farm marketing and, 39; hogs and, 160, 188, 219–22, 225; large-scale farming and, 28; turkeys and, 177. *See also* vertical integration

control, 2. *See also* government programs

cooperatives: cotton, 246–47; egg production, 147; Florida Dairy Farming Co-op, 93–94; Fort Recovery Equity Exchange, 162; hog production, 159–60; North Alabama Poultry Cooperative, 127; resistance to change and, 97–98; Rockingham Poultry Marketing Cooperative, 178; ValAdCo, 222–25; vegetable crop, 250, 251. *See also* alliances, farmer

corn, biotechnology and, 17–18

Corn Belt: farm ownership, 20–22; farm product sales, *27, 29;* farm size, 16, 20, *21, 23;* hog production, 187, 191, 263; mixed farming, 15, *24;* transformation case studies, 28–39

corporate farming: acceptance of, 210; criticism of, 229–31; failure to adapt to, 97–98; government programs and,

261–62; management and, 28; restriction of, 201

corporations: criticism and distrust of, 231–33; family farms as, 10–11, 33–34; rural communities and, 261; vertical integration and, 35

cost of production: broiler, 120–21; Corn Belt farming, 16–17; egg production, 150; failure to adapt and, 108; farm machinery and, 18–20; farm size and, 4–6; food-supply chain and future, 260; gross return per acre, *242;* insect control and, 245–46; prices and, 8; turkeys and, 173, 175; vegetable crop, 250

cotton, 57–58, 243–47

cow/calf operations. *See under* beef cattle

crop production: economy of scale, 11; farm size and, *9;* livestock and irrigated, 49–51; mixed farming, 14–16; plant breeding and, 17–18; resistance to change and, 38–39; vertical integration and, 12–13

crop rotation, 14–16

Cuddy, Bruce, *169,* 181, 183

dairy industry: California, 67–71, 82–84, 184; concentration by state, *81;* cooperatives in the, 64, 97–98; Corn Belt farming and, 63; farm size in the, 65–66, 80–82; Florida, 90–95; Kansas, 84–90; Midwest, 96–98, 106; Minnesota, 101–10; price support programs, 67; South Dakota, 98–101; transformation of, 68–79, 262–63. *See also* livestock production

D'Arrigo, John, 251–56

Delaware: broiler production, 114–16, 125; vegetable crops, 247

Delmarva Peninsula. *See* Eastern Shore

Devine, Don, 56–58, 60

Dewey, Tim, 88–90

disease control: antibiotics and, 229; egg production and, 155; hog, 193, 195, 212; vegetable crops and, 249

diversification: business, 135–36; consolidation and, 254–56; farm, 2–3; Harris Ranch, 58–59; hog production and, 191–93, 197, 209–10; specialty products and, 239; Tyson Foods, Inc., 144

dry-lot dairies, 69–70, 80–82

Eastern Shore, 114–16, 263. *See also specific states by name*

economic development: agricultural transformation and, 85–86; broiler industry and, 135; dairy industry and, 97–98, 106; hog production and, 198–99, 201–6, 211, 214–15

economy of scale: beef cattle business, 42–48, 61; consolidation and, 2, 254–56; crop production, 11; food-supply chains, 257–60; livestock and, 11; technology and, 7–8; turkeys and, 175

education, 60–61, 137

egg production: case studies, 156–68; early development of, 146–48; food processing, 149–50; industry concentration, *151;* management of, 152–55; Perdue Farms, Inc., 141; transformation of, 263

embargoes, import, 17–18. *See also* export markets

entrepreneurs: in American agriculture, 1–2, 260–62; broiler production, 119–20; Earl Brookover, 48–55; Jack Harris, 55–61; hog production, 187–99, 209–10; management and, 167–68; Warren Monfort, 42–48

environmental issues: dairy industry and, 95; genetically modified organisms (GMOs) and, 17–18; hog production and, 195–96, 201, 263; insect control and, 245–46; manure handling, 100–101, 103–5, 159, 223–25; poultry industry and, 155–56; turkey production and, 174; urban encroachment and, 78–79, 84; wastewater as, 74, 84, 89–90, 93; water projects, federal, 250–51. *See also* pollution; waste management

estate planning, 33–34, 108–9, 229–30

Everglades agricultural area, 247–51

export markets: broilers and, 121; General Agreement on Tariffs and Trade (GATT) and, 210; genetically modified organisms (GMOs) and, 17, 35–38; hogs and, 197–98, 210–11, 214; North American Free Trade Agreement (NAFTA) and, 210; turkeys and, 176; vegetable crop, 252

Falwell, Larry, 85–88

family farms: contract production and, 219–22; defined, 4–7, 22–23; farm subsidies and, 261–62; gross return per acre of, *242;* incorporation of, 10–11; intergenerational transfer of, 28–39, 107–9, 158; resistance to change and, 206; technology and, 229; vertical integration and, 13

Farm Bill (1985), 34

farm income: off-farm jobs and, 6; prices and, 8; resistance to change and, 27–28, 38–39; self-sufficiency and, 2–3; 265 n. 1:1

farm machinery, 18–20

farm product sales, Corn Belt, *26, 27*

farm size: commodity production and, *9;* consolidation and, 8–10, 230–31; Corn Belt farming and, 16, 20, *21;* dairy industry and, 64–66, 80–82; farm subsidies and, 261–62; machinery and, 18–20; specialization and, 4–7

farm subsidies, 261–62. *See also* government programs; price support programs
Farr, W. D., 43–48, 60
federal water projects, 58, 250–51. *See also* irrigation
feedlots: California, 55–61; Corn Belt, 41–42; High Plains, 48–55; Warren Monfort and, 42–48. *See also* beef cattle; livestock production
fertilizers, chemical, 18
Florida, 247–51; corporate farming, 10; dairy industry, 90–95; vegetable crops, 247–51, 263
food processing. *See* processing, food
food safety and biotechnology, 17–18, 238
food-supply chain, 257–60. *See also* vertical integration
forward integration. *See* vertical integration

Gaddis, Fred, 134–37
Garcia, Frank, *80,* 83–84
General Agreement on Tariffs and Trade (GATT), 210
genetically modified organisms (GMOs): animal rights and, 237–38; biotechnology and, 17–18; cotton and, 245–46; soybean marketing and, 38; vertical integration and, 35. *See also* biotechnology
genetics. *See* breeding
Georgia: broiler production, 116–17, 122–23, 125, 132, 263; cotton, 243–44
Gilland, Roger, 24–25
global agriculture, 27, 35, 264
global positioning system (GPS), 19
GMOs. *See* genetically modified organisms (GMOs)
Gold Kist, Inc., 124, 130
Gore, Fred, 93–95
government, criticism and distrust of, 231–33
government programs: corporate farming and, 261–62; cotton and, 57, 246; dairy industry and, 67, 97; insect control and, 245–46; irrigation and, 58; 1985 Farm Bill, 34; production control, 123; tobacco, 139. *See also* price support programs
grain storage, 19
Grant, Marshall, *239,* 245–46
Great Depression, farming and the, 28
greenhouse and nursery crops, 239–43
Greenpeace, 238
grocery business. *See* supermarkets

Harris, Jack, 55–61
harvesting, 18–19
health concerns: antibiotics, 229; beef and consumer, 47; dairy industry and, 78–79; dairy products and, 66; eggs and, 148–49; future and the food-supply chain, 258; genetically modified organisms (GMOs) and, 17–18; hog production and, 195–96, 223–24; meat packing industry and, 55; pollution and, 228; pork industry and, 187; poultry industry and, 121, 123, 155; turkey production and, 174–75
herbicides, biotechnology and, 17–18
hog production: case studies, 187–99, 201–25; contracting of, 37; cooperatives, 159–60; Corn Belt farming and, 15–16; early development of, 186–87; industry concentration, *188;* per capita consumption, *121;* transformations in, 262–63; turkeys and, 191–93; Tyson Foods, Inc., 144; vertical integration and, 12–13. *See also* livestock production
hybridization, corn, 17–18

Idaho, dairy industry, 75, 262–63
Illinois: corporate farming, *10;* hog production, *189*

immigrants. *See* migrant workers
income: off-farm jobs and farm, 23–24; self-sufficiency and farm, 2–3, 265 n. 1:1
incorporation: family farm, 33–34, 229–30; farm ownership and, 10–11, 108–9
independence, farmer: beef cattle industry, 60–61; broiler production and, 124; farm marketing and, 39; of individual farmers, 2; large-scale farming and, 28; vertical integration and, 12–13
Indiana, hog production, *189*
innovation, economy of scale and, 7–8
insect control, biotechnology and, 17–18, 245–46
integration, 18–20, 61. *See also* vertical integration
Iowa: corporate farming, *10;* dairy industry, 106; egg production, 167; hog production, *189,* 191, 201–2, *217, 218, 263;* turkey production, 170
irrigation: aquifer depletion, 88–89; cotton, 246; government subsidies for, 58; livestock production and, 49–51, 54, 55–61

Jerome, Wallace, *169,* 179–81
Jewell, Jesse, 116–17
Johnson, Marvin, 181–82

Kansas: beef industry, 48–55, 210, 262; dairy case studies, 85–90; dairy industry, 84–85
Kislingbury, Kent, 216–19
Koetsier, Edwin, 84

large-scale farming: animal rights and, 235–38; animal welfare and, 233–35; broiler production and, 124; criticism of, 229–31; dairy industry and, 96–98; dry-lot dairies and, 69–79, 80–82; egg production and, 168; gross return per acre of, *242;* hog production and, 187–91, 216; livestock production and, 60–61; management of, 28; Midwest dairy, 106; pollution and, 227–29; rural communities and, 261; transformations in, 262–64; turkey production and, 171, 185; of vegetable crops, 247–56
leadership, community, 38–39. *See also* rural communities
Leeuwen, Arlen van, 71–74
legislation: dairy price supports and, 67; environmental regulation, 223–25; resistance to change and, 27–28, 187, 264; vertical integration and, 12, 28
legumes, crop rotation and, 15
lifestyle, farming as a: large-scale farming and, 229–30, 259; self-sufficiency and, 5; subsidies and, 261–62
livestock production: agricultural consolidation and, 8–10; animal rights and, 155–56, 168, 195, 235–38; animal welfare and, 233–35; antibiotics and, 229; Corn Belt farming and, 15–16, 24–25; cyclic prices of, 123; economy of scale, 11; farm size and, *9;* irrigation and, 49–51, 54; large-scale, 60–61, 262–64; meat per capita consumption, *121;* mixed farming and, 14–16; regulatory impact on, 24–25; specialization, 3–4; value-added products and, 11–12. *See also* beef cattle; broiler production; chickens; dairy industry; hog production
Livingston, John, 127–32

machinery, farm, 18–20
Magnus, Doug, *14,* 35–39
management: entrepreneurs and, 167–68, 221–22, 260–62; farmer alliances, 216–20; large-scale farm, 28, 110–11; mishandled, 222–25; poultry, 122–23, 137, 152–55

manure handling. *See under* waste management

marketing: broiler, 113–15, 117, 121, 135; cash-crop farming, 32; cooperative, 64; egg, 147; global, 27; industry fragmentation and, 60–61; niche, 23; promotion and, 117, 141–42; United Soybean Board, 38; value-added products, 239

Maryland: broiler production, 114–16, 141; vegetable crops, 247

Mather, Ken, *14,* 28–35, 39

McArthur, James, 90–93

McCarty, H. F., Jr., *125,* 135–39

McDonald's, 134, 234

meat packing industry: food quality and, 59–60; Harris Ranch and the, 55–61; transformation of, 54–55; vertical integration in the, 11–13, 46–47. *See also* livestock production

meat per capita consumption, *121*

Meyers, Harold, *200,* 207–9

Midwest: dairy industry, 65–66, 96–98, 106; hog production, 187, 191, 215; turkey production, 173. *See also specific states by name*

migrant workers: dairy industry and, 78, 91–92; egg production and, 155; food industry and, 231; future and the food-supply chain, 259; hog production and, 205; meat packing industry and, 55, 198, 211

milk, 67. *See also* dairy industry

Minnesota: dairy industry, 62, 96–97, 101–10; egg production, 156–60, 166–68; hog production, *189,* 210, 215–29, 263; turkey production, 170, 178–81

minority workers, 55. *See also* migrant workers

Mississippi: broiler production, 132–39; cotton, 243–44

Missouri: corporate farming in, 201–2; expansion of hogs in, 187, 191; hog production, *189,* 202–9, 263

mixed farming: Corn Belt, 24; defined, 14–16; shifts in, 262–64. *See also* cash-crop farming

Monfort, Warren, 42–48

monoculture, specialization and, 2–4

Murphy, Wendell, *186,* 187–91, 196–98

National Academy of Sciences, 17–18

Nebraska, hog production, *189,* 200–201

New Mexico, dairy industry, 75

New York: dairy industry, 62, 64–65; vegetable crops, 247

niche markets, 23, 59. *See also* specialty products; value-added products

North American Free Trade Agreement (NAFTA), 210

North Carolina: broiler production, 132, 139–41, 142; cotton, 243–44; hog production, 187–98, 263; turkey production, 137, 171, 181–83

nursery and greenhouse crops, 239–43

off-farm jobs: beef cattle and, 40–41; broiler production and, 119; dairy industry and, 65; farm income and, 6–7, 23–24

Ohio: egg production, 161–63; hog production, *189*

Oklahoma: beef industry, 48–55, 262; hog production, 187, 191, 209–15, 263

Olson, Earl B., 178–79

ownership, family farm: Corn Belt and, 20–22; farm size and, *21;* incorporation and, 10–11, 229–30; intergenerational transfer of, 107–9, 158

People for the Ethical Treatment of Animals (PETA), 236–38

Perdue Farms, Inc., 124, 141–42

Perico, TX, 206–9
pesticides, biotechnology and, 17–18
Pires, Joe, *80*, 83–84, 98–101
plant breeding. *See under* breeding
politics: animal rights and, 235–38; biotechnology and, 17–18; criticism and distrust of, 231–33; dairy price supports and, 67; environmental regulation and, 196–97; farm subsidies and, 261–62; resistance to change and, 27–28, 97–98, 264; vertical integration and, 12, 28; water and, 250–51. *See also* government programs; price support programs
pollution: controls, 103; future and the food-supply chain, 258; hog production and, 195–96, 224–25; manure handling, 227–29. *See also* environmental issues; waste management
poultry. *See* broiler production; chickens; egg production; turkey production
Premium Standard Farms, 201–9
price support programs: agricultural transformation and, 264; cotton, 246; dairy, 67, 97. *See also* government programs
processing, food: broilers and, 117, 120–21, 124; ConAgra Foods, Inc., 47, 124; dairy and, 106; eggs and, 149–50; future and the food-supply chain, 258–60; Gold Kist, Inc., 124, 130; Kentucky Fried Chicken, 121; McDonald's, 134; Perdue Farms, Inc., 124, 141–42; turkeys and, 170–71; Tyson Foods, Inc., 124, 137–38, 143–45
production. *See* agricultural production; cost of production; livestock production
profits: in agricultural commodities, 58; in beef cattle business, 42; in Corn Belt farming, 16; cost of production and, 8;

gross return per acre, *242;* vertical integration and, 117. *See also* asset turnover
promotion marketing, 117, 141–42

racial tension, rural communities and, 55. *See also* migrant workers
railroads: dairy industry and, 64; unit trains, 122, 262
Ralston Purina, 128–32
Ramsey, Bill, 253
Ramsey, Dennis, 139–41
regulation: criticism and distrust of, 231–33; environmental, 185, 196–97, 226–27; farm transformation and, 24–25, 212, 251, 254; urban encroachment and, 79; violations, 155–56, 223–25
resistance to agricultural transformation, 226–38
Rogers, Bennie Clyde, 132–34
Rogers, John, 134
Roth, Rick, *239,* 249–50
rural communities: decline of, 229–31; future of, 259, 261; transformation of, 55; urban encroachment and, 240–43
Rydzewski, Bob, 91–93

safety, worker, 55, 155–56
Salinas Valley, 251–56
Schimpf, Nick, 160–61
science, biotechnology and, 17–18
Seaboard Farms, 209–15
Seifring, Bill, 161–63
self-sufficiency, farmer, 2–3, 265 n. 1:1
Singer, Peter, 235–36
social activism. *See* activism, social
South Dakota: dairy industry, 98–101, 106; hog production, 191, 201
Southeast United States: broiler production, 116–17, *126,* 263; cotton and, 243–47, 263; egg production, 152;

turkey production, 173. *See also specific states by name*

soybeans, 17, 35–38

Sparboe, Bob, 166–68

specialization: Corn Belt farming and, 22–23; custom cattle feeding, 51–54; self-sufficiency and farm, 2–4, 265 n. 1:1; standardization and agricultural, 11–13; technology and farm, 7–8; transformation and, 216, 252

specialty products: agricultural production of, 263; family farms and, 23; irrigation and, 58; nursery and greenhouse, 239–43; vegetable crops as, 247–56. *See also* niche markets; value-added products

standardization, specialization and, 11–13

Staples, Dave, 163–66

storage, grain, 19

subsidies, farm. *See* farm subsidies

supermarkets: beef and consumer, 45–47; broiler production and, 120; consolidation of, 252–53; egg production and, 148, 160; food-supply chain and, 258–60; profit margins and, 8; specialty products and, 242–43; transformation and role of, 257–58

Tanimura, Gary, 252–54

taxation: custom cattle feeding and, 52; economic development and, 99; family farm, 33–34; urban encroachment and, 71–79

technology: bar-code scanner, 258–60; beef feedlot, 48; Corn Belt transformation and, 18–20; cotton and, 246; dairy industry and, 67–68, 70–71, 96–98; economy of scale and, 7–8, 175; egg production and, 150; failure to adapt to, 107–8; hog production and,

210–11; large-scale farming and, 229–31; transformation and, 264; waste management, 103–5

tenant farmers, 21

Texas: beef industry, 48–55, 262; broiler production, 125; corporate farming, 10; cotton, 243–44; dairy industry, 75, 262–63; hog production, 206–9

tobacco, 139, 181

Tobkin, Ron, *96,* 111–16

transformation: of American agriculture, 1–2, 262–64; beef cattle production, case studies of, 42–61; of broiler production, 118, 124, 145; to cash-crop farming, *26;* complacency and, 25–28; Corn Belt case studies, 28–39; of Corn Belt farming, 16–17, 24–25; cotton, 243–47; criticism and distrust of agricultural, 226–38, 264; of dairy industry, 68–79, 80–82; as economic development, 85–86; of egg production, 146–47, 150, 168; entrepreneurs in agricultural, 260–62; failure to adapt to, 96–98, 107–8, 138; of hog production, 186–87, 215–16; of meat packing industry, 46–47, 54–55; rural communities and, 261; urban encroachment and, 240–43; vegetable crops, 247–56. *See also* case studies; consolidation

transgenic crops. *See* genetically modified organisms (GMOs)

turkey production: broiler model of, 172; case studies, 177–85; early development of, 137, 169–70; hogs and, 191–93; industry concentration, *171;* transformation of, 171, 263; vertical integration and, 12–13. *See also* livestock production

turnover, asset, 109–10

Tyson Foods, Inc., 124, 137–38, 143–45

United Soybean Board, 38
urban development: dairy industry and, *68*, 71–79; egg production and, 147–48
Utah, hog production, 187, 198–99, 263

ValAdCo, 222–25
value-added products: agricultural production and, 11–12; beef cattle as, 47, 56; broilers as, 120–21; Coolidge Dairy, 88; egg production, 149–50, 164; farm marketing and, 39; future and the food-supply chain, 259–60; Harris Ranch, 58–60; specialty products, 239; turkey as, 175, 185; Tyson Foods, Inc., 144; vegetable crops as, 253–54. *See also* niche markets; specialty products
vegetable crops: farm size and, *9;* industry transformation, 247–56, 263; urban encroachment and, 240–43; as value-added products, 239; vertical integration and, 12–13
Verhoeven, Martin, *62,* 69, 73, 75
Verhoeven, Ron, *62,* 75–78
vertical integration: of agricultural production, 11–13; of broiler production, 116–18, 124; of dairy industry, 93; farm management and, 28; genetically modified organisms (GMOs) and, 35; of turkey production, 171, 176–78
Virginia: broiler production, 114–16, 142, 178; hog production, 192; turkey production, 170, 177–78

waste management: broiler production, 119, 135; by-products, 100–101, 103–5; composting as, 158–59, 160–61; egg production, 153, 163; hog production, 195–96, 201, 222–25; manure handling, 45–46, 70, 74, 77, 89–95, 199, 208–9, 216–17; turkey production, 174. *See also* environmental issues; pollution
water projects, federal, 58. *See also* irrigation
wheat, dairy industry and, 62–63
Wisconsin: dairy industry, 62, 64–65, 96–97; egg production, 160–61, 163–66; turkey production, 179–81
women: in American agriculture, 113–14, 134, 147, 168; as farm labor, 33, 36–37, 108, 162, 184, 266 n. 2:5; farm ownership and, 20
Wood, Dave, 59–61
worker safety, 55, 155–56, 211

Inset Photographs

Page 14: Doug Magnus in 1983 (inset left); Ken and Alan Mather in 1999 (inset right)

Page 40: Bill Baxter, President of the Brookover Companies, 1997 (inset)

Page 62: Dennis, Martin, and Ron Verhoeven in 1998 (inset)

Page 80: Joe Pires and Frank Garcia near Tulare, 1998 (inset)

Page 96: Linda Allen, 1999 (inset left); Ron Tobkin, 1999 (inset right)

Page 125: H. F. McCarty, Jr., 1997 (inset)

Page 146: Amon Baer, 1999 (inset left); Amos and Amon Baer, 2000 (inset right)

Page 169: Wally Jerome, 1998 (inset left); Bruce Cuddy, 1995 (inset right)

Page 186: Wendell Murphy, 2000 (inset)

Page 200: Harold Meyers, 1997 (inset)

Page 239: Rick Roth, 1983 (inset left); Marshall Grant, 1995 (inset right)